AFTERMATH

Confederate Soldier Returns to Devastated Homeland

Paul St.Cyr

Sept. 2019

To all who fought then and now

Acknowledgements

Thanks to Janice, Chris, and Cheryl for providing their time and energy with thoughtful comments and creative suggestions.

Author's Comments

The events and individuals identified in this story are presented with partial accuracy defending the basic theme. The fictional characters that make up this novel appear in actual historical events.

One

APPOMATTOX

They considered themselves Americans, one from Ohio, the other from Virginia. They both read the same Bible and believed in the same God. Both were highly respected experienced soldiers. Both graduated from West Point, one in the middle of his class the other ranked second. Both fought in the Mexican War. Both were brave proud men. Both were weather beaten from years of travelling, strategizing, and leading. And both were tired of fighting and killing.

Both men sat peacefully a few feet apart facing each other in the living room of a southern home. They read from their respective hand written copies of their previous correspondence of the settlement. They had been corresponding with each other over the previous few days to finalize their thoughts, their beliefs, their commitments to their respective soldiers, and ideas for peace.

One wore a complete gray uniform, the other a dusty blue outfit. One was dressed as if he were attending a military ball. The other looked as if he had just crawled fifty yards thru dust and dirt. One was barely five and half feet tall while the other stood six inches taller. It was April 1865. I was in Washington DC and reading the fast breaking news, alone, and attempting to complete my personal questionnaire. I grabbed my journal and made some entries.

John Trenton McMurtree

My name is John McMurtree. JT for short! I was born in 1844 and raised in Boxford Forge located in the northeastern corner of Tennessee where union support was present in 1861 when the War Between the States started. My family was somewhat religious with Sunday attendance at the local church. My pa and older brother and me worked the small farm where I learned values and priorities common in that section of the south and my family never owned slaves, besides, my best friend was black! I loved my early childhood, even though I was given great responsibilities when pa and my older brother left in the late 50's. I grew up quick after pa left, but nothing was to compete with my transition from adolescence to adulthood, as did the time I spent in the Confederate Army during the war. As innocent and naive as I was, it was during the early months of 1862 when I ventured to Clinton and proudly enlisted believing I was completing my responsibility as a true southerner.

I spent the last three years as a Confederate soldier, had risen to the rank of sergeant, and fought in many battles such as Second Manassas, Fredericksburg, and Gettysburg. After battlefield wounds, diseases, and pneumonia that led to long recoveries, after considerable personal struggles with tragedy on the home-front in Tennessee, and after changes in my assignments from front line soldier to prison guard, I decided, like many, that the lost cause of the Confederacy was approaching and I simply walked away from the war. That was early 1865!

But before leaving, some say deserted, I met many interesting soldiers. My life as a Confederate soldier was interesting to say the least. I met and fought with soldiers from every southern state, most with no formal education, and all with stories that were sometimes as ridiculous as "jumping over the moon" or as funny as listening to soldiers bet on "cockroach races." Battlefield experiences, the horrors of hospitals and prison life were extremely emotional and personally damaging. Most Confederate soldiers were not even twenty years old! I was 18 when I said I would defend the southern cause. I never wore anything resembling a rebel gray uniform as promised upon enlisting. Food was always tasteless and living conditions in most cases were deplorable, especially during marches or in camps.

Over many months with varied audiences I watched and listened as soldiers from every walk of life detailed their life on small farms, in small towns, or in some cases men and women from huge cotton or tobacco plantations located in Mississippi, Alabama, South Carolina, or Georgia. I listened to soldiers brag about brutal experiences of torture to slaves or freed blacks. For some their home life and behavior before the war never wavered during their responsibilities as soldiers when they continued their brutal attacks on the "inferior race" as they referred to blacks.

Soldiers talked all the time about their wartime experiences. Some enjoyed the fights and described the battles. Others spent more time complaining about camp conditions, lack of medical supplies or treatment, and a few always had stories of their travels to the outskirts of the camp to meet the local girls who had something to offer. On many nights as the campfire warmed us, tired and cold bodies bragged about the nightlife in the big cities of Washington or Richmond. This helped relax the mind with exciting sexual experiences or wishful thinking.

I met soldiers from the Union side and listened as they explained their life with hopes and dreams outside of the war. One interesting fellow from Rhode Island described his early experiences when a small group of rebels and me got disconnected from our unit and lost for a few days. I think his name was Brian, I forget his last name, as we spent an evening trying not to kill each other by talking and listening. We were on a small farm miles from any battle. We settled our disputes and returned to our respective units.

The war was really strange! Yankees talked with Rebels! While just yards apart, we bathed in the same streams and rivers simultaneously hollering insults to each other, as we stood naked as newborn babies! After many battles opposing forces gathered on the battlefields to secure the wounded and bury the dead followed by more fighting within days. Acquaintances' one minute, enemies the next!

Stories were always interesting, some more outrageous than others as was the one rebel soldier who decided that any killing was acceptable and described his brutal nightly attacks on Yankee guards. He was proud he had carried out such killings, but unfortunately his life was taken in the next battle in Sharpsburg.

Sitting around a campfire on another night, a young soldier informed me he could not hear and I remember being somewhat dumbfounded by responding, "You can't hear?" Actually, he had lost his hearing after spending the previous day loading cannons on a hill overlooking Yankees in the cornfield a short distance from Antietam Creek. He said, "I loaded the cannons all day." He described the day as I listened. I really felt bad. He was too young to have lost his hearing. He wasn't even twenty! We talked for some time before I was able to get his release as his army life was over and he returned to his home in Mississippi.

During my war years, I spent time writing letters home, reading newspapers and magazines, and talking with preachers. I didn't receive many letters from home, but I was lucky enough to get a few from Samantha, grandpa, and Mary Lou. When I wrote home, I spent time detailing my army life either around the campfires, battles, or hospitals but in most cases I refrained from the gory details. Letters from home reported family issues including ma's death and the Yankee destruction of our small Boxford Forge farm. Lonesome, probably described me best as I complained about many of my concerns. My early letters home described me complaining about everything from inadequate, unhealthy food, lack of warm winter clothing, especially boots, and in one correspondence, I complained excessively about everything wrong about the conduct of the war, the politics, and the stupid mistakes made by generals on both sides of the conflict.

But, one of the most damaging pieces of mail I received was my brother's journal detailing his imprisonment. He had joined the Union Army, was a captain, and had been captured in northern Virginia. He had been transported to Macon, Georgia, and eventually died while incarcerated. His journal detailed his prison life. Needless to say, I was devastated! Today, I carry that journal everywhere!

Luckily, he and I had met on two occasions during the war when I was positioned on picket duty and he discovered me where we talked extensively about life in the north after he and pa left the farm in 58. And I spent a lot of time reading!

My reading was basic. Sometimes I was fortunate to grab an old Washington or New York paper. Stories were always interesting as northern editors continued throughout the war to blast Lincoln's Generals for lack of aggressiveness, or find fault within congress. Southern newspaper editors always blamed the north for the war by invading southern territory. 'The War of Yankee Aggression," said many. Charleston and Richmond writers openly disagreed with Davis, his dysfunctional cabinet, or found fault with state government that lacked leadership. Governors fought over everything from railroad control to placement of soldiers. Southern executives argued whether it was more important for rebel soldiers to defend their states or become part of the Confederate Army. Many governors refused to allow their units to leave their respective states reducing the numbers on major battlefields in Lee's armies in Virginia or Hood's armies further south.

Governments and newspaper editors fought over varied issues and interests while young soldiers struggled simply to survive. The entire three years were extremely confusing as strange events take place in wars!

For example, as I briefly mentioned earlier, after many battles soldiers from opposing sides waved a flag of truce, met, shook hands, told stories, exchange trinkets, recovered their wounded and dead buddies and returned to their unit to fight another day. Competing for attention across a river or positioned on surrounding outskirts of small towns, Yankees and rebels alike played musical instruments refining their talents while displaying horrible examples as musicians. Within earshot, soldiers listened as the instruments brought forth a bombardment of unexplained or unrecognizable musical notes. Basically, the music was bad! When the musical instruments rested, the bored and tired picket soldiers spent the rest of the night harassing and intimidating one another across open fields or across a riverbank.

Boredom was common with thousands as soldiers became restless and on many nights they resorted to other tactics such as robbing the local farmers or businesses of their products. Many left the tenting area, never to return. Since food was always in short supply, the locals in small towns and rural communities were fair game and soldiers helped themselves. Occasionally, when push came to shove, someone died. Usually the soldiers won! By the middle of 64 southern civilians became fearful of anyone they did not recognize as women, children, former slaves, former plantation owners, businessmen, and local leaders paid the price. As the war was coming to an end, the landscape suffered when anxiety escalated.

Another characteristic that threatened my young life was my attention or lack thereof of religion. I had practically abandoned religion during the war. However, during many difficult times when my mind drifted to home, a recent battle, or prison experiences overwhelmed me, I discovered preachers who listened to my complaints.

Initially, I voiced my opinions about the lack of letters from home. Then I hit the need for boots and good food. I complained about marching. I complained about my health. I complained about "stupid battles and horrible deaths". And the preachers listened as I told stories of watching soldiers die from direct gunshot wounds to the head or stomach or of the horrific deaths I described in prisons.

Preachers educated me on varied topics that emerged during candle lighting time as we discussed my next crisis. Discussions regarding dedication to the Confederate cause surfaced on many occasions. Even while southern pulpits were convinced that God was on our side, I questioned preachers who either defended the same ideas or blasted the thinking. The southern God praised the Confederate Army when we won major battles saying that God had provided the motivation, while in defeat, soldiers did not live up to God's expectation. Many times confusion overwhelmed me and I simply left the tent to retire and digest whatever was discussed. Whose side was God on? My most influential meeting with any preacher came when I was at Camp Sumter, in Andersonville, Georgia.

Isaac Pritchard was a local eighty-three year old Baptist preacher who came to Camp Sumter to comfort prisoners and on a couple of occasions we sat and talked. He convinced me the need to move "into the future" he proclaimed, with my life and climb the mountains that prevented me from any forward progress. We had long talks about family, as I mentioned pa, my brother, Samantha, and Mary Lou. One day he asked about Jonas. I had no answer. With God in mind, Mr. Pritchard reminded me of my responsibility and decisions I had made over the previous three years.

But, it was my decision to leave and when I left Georgia that cold winter and returned to Clinton, Tennessee to visit Mary Lou and Samantha, I had many questions to answer. During the long exhausting walk home, I had the opportunity to revisit many events of the previous years.

While 1864 turned drastically destructive in northern Virginia with major battles and mounting casualties, Tennessee, Alabama, Georgia and South Carolina, witnessed some of the most physical damage to the southern landscape that one could imagine. In both the north and the south, the Union Army was almost twice the size of rebel forces. In northern Virginia, thousands of Union and Confederate soldiers lost their lives or were severely injured for life in battles at Cold Harbor, The Wilderness, Spotsylvania, Cedar Creek, and the long lasting siege at Petersburg. But the southern landscape was battered!

In the south, generals moved soldiers to and from strategic locations to win decisive battles to further their cause. The Total War concept, endorsed by Abe Lincoln and his generals, specifically Grant and Sherman, produced devastating results. As extensive agricultural productive areas were being overrun by aggressive and destructive Yankee soldiers newspaper accounts reported thousands of innocent civilians and freed blacks became victims. Isolated, lonely, and frightened women and children were not exempt. Cities and small towns were demolished. Plantations and small farms that once produced tobacco or cotton were destroyed. Forests or fields covered with unpicked cotton were burned to the ground. Mills, factories, banks, businesses, government structures, hardware stores, and more were completely abolished. Important railroad centers like Atlanta, seacoast centers such as Savannah, and state capitals, especially Columbia, were recipients of the brutal Union onslaught.

While blood was being drained from tired soldiers during the 64-65 campaigns, my life centered around guarding prisoners at Belle Island and Libby Prison. Both encampments were located within miles of each other, one located in the middle of the James River, the other in the middle of the Confederate capital, Richmond. Captured enlisted Yankees were incarcerated on the island while Libby, a former warehouse, was home to thousands of Union Officers, northern newspaper reporters, and political leaders whom the south considered threatening. I went from a short stay at Belle Island to Libby before I ventured south on a long train ride to the most gruesome experience of all at Camp Sumter, located in the small community of Andersonville.

During the short life of the southern prison, located in southern Georgia that was built to hold less than 8,000 Yankees, thousands died needlessly. At one point during the summer of 64, upwards of 33,000 northerners were imprisoned in the 16-acre open stockade structure that eventually doubled in size. Make shift shelters from cloths, rags, or branches gave little respite as most of the incarcerated men lived in the open with no cover during the hot steamy summer days and the cold winter months before thousands escaped and the prison closed. For guards and prisoners alike, food was always in short supply. The lack of adequate food from the southern government led to competition between local farmers who profited with increased prices to prison leaders.

Widespread diseases circulated throughout the prison as flies, contaminated water, and lack of medical supplies produced immediate deaths that numbered over one hundred daily and the constant trek to the cemetery as comrades watched as emaciated bodies were loaded onto wagons for the ride. Following shortly, the workers themselves would be carried to the cemetery to be placed in ditches where their fellow inmates had previously been tossed.

Indiscriminate killings occurred daily among prison gangs or guards who shot prisoners from crossing the "Dead Zone." The sheer numbers tell the story! When the final tally was counted, over 13,000 Yankees died as a result of the brutal conditions. They are buried in a cemetery a short walk from the prison wall.

As a prison guard, I was a wreck!

During the three years away from my childhood home in Boxford Forge, Tennessee, Yankees destroyed my home, the barn, and surrounding structures. I eventually discovered my parents had died, my ma from a "broken heart" and my pa from a horrible paper mill accident in New York. I sadly determined my older brother, who had left home with my pa heading north before the war, had died in a southern prison. I asked myself on many occasions if life could be more hurtful. My brother's accounts of his incarceration are recorded in a journal I keep close by! One of my younger sisters had also died from a horrible disease. My two young sisters and ma are buried in Tennessee. My pa is peacefully resting outside of Albany, New York and my older brother in buried in some red Georgia clay near Macon. The only people left in my life are my younger sister, Samantha, Captain Steele, my closest childhood buddy Jonas, and my sweetheart, Mary Lou.

During my experience at Camp Sumter (Andersonville), visits to talk with the local preacher helped as I grew up from the 18 year old kid who entered the army in 1862 to a determined young 21 year old man. The time I spent with preachers seemed to help while other times I became confused and overwhelmed with their comments. Often I questioned my decisions, commitment, and questioned the southern belief that God was on the side of the Confederacy. Still, I was a young innocent proud soldier with many questions about the south's future.

The Treaty

Ulysses S. Grant and Robert Edward Lee sat discussing the peace arrangements that Palm Sunday afternoon in early April 1865. Union soldiers gathered outside relaxing while discussing former battles and planning the future. Rebel forces were a short distance away starving and awaiting word of their fate. Abraham Lincoln and his wife Mary were discussing reconstruction plans while Confederate President Jefferson Davis was on the run escaping through North and South Carolina. And as the two gentlemen recalled their meeting in the Mexican War, they completely understood their similarities and differences. Their backgrounds were different, but their mission was built around one theme-"peace".

General Grant came from the mid-west, Ohio specifically, while Lee came from a history rich area in northern Virginia. Grant had graduated from the U.S. Military Academy, went to fight, eventually ending up in California before the war. On the other hand Lee moved up the ranks and eventually became Superintendent of the U.S. Military Academy at West Point. By 1861, Grant had faltered in Midwest business adventures and was financially struggling while Lee was living handsomely in a beautiful home located on a hill across the Potomac River overlooking Washington DC and the US Capitol.

At precisely one o'clock in the afternoon of the 9th, the General of the Confederate Army, Robert Edward Lee, entered the parlor of Mr. Wilmer McLean's home in Appomattox Court House and waited for the northern general. Unusual as it may seem, Mr. McLean had owned a home near Manassas Junction where the first battle of the War Between the States took place and would now own a structure where the war would end. Located within a few miles of Lynchburg, Virginia, the McLean home near Appomattox Junction had no military significance to either army. Both armies had lost a significant number of men in the previous days and were within feet of one another. For the most part, the fighting had stopped. Lee waited, as his horse Traveller rested outside awaiting its master's return.

Over six feet tall and handsomely dressed for the occasion, 58 year old General Robert E. Lee wore a full dress gray uniform with highly polished boots, a scabbard holding a ceremonial sword, and around his thin waist was a brilliantly colored red sash. Even as Lee thought about his depleted and starving soldiers, their physically and emotionally tired bodies, and the lost southern cause, he was not going to meet Grant without demonstrating the utmost gentlemen respect and honor. Lee's reputation would not falter even if he were surrendering his army. Integrity, honor, discipline, loyalty, and religion rested comfortably inside the southern gentleman. Even though he was ruthless during the war, his pride and deep emotional ties with strong family values, Lee always demonstrated concern about the safety of his men. Proud that they had done their best, he would represent them with the greatest example and presented himself in the most celebratory fashion.

The Union General arrived thirty minutes later wearing nothing that resembled his position except the general's stars on his shoulders. 43 years old and a strong unionist dedicated to the army, Grant removed his hat. He entered wearing an open blouse, basic trousers, and mud stained boots. Except for the stars, he could have been mistaken for a private in any man's army. General Grant was a man with strong convictions, was always confident, and most of all, he was a sensitive man who believed the fighting was over and reconciliation would follow. No punishment was necessary! They shook hands and sat!

Grant had conferred with his staff and present in the room were about twelve of his subordinates including Captain Robert Lincoln, the president's son. Nearby the Confederate leader was with one assistant. The leaders talked!

When the discussion got a little sidetracked by events of previous fought battles some 20 odd years earlier, General Lee asked for treaty specifics and General Grant, with a complete understanding of President Lincoln's post war agenda, informed the southern commander of the following.

First and foremost, there would be no retribution, retaliation, or revenge. There would be no allegations of treason. There would be no trials as rebel soldiers could go home peacefully. Basically, soldiers are to surrender their arms, ammunitions, and supplies. Soldiers will be paroled. Officers would be allowed to claim their horse and return home without any imprisonment. Soldiers who needed horses or mules for spring planting and farming would be allowed to keep their respective animals. There would be no more killing. Soldiers were to return to their homes without any punishment.

The war was over. The Union generosity, espoused by Lincoln, was obvious when the treaty was complete. The Confederate Government was to return to the union and the country would again be identified as the United States.

General Lee asked that formal notes be written and copies be made for both parties. The southern general asked that food be provided for the starving 25,000 soldiers nearby and Grant answered in the affirmative. The meeting lasted over three hours as Grant and Lee reviewed and edited the document.

Together the men exited the McLean home. As both parties left the premises, they shook hands and said their goodbyes. Lee walked down the steps, mounted Traveller, acknowledged the union leader and departed. Both generals immediately returned to their men.

As the southern general approached his men Lee told them he was extremely proud of their achievements, devotion, and commitment. He told them to return home and start a new life. Lee said, " I have done my best. The war is over."

In the Union ranks, soldiers fired rifles in a celebration of the most recent events, but when Grant heard the surrounding explosion, he instructed his men to refrain from shooting as the war was over and "they are our friends". Within hours men from opposing armies laid down their weapons, shook hands, and started reminiscing of their wartime experiences. And one ingredient was common.

Now, they were all Americans, again. Within days General Joshua Chamberlain and his staff received the formal surrender agreement, distributed food to rebel forces, and everyone disbursed. Many returned home to loved ones. Some wandered north or west! Appomattox Court House was for many, the last stop on a wartime experience no one wished to repeat!

Captain Edwin Steele and I had just met and I was looking forward to some peace and quiet. And I knew Mary Lou Gant, my sweetheart, was waiting for me in Clinton, Tennessee. We planned to get married when I returned. Plus, I needed to see my buddy, Jonas!

Two

WASHINGTON DC
APRIL 14, 1865

I arrived in Washington shortly after the treaty had been signed on April 9th. I had walked away from Camp Sumter, located in the small isolated town of Andersonville, Georgia. When I left the Confederate army, I headed north to Clinton for a short visit before visiting pa's grave in Albany and making my way to the federal capital by way of New York City and Baltimore. Then I educated and refreshed myself with newspapers while listening to northerners explain their views about the War Between the States. I just listened and tried to avoid any confrontation or disagree with anything they said. But, the war was over, or at least I thought it was!

Washington, DC was an ugly sight! Pigs roamed freely. Cows circulated the unfinished Washington Monument. Dung was everywhere! Small army tents were full of former soldiers still in uniform. Young and old veterans missing an extremity ambled around while leaning on a cane. Dilapidated buildings surrounded the outskirts of the city. Civilians from all walks of life roamed celebrating the end of the war. Beer toting drunks were everywhere as bartenders helped patrons to their next saloon.

Farmers in overalls, well-dressed businessmen and bankers, politicians, laborers, and rebels walked the streets and filled the saloons and hotels. People in the north continued to refer to the war as the "Civil War." I still thought of it as the "War of Yankee Aggression." And to make matters really complicated, spring rains never stopped and mud, ankle deep, covered the roads. Just getting around was cumbersome!

From the day the treaty was signed on Palm Sunday until I arrived in DC, the population of the city had multiplied and Lincoln was a hero. Citizens wanted to hear the president speak. Yankees demanded quick action. Many hollered, "We won." "Kill Davis," some shouted! "Put Lee behind bars," others insisted. Punish! Punish! Punish! Hurray for Sherman!

The Union President had given a short speech on the front porch of the White House on Tuesday. He described his ideas, but many in the crowd were not happy. His goal was to restore the union with no blame placed on either side as he felt both the north and south share equal responsibility for the previous four year's destruction and each should pay for the restoration. However, there were elements within the north as well as the south that viewed the outcome differently. Some wanted peace while others wanted the south to pay for the destruction. After returning to his family quarters in the White House, Lincoln simply told Mary, his wife, that the speech was not well received, but he refused to punish the south. He simply said, "They are our neighbors and we should treat them as such."

Around noon on Good Friday, I found my long lost Confederate friend, Captain Steele. We had met during the war. He had lost his entire family to Yankees when they invaded the northern section of eastern Virginia. His land was destroyed. His livelihood was gone and he was angry. But through the war we talked, grew up, and with many questions accepted the disasters. In 63, we separated and went different ways. Eventually, I discovered he was my conduit to questions about my brother. He was responsible for sending me Thomas' journal that confirmed his imprisonment and untimely death. But, that Friday afternoon was special!

We shared our family losses. He introduced me to his girlfriend who he planned to marry soon. We laughed about similar stories. I was more emotional than the former captain when describing special events. I mentioned my experience with my brother's girlfriend in Vermont and how I had to explain his death. The captain understood. He was almost thirty and much more mature! At least, that's what I thought! Over some BBQ and beer, we talked about our respective war experience, shared future plans and goals, and agreed to meet the next morning. We had plans to visit the president's home and maybe shake his hand.

Abraham Lincoln had been re-elected in November of 64. The 13th Amendment to the Constitution had been passed by Congress and waiting ratification from the states. And Lincoln's second inaugural address had reconstruction ideas throughout! He closed that March day with:

"With Malice toward none, with charity for all, with firmness in the right, as god gives us to see the right, let us strive to finish the work we are in, to bind up the wounds, to care for him who shall have borne

the battle, to do all which may achieve and cherish a just and lasting peace, among ourselves and with all nations."

The last year of fighting leading to Appomattox was more brutal than the previous three years of the War Between the States. By April 1865, the northern army controlled major cites, railroad routes, and had enlisted forces far superior in numbers to the dwindling rebels. The Confederacy was falling apart and the end was quickly approaching with greater speed. Union leaders were controlling northern battlefields around Richmond and Petersburg. Grant and Lee had battled fearlessly and were tired. Confederate desertions increased daily. Thousands of men simply walked away! Me included! My mind was spent! I was a physical wreck! My family had vanished!

As the end of 64 approached and the calendar turned, food and necessary war materiel were in short supply in both armies, but the northern camp's supply totals were far superior to that in the Confederacy. The Shenandoah Valley, the Confederate breadbasket was controlled by Union General Sheridan's forces and further south, General Sherman controlled the eastern corner of Confederacy. But, both armies were mentally and physically tired. Enlisted men were drained! Officers were ready for a stoppage! Each army had lost important leaders, like generals Jackson, Stuart, and Armistead in the south, and from the north, Kearny, Reynolds, and Sedgwick.

As Easter approached, Southern President Davis destroyed Confederate documents and had escaped Richmond, as it burned to the ground in early April. Grant chased Lee southward. Sherman and Sheridan closed in on central Virginia. By April 9th and the treaty signing, nothing was left of the Confederacy except to feed the starving army and send them home.

On Good Friday, President Lincoln met with his cabinet, asked General Grant and his wife to attend the theater, and had taken a carriage ride with Mary before the sun went down. General Grant had refused the theater invitation on a recommendation from his wife who wished to visit family in New Jersey. Another couple accepted the invitation.

I put the daily paper on the bedside table and went to sleep. It was 10pm, April 14, 1865.

Three

FORD'S THEATER

Saloons, boarding houses, brothels, and hotels were full to capacity! Everyone was in a festive mood! Washington, DC was crowded! Streets were covered with joyous citizens celebrating the war's end! Former army friends and foe reunited to share stories! Some good, some bad, all interesting! As I entered my quarters and walked by the bored desk clerk who was trying not to appear obviously segregated from the fun, I noticed a sign in the boarding house lobby that simply said, "Lincoln to Attend Ford's Theater Tonight."

Extremely tired and wishing to head back to Clinton in the morning, I climbed three sets of stairs to the third floor, and entered my small room. I looked at my journal and made a few entries. I reread a few pages of Thomas' prison journal and thought about my special Amish coin. I went to sleep that April night just a short walk from Ford's Theater thinking about my future with Mary Lou and our approaching wedding. I needed to find my childhood friend Jonas. A cold light rain hit the window as I drifted away.

I had just fallen asleep when I abruptly woke up and thought I was dreaming. I could hear loud noises through the now pouring heavenly liquid. I looked out! Commotion covered the street. People were running and shouting! As I watched people scurrying about as if to hide or question anyone, I wondered what was the fuss! Shielding my eyes and getting wet, I opened the window. Ear piercing screams and yelling controlled the surrounding area. Confusion circulated as strangers questioned others as to the accuracy. I looked further down the street as I watched crying women grab one another asking for answers. What was going on, I asked myself. I grabbed my jacket, went flying down the stairs, walked briskly by the somewhat comatose desk clerk, brushed the Lincoln sign in the lobby, and left the boarding house. I didn't even know where I was headed! I joined the melee'.

As I exited the front door, a black man bumped me saying, "He dead!" I tried to ask him a question, but he left quickly as he grabbed his friends and continued around the corner. What was he talking about? I tried to get an answer from anyone. I grabbed a lady wrapped in a shawl and somewhat drunk as she swung her arms and pushed me away as she continued her swaying down 10th street. I bumped into another fellow dressed in blue and carrying a rifle when I tried to get a response. He simply said, "Those bastards from Dixie killed the president." The crowded street did not allow much movement so I decided to stand still and question anyone willing to answer my questions. That didn't pay off, so I left the area and started looking around. I thought of Captain Steele and his friend. Where did he say he was staying?

The rain finally eased, but mud covered the streets. With all the confused traffic, hundreds of innocent bystanders, idol wagons going nowhere, and too many questions yet to be answered, I slopped along through the ankle deep mud. Within two minutes I was covered with mud and dung from my ankles to my knees.

People were stunned. Innocently, I stopped. Chaos, confusion, sad faces, crying, and worried celebrating citizens asked why. Some stood still in complete shock. Strained faces spreading tension appeared throughout the small and congested streets. People seemed paralyzed with many unable to move or answer even basic questions. I walked around the corner and noticed a small group of congregating blacks. They were angry. Women within the group continued crying and asking why. One huge black man hollered, "Mr. Lincoln gone. What next? Weed goin back?" Someone fired a rifle as Union soldiers hurried up and down 10th street. It was 10:30pm, "Good Friday".

Across the street and up from Ford's Theater, the confusion and noise quickly spread with increasing volume and madness. Mass numbers of people covered the street outside the building.

Eventually, I discovered the president had indeed been shot. Inside John Ford's Theater a young doctor, fresh out of medical school, had tried to stop the bleeding from a head wound. The president had been shot while watching a production of "Our American Cousin" sitting beside his wife and positioned in the presidential box just a few feet away was an Army Major and his young date.

Word quickly spread that nationally known actor John Wilkes Booth, had entered the presidential box and shot President Lincoln with a small .22 caliber pistol. Before attempting to escape over the presidential box, Booth attacked Major Rathbone with a knife causing serious arm injuries before jumping onto the stage and leaving the theater through the back door. Within minutes reports told the story.

Eventually the young doctor cleared the wound and the semi-conscious president was carried across the street and placed in the back room of the Peterson House. Since Lincoln was over six feet tall and the bed was considerably small, the president was place diagonally in the bed as he suffered with the bullet lodged behind his right eye. Labored breathing quickly overcame the president, as blood loss was severe from the massive wound while Mary Lincoln, the President's wife sat uncontrollably crying beside the bed.

Immediately, a massive manhunt got under way. Roads, streets, and bridges around the capital were secured. Military guards were placed around government buildings and a search started for the actor. Rumors started! Hearsay became factual! Anyone within the immediate area had an opinion of the circumstances! Fear of a widespread conspiracy circulated and Vice President Andrew Johnson found his residence under heavy guard.

Not far from the theater, Secretary of State William Seward, was fighting for his life as another assassin was attempting to kill him. Louis Paine, also known as Powell, used a knife attempting to assassinate him as he lay sick in his upstairs bedroom almost directly across the street from the White House. After severely injuring the secretary and his son, Paine escaped. The conspiracy spread to Vice President Andrew Johnson, but the assassin, George Atzerodt, decided otherwise and never made an attempt on Johnson.

I looked for Captain Steele. The confusion continued. It was long passed midnight when I found the captain and we tried to understand what was happening! In the Peterson House Lincoln lay struggling to stay alive. Visitors, friends, government officials, cabinet members, Robert and Mary Lincoln, and others looked in on the dying 56 year-old President. During his escape, Booth had convinced bridge guards that he was an actor headed home from work and they let him through without any trouble. Little did they know, Booth had just attempted to assassinate the President of the United States.

Captain Steele and I talked through most of the night trying to digest what had taken place. We watched as the citizens of the Nation's capital tried to understand what had just transpired. No one had any answers. Rumors spread!

By noon on the 15th of April, Lincoln had died and his body had been transferred to his home. Andrew Johnson had been sworn in as the new President. Booth had escaped the city as the massive manhunt continued. A huge reward was placed for his capture. Like thousands, the captain and I searched for answers and questioned what the future would bring. Basically, we came up blank!

Throughout the day citizens, government officials, and cabinet members attempted to keep the country together. Grant was contacted by telegraph in New Jersey and returned to the capital to command the army. Initially, Secretary of War Edwin Stanton had taken command, but was short lived when Johnson was sworn in.

The captain and I grabbed something to eat at the Royal Saloon. Nothing tasted real good, and we swallowed hard. At that moment, it seemed like the last four years were a complete waste. Everyone, including rebels like me, was looking forward to a peaceful future. Fear set in! "What next," questioned Alley as she served up the cool beer?

I had read many versions of the president's plans for rebuilding and believed he was the foundation that would keep the country together. Was I wrong? Was I too innocent to comprehend the complexity of the situation? I had no answers! My mind wondered. I could not escape my concerns for Jonas! Were plans for former slaves and freed blacks well established?

I asked the captain if he had heard anything that might damage future plans when he said, "JT, the only thing that will harm and interrupt a return to peace will be the countries inability to come together and agree to reunite. Lincoln wanted a United States! Not a Disunited States! Everyone will have to work together. Northern and southern views will have to compromise on political and social plans. Local, state and the federal government will need to make plans that will put people back to work. Slavery is gone! How will we, as a people handle and deal with thousands of blacks, who are now free to live and work where they wish? The way everyone treats one another will be extremely important." Without any specific explanations or examples, I listened as the captain continued.

"People here in Washington will need to lay plans for economic growth without blaming southern leaders or soldiers for the war. You know that Union soldiers were given provisions and small amounts of money when they separated from the war while southern soldiers returned home with no government support. Somehow, rebels will need help. Thousands of wounded, angry, disabled men are roaming the south. Homes, farmland, small towns and large cities have been destroyed and will need to be rebuilt. Where will that money come from?"

Captain Steele took a breath and continued, "The Confederacy is gone. The southern government no longer exists. Lincoln talked about no retribution. Will his plans be enforced? And what are the ideas of the new president? Lincoln was a republican. Johnson is a Democrat. Does he believe like Lincoln? I don't know what Johnson thinks!"

I looked across the saloon floor and saw people with puzzled expressions who seemed as confused as me. Too many questions and very few immediate answers!

We each grabbed another beer, slopped over to the crowded half completed Washington Monument where hundreds who lived in tents discussed the tragic events, and we looked across the Potomac River to Lee's former home now surrounded by tombstones. I murmured, "The south." Cows, pigs, and dogs splashed around in puddles as unconcerned as the still monument!

Everywhere we walked, crowds continued to discuss what had taken place. So did the captain and I! We looked around to see soldiers posted in front of civilian homes, hospitals, government offices, including the White House, and businesses. Everyone was nervous! Normal people continually ran yelling hysterically. Someone hollered, "Catch the bastard." We headed to the capitol building.

With widespread fear that was very obvious, I asked the captain what he thought about rebels who had expressed a willingness to continue to fight in 'hit and run tactics'. Newspapers from Richmond and Charleston had been reporting there was plenty of anger with planters and businessmen in the south over the destruction of their livelihood. "JT, I think those few individuals will eventually find other means of addressing the war's end. Those few guerillas will stop eventually! I hope anyway! I am hopeful all southerners, including leaders of the new south will structure a society that will function not as a south or another part of America, but as a united country." He really sounded like a preacher or politician.

I finally responded with, "Captain, are you kidding me? People everywhere are angry. Northerners want the south to pay. The south is no more. Northerners will invade the south again. How will we as southerners be able to rebuild? Where will we get supplies, farm equipment, or where will I be able to get any money. My confederate notes are worthless! People in the south want help.

And while I was looking for you last night, I met an older man named, Frank, from Baltimore, who said the capital is full of rebel spies who are ready to disrupt anything. He said he heard of a plan to plant bombs in the capitol building and kill more Union soldiers. He said the spies could care less about northern plans. They just wanted to create havoc wherever they could. They wanted to destroy the northern land and cities. They wanted to kill some congressman named Stevens. They said Stevens was from Pennsylvania and spies wanted to kill him because he was from the same state where Gettysburg is located. Is that stupid or what?

I was just getting started when I continued with, "Captain, people are crazy! That makes no sense! Are those spies really that stupid? Look around, captain, there are military patrols everywhere. And you can't get out of the city because all exits are guarded."

I looked at the captain and asked, "And who the hell is John Wilkes Booth?" He responded with, "I don't really know, but we can find out."

Quickly rumors circulated that a rebel conspiracy, designed by southern sympathizer John W. Booth, was taking place. Based on their pro-southern beliefs coupled with their hatred for union control, Booth and others wished to overthrow Lincoln's plans for reconstruction and disrupt any further movement on a union agenda. Booth, a devout southern sympathizer who hated blacks, had initially devised a plan to kidnap the president and exchange him for money that would demand the freeing of southern prisoners. That changed when the war ended!

Booth, the brother of Edwin Booth the famous well-known actor with fame that had spread across this country and Europe, was a fanatic who craved notoriety. John never lived up to the equivalent of his brother! Word circulated the white supremacy racist had attended Lincoln's Second Inaugural Address and watched as Lincoln took the presidential oath. Booth angered even more! Many citizens reported Booth had attended the short speech the president had delivered the previous Tuesday welcoming southerners into the union. Booth wanted revenge. He hollered, "The North invaded the peaceful south."

The government and citizens quickly discovered the conspiracy involved Booth and others. Fear and confusion continued in the capital when Mary Surratt, owner of a boarding house where conspiracy plans were discussed, was implicated and arrested. Mary's son, John, was implicated, but was in Canada at the time. David Herold, the youngster who held Booth's horse outside the theater and had escaped with him, was identified.

By late afternoon, DC citizens and visitors continued to question everything as fear and anxiety spread. Citizens questioned newly installed President Andrew Johnson, who was being guarded with utmost care. What were his plans for reconstruction? Was he a Lincoln follower or were his plans significantly different?

The captain and I listened as citizens jokingly expressed concerns about Mary Lincoln, as her passed emotional problems had been the focus of many editorials during the war. Apparently, she was a thorn in Abe's side! Cartoons had appeared regularly in newspapers showing Mrs. Lincoln on shopping sprees in New York City with her son Tad where she spent lavishly buying gowns and considerable pairs of shoes. Steele commented, "She may go nuts!" And editor of the Tribune, Mr. Greeley always was front and center with his opinion! Northerners could always depend on him to bring things to life!

Easter Sunday wasn't much better as the anxious city of Washington watched and waited. As the sun went down that evening, I had spent two days with the captain and tried to digest all of the newspaper coverage that described the killing and escape. There were detailed descriptions of events at Ford's Theater and the attempted assassination of Secretary of State William Seward. Explanations and editorials on John W. Booth covered the front pages. There were reports of the capture of some of those responsible for the catastrophes. Mary Surratt, Louis Paine, (Powell), and George Azterodt had been apprehended. Booth and his accomplice were still on the loose.

Even preachers got into the act with comments about the future.

Four

ON THE RUN

Since I was a prisoner in the city, I decided to try relaxing and make some entries in my journal. They were not happy entries, but they covered the events of the previous week. Resting peacefully for a few days gave me some satisfaction that I was alive and would eventually get back to Clinton and Mary Lou. Again, I wrote about Jonas as many sleepless nights covered my mind with his safety. Like many, I didn't feel good about the future. Lincoln's agenda would be debated on the streets of America, in the halls of congress, and the living rooms of average citizens.

By mid-week I had followed the events in Washington and was aware of the funeral and circumstances surrounding removal of Lincoln's body from the city. A long ride back to his home in Springfield, Illinois was planned. Apparently, a nine car train would carry the fallen president westward for a fourteen day circuitous trip with stops in big cities like Philadelphia, New York, Albany, Buffalo, Cleveland, and many more before arriving. I found preacher Jonathan Wakefield from Overland Park, Illinois sitting on a bench near the White House one day and we talked at length about many things. I wasn't searching for a man of God. He was just there!

Preachers seem to have a knack for putting things in perspective. Or that was what I thought! Even at 21 years old, I had learned a lot, but I could always use a good cleansing and reminders of what is really important. I had remembered some of the comments from preachers during my war years, but Mr. Wakefield opened my eyes to other conflicting personal concerns. Initially, he sounded ok, but confusion and questions followed!

One of the first comments he brought forth was one similarly made by grandpa about the difference between what God wants and what man wants. Grandpa had made the comments to me in a letter I had received while fighting those mean Yankees. The letter is sitting in Clinton, but I remember what grandpa had mentioned about how man had let his warped mind get in the way of his human misguided wants. Grandpa said man had a way of making a mess of his life!

Mr. Wakefield asked me to think of where I have been, how I survived the war, and where I was headed. Man, he sounded just like grandpa! Neither of the two men was complicated. They both expressed views in simple terms. And if anybody needed simplicity in his life, it was certainly I. So I listened, but things were not as simple as I thought.

Many of his comments I had heard before, either from wartime preachers or from church preachers from Boxford Forge before I enlisted. Boxford Forge that little peaceful town stuck in the corner of Tennessee where simple is truly simple! Mr. Wakefield mentioned things like responsibility, honesty, values, God, stories of Jesus, devotion, and the list never stopped, and as someone looking for answers, I just sat. Since I enjoyed listening to most preachers and wanted to know more about the north, I figured I would change the subject and try to discover other interesting aspects of northern life. That's when I realized simple was truly Not simple!

Eventually, I asked the preacher about Illinois, when he said, "Great place to live. No better state in the north! Great friendly people! Lots of people from Sweden and Norway." "Where is that?" I asked. "Across the Atlantic," he responded. He related stories of his hometown of Overland Park. He described life in the small town that I compared with Boxford Forge, except his small community was located next to a cotton mill where former slaves were taking over the work force. "Too many blacks," he commented. That's the way he described it, 'blacks had taken over the mill.'

I asked him what he thought of the blacks working in northern states when he quickly said, "I guess if they work hard and mind their own P's and Q's everything will be just fine." At that point, he seemed somewhat unsure and I questioned his next comment. I discovered he really wasn't convinced that blacks could adjust to the northern lifestyle. "But they don't fit in," he said. I reached for my journal as he continued.

With a determined look on his face, he described events in a neighboring community. He said, "You know John, there is a large anti-black population here in the north specifically in a section of Brownville, over the river in Indiana. The small town of about 8000 people have rallies every Sunday to protest the invasion of blacks into the north." 'Invasion of former slaves,' I said to myself as he continued. "Some of the whites in the town of Brownville lived in the south before the war and now want nothing to do with blacks. They consider all blacks slaves, and think all blacks deserve nothing from the superior white population." I found that comment about the 'superior whites' disturbing, but I let him continue.

"Mr. Chandler, the local mayor, wants to see his town free of blacks and has encouraged the local citizens to drive the blacks back south. Matter of fact, Mr. Chandler came to Indiana from southern South Carolina where he once owned about 50 slaves on his tobacco farm." With some idea of where he was headed, I questioned the preacher about the 13th Amendment.

He said that certain things the federal government passed over the last few years have been wrong. 'Wrong, I said to myself!' If the preacher was trying to hide his anger about blacks, he surely was doing a poor job! Was he preaching his warped ideas on Sundays?

I jumped up angrily asking, "You mean to tell me that you think freeing the slaves and giving them an opportunity to live in a society where they are treated as equals is wrong? I can't believe you said that! What are you saying? Do all northerners feel this way? How big is the black population in Indiana anyway?"

"Hold your horses JT!" he responded. Almost instantly, my mind exploded with anger as my face turned red. He tried to continue, but I refused to let him speak when I flung my arms in the air and yelled, "I thought you were a man of God where the Bible is more important than any man made laws. Does the Bible tell me that whites are better or superior to blacks? If so, show it to me. Does your God tell you to hate blacks or not treat them fairly? What does your God tell you to do with your 'so called' inferior race? You sound like some angry southern preacher who wants white control. I thought your responsibility was to preach and teach goodness. You seem to be saying one thing one moment and something entirely different in the next. Why should I listen to you? You are no better than former plantation owners. Nathan Bedford Forest would love to have you in his ranks."

Mr. Wakefield sounded like an imposter, as he is no better off than some hateful rebel or misguided Yankee. First, he talks about God. Then he says the north is a great place to live, while he tries to convince me that freeing blacks is bad. I reckon his small town may be considerably different than my little Boxford Forge! From that moment on, I did not feel real comfortable with the preacher and eventually said I needed to find some friends. I had had enough slanted views of blacks! Maybe, he wasn't even a preacher! I walked away and never looked back.

"See ya," I said as I quickly separated myself from the deranged stranger and his conflicting lifestyle. I'm glad I didn't belong to his church or have to listen to him every Sunday. I wondered if the blacks in his town were any better off than the blacks across the river. I mumbled to myself! Is the rest of the north so focused on blacks in their individual state that they cannot see the big picture? What is the big picture, anyway? Are northerners ready to move forward after this destructive war has ended? How many other Yankee towns and big cities have similar ideas spreading among its population? Are his comments widespread or are there small pockets of anti-black sentiment?

Maybe I need to get out of DC and get back to Clinton, Tennessee where life is a lot simpler! I thought about my childhood black friend, Jonas, and began thinking about his safety. 'Sweet Jesus!' I mumbled.

I grabbed my floppy hat and proceeded back to Pennsylvania Avenue where a parade had just departed near Lincoln's home headed to the capitol. The former President's body was in a wagon pulled by slow moving tired mules headed uphill.

Surrounded by thousands of onlookers standing on the sidewalks and in windows, a black northern infantry unit led the parade, followed closely with the wagon carrying the fallen president. Immediately behind the wagon were the president's two sons. Robert, the Harvard student and recently promoted Union Captain, walked hand in hand with his younger brother Tad. Mary was not in the parade as depression had overcome her and she was resting at the White House dressed in black, the color she would eventually wear until she died. Also in the long parade were wounded soldiers wrapped in rags or medical cloth! Seemed like everyone wanted to be part of the activities! Flags were flown at half-staff on all government buildings and in many private businesses.

Looking up and down Pennsylvania Avenue, I could see farmers in overalls, beggars looking for a handout, average citizens, saloon owners, and more citizens just trying to be part of the ceremony. Citizens shoved and maneuvered just to see the president! Other people were positioned in business and government buildings or on top of buildings attempting to simply get a look at the parade. Some stood in wagons to see better while others were mounted on horses or mules to get a peek. This parade had special meaning to practically everyone, man, woman, black, white, Catholic, Protestant, Jew, rich or poor. No one wanted to be left out! Former combatant in union blue or butternut Carolina overalls stood side by side. I spotted Captain Steele and his girlfriend who were standing in the middle of a crowd near the Old Post Office watching as soldiers from New York, Pennsylvania, Massachusetts, Maine, Rhode Island, Ohio, Illinois, Maryland, and a small unit from Indiana marched in step on their way forward. When I saw the unit from Indiana, I recalled what that preacher had just said! I wonder what Lincoln would have thought of that man of the cloth's comments!

Finally, I mentioned to Captain Steele where I had been and expressed my dissatisfaction with what I had discovered as the three of us watched soldiers march and bands played. By the time the body and rest of the parade had reached the capitol, another light rain started and those interested in seeing the casket formed lines that wound around the Capitol and down the street. People wanted to pay their respects to the former president now resting in the center of government.

Booth

Miles away in the forest and countryside of Maryland, the assassin, John W. Booth was trying to stay alive.

Two hours after his theatrical performance in Ford's theater and a successful escape out of Washington, Booth stopped at the Surratt Inn to pick up some needed supplies, including weapons and ammunition. Booth and David Herold were on the run and the government placed a huge reward on Booth's head. The pair continued riding through the woods of Maryland! Booth's leg had broken when he jumped from the presidential box as his heel got caught on an American flag and he fell awkwardly to the floor. It required some medical attention.

Booth needed help and upon arriving in the middle of the night at the farm of Dr. Samuel Mudd on the 15th, he received care. Dr. Mudd set the broken leg. Booth shaved his beard and rested. Within a few days, with the help of David Herold, Booth thanked the doctor and left heading to the safety of the dense woods.

By the end of April, I was running out of money. Newspaper accounts detailing events of the previous month were being consumed and read by all Americans. Greely and his reporters at the Tribune tried to find some comfort with supporting the new Johnson administration, while General's like Grant attempted to settle the turbulent waters within the military. General Sherman and Confederate General Johnston finally ended their fighting in Carolina and agreed to outrageous terms outlined by the northern general. When the news of the impending treaty reached Washington, it was obvious corrections needed to be made.

William Tecumseh Sherman had designed a treaty that in part gave southern planters the same personal property they had before the war. That simply meant slavery would be reinstituted. Secretary of War was outraged as was the entire former cabinet, even Johnson. With the help of Grant and others in the new administration, the so called 'Sherman Treaty' was rewritten to resemble what Grant and Lee had signed at Appomattox in early

April, basically giving pardons to those who had opposed the northern invasion and those soldiers who fought for the Confederacy. However, there were a few exceptions!

I continued to make detailed entries in my fattened journal! Many were down right disturbing! Editors in Richmond never stopped their coverage of the aftermath. The war and the assassination took front stage and souvenir seekers were everywhere!

Magazine stories from the south described over anxious soldiers ransacking the Wilber McLean house after Grant and Lee departed stealing tables, candlestick holders, upholstery from chairs and sofas. Souvenir seekers were everywhere! The table where Grant and Lee sat to sign the treaty simply disappeared. Celebrations took on many forms as souvenir seekers escaped with goods from the Peterson house, including wallpaper, and stripped items from the bedroom where Lincoln died. Minutes following the murder at Ford's Theater, to preserve history, rambling unworthy citizens ransacked the entire 10th street building taking whatever was not tied down, including chairs, boards, and pictures. Quickly, John Ford closed the theater.

In other parts of DC, citizens ripped apart Yankee and Confederate unit flags to preserve a small article of war. Any government building was at the mercy of roaming thieves as ink wells, cups, saucers, documents, curtains, tokens, military uniforms, belt buckles, caps, counterfeit money, and horse bridles disappeared. And uncertainty and turmoil continued as pigs and cows ran wild through the tenting muddy area between the Washington Monument and the legislative branch of the new United States.

While the new government was reorganizing in DC, northern newspapers daily reported Yankee hatred of the south. 'They caused the war,' was the call. Civilians blamed the south for killing Lincoln, and wanted the south to pay. The constant demand for the capture and hanging of the Confederate President was discussed in saloons and written about in all newspapers. April was coming to an end, but there was nothing in the country that appeared peaceful. Everyone had an opinion and wished to express them selves!

While the northern pulpit attempted to calm congregations, riots spread in many cities calling for abusive tactics and laws to control those rebels. Angry congregations formed secret societies to deal with issues. Unhappy citizens approached state capitols to protest. Some state legislatures wanted laws to control the movement of former slaves into their respective states, while others wanted laws to create better working conditions in factories and mills. Some states wanted the federal government to protect them from outlandish taxes that were imposed to help pay for the war. And throughout the land unhappy physically and mentally handicapped veterans returned home with little to offer their community.

As the month came to a close, John W. Booth had been killed in a shoot out, on the farm owned by Mr. Garrett. Booth had arrived at the farm on the 24th. During the afternoon of the 26th, federal troops arrived. When the assassins were asked to surrender, David Herold, Booth's accomplice walked from the barn. With Booth inside and refusing to surrender, the barn was set on fire. Gunfire erupted. Federals fired continuously. Booth fired back. When the shooting finally stopped, Booth was severely injured and taken to the porch of the house where he died and Herold was returned to Washington to stand trial.

With Booth's death and the arrest of eight others, the stage was set for an interesting turn of events, as a military tribunal was assembled to prosecute the conspirators. David Herold, George Azterodt, Louis Powell, Mary Surratt, Michael O'Laughlin, Edward Spangler, Samuel Arnold and Dr. Samuel Mudd would stand trial for conspiracy and the murder of Abraham Lincoln.

As Lincoln's body was arriving at his home in Springfield, Illinois, I located Captain Steele and we talked for hours. "Much too much happening at such a rapid pace," I complained. "DC's a mess." Captain Steele swallowed and simply said, "John Trenton McMurtree, we all have a cross to bare. Lets get out of Washington." I responded, "I agree, captain."

As I was recording recent information in my journal that night, I recalled the small town of Port Royal where Booth was killed, was just a short walked from Fredericksburg. That reminded me of the battle of Fredericksburg in the winter of 62-63 and the horror of war. 'The Sunken Road' 'Mayre's Heights' 'Slaughter.'

With May on the way, I was looking forward to getting back to Mary Lou. My wedding! Samantha! Jonas! Cecil! Washington had given me more than I asked for! I tried to focus more on my future. I was tired. I wanted some peace and quiet and even made a few entries in my journal about more promising days, but similar to military days where events change quickly, I learned there was more excitement and turmoil close by, plus I was fighting another bout of pneumonia!

Five

DEVASTATED CONFEDERACY

Eventually, I realized too many days in the north had drained me. As I watched the events unfold in Washington where confusion and disarray exploded with considerable uncertainty, I welcomed a change and wished to return to the south. Exhausted and looking for concrete answers about my future, I needed to make some entries in my journal. Maybe that will relieve some of my anxiety, I thought.

Journal Entry April 28,1865

Just a few comments! My thoughts are running ragged. Captain Steele is close by in a saloon with his girl friend. He said they plan on getting married shortly. He wants to move to southern Virginia, raise hogs, and farm. He said his military days are over and wishes never to see another Yankee or rebel uniform. He mentioned he may try some schooling but he wasn't sure. Some school named Washington. News has just come in that John Booth has been killed and people want a trial for those captured who are still behind bars. And they want it now! Many say rebels are causing all the trouble. Jack, a former soldier from New Hampshire, said that more control over the blacks is needed here in the north and he does not want any more niggers coming north. First the preacher, now Jack! For me, I'm confused, but I don't like to complain. Seems like everyone has an opinion about blacks and where they fit in!

I still have regretful thoughts of leaving the beaten rebel army when I left Andersonville. I remember feeling angry the way prisoners were treated! Captain Steele said to forget it and go on with my life, but

39

I find it hard to concentrate and continually think I made a terrible mistake. I think about the friends I left behind. I just walked away! I think about abandoning my responsibilities. Did I show no respect for the Confederate Army and what it stood for? Could I have done more? And I think of the hundreds of thousands on both sides who did the same. James, Willard, Harvie, Darrell, Guilford, Prentiss, Chandler, Harris and more left unannounced. I wonder if they made it home or where did they go? I still think of the prisoners who left Andersonville on what they thought was an exchange program, only to die in some swamp in Alabama or get shot by angry roaming mobs. I wonder what happened to the sketch artist from Chicago. I think his name was Jon Sanborn! I hope he made it home.

When I talked with the captain, I mentioned I was tired of war and seeing all the destruction, tired of watching people die needlessly, tired of watching state governments fight among themselves and tired of broken promises like better food, getting a new uniform, or that train ride that only came when I headed to Camp Sumter. One thought haunts me, my pride to be a southerner. I love my land. I long for the day when I can raise a family, work my own farm, and reside peacefully with loving neighbors. I love my family, even if it is no longer of the same dynamics and composition as it was when I left in 62. At times for a few years, I loved to be called a confederate soldier. But now, I look forward to returning to my home and am fearful of what lies ahead.

The following are some of my thoughts regarding the assassination of Abe Lincoln. I remember saying to the captain that we had planned on going to see him the next day as we retired on the 14th. I had looked forward to that experience. First, I thought, he was on the right tract to rebuild the south. I like what I had heard, even when others questioned him. He sounded like a thoughtful human who wanted peace in the country with everyone working together. I liked what I had read in his speech at Gettysburg in 63 and his comments at the capitol earlier this year in March. When I heard of the agreement at Appomattox, I was satisfied the two generals had made the right decisions and Grant was siding with Lincoln's plans for rebuilding the south.

But I still am not convinced the North is ready to lend a hand to help the south. Too many people with strong opinions who are in power don't want to sit and talk things out. They're arguing now! And when decisions about the former confederacy are clearly defined, who will answer? Will it be any southerner? Will it be all blacks? Will former planters be safe from northern policies and laws? Or will lost souls like me, Samantha, and Mary Lou who are as innocent as any person in Tennessee or any other southern state, have to answer to abusive northerners who are invading the south. Selby Travers, a businessman from somewhere in New York, said he was headed to Georgia to help clean up the mess. That's what he called it, "Clean up the mess!" He bragged about owning a clothing store.

I'm beginning to trust very few people. Preachers of the north have left too many questions about their sincerity. Even though, the new President Johnson is from Tennessee, I'm not sure he is in agreement with others about rebuilding the south. He is reported saying that blacks are lesser folks than whites. That comment is not right! I have some real bad feelings about rebuilding my little farm in Boxford Forge.

My confederate notes in my pocket are worthless. I have very little money left from what Mr. Adams gave me; maybe just enough to catch a train ride home.

Like the captain said the other day, I need to get on with my life. I need to get that train and head south. I'll write more later.

JT

The next day I met Captain Steele and his girl friend at the train station and said goodbye as he reassured me things would be ok. I told him not to worry about me and I would write when I was safely home in Clinton. He tried to assure me he was fine, would be married shortly, and ready to go on with his new life. Again, he made everything seem so simple.

As I said so long to DC, I paid my eight dollars and boarded a train near the capitol with newspapers in my sac. Hundreds of lost souls did the same thing. Men who guarded bridges and major roads after the assassination were no longer positioned or needed as a somewhat relaxed atmosphere now overcame the capital. Hundreds, who had been stuck in DC since April 14th, wanted to get out as soon as possible while others were demanding punishment for the co-conspirators who awaited trial.

April had been a critical month with the Confederate government evacuating Richmond, the peace treaty signing at Appomattox, Lincoln's death and the capture of the assassin, while in the west Yankee and rebel forces still engaged one another. And to make newspaper writing more exciting, Jefferson Davis was still on the run and being hunted by Union soldiers in the Carolinas and Georgia.

Whites dressed in their Sunday best, blacks with sacs over their drooping shoulders, many former soldiers dressed in rags with gray caps and saddened faces, and normal citizens looking for a return to a peaceful atmosphere took seats in the former military transport. The Union 4th Infantry Regimental Black unit from North Carolina was headed south to return home after suffering huge losses when over eighty percent were killed in the last three months of the war. Many stood! A few sat!

Some union soldiers scrambled aboard to find superiors as their responsibilities were not finished and were expected in Richmond to assist in the recovery effort. There was a little shoving, swearing, and pushing, but generally everything went peaceful. Located near the back of my car were about ten blacks all standing except one! I eyed a vacant seat and sat next to a tall black man! Everyone was talking! No one listened as the noise level increased!

Richmond, the former capital of the Confederacy, was a few hours away and after reading a sad story on page one about three orphans who were beaten and abandoned by their parents, I turned to page three of the Washington Daily and read that by the end of April, all Lincoln conspiracy prisoners had been transferred to the Arsenal Prison. Soon after their capture they had been placed on Ironclads, positioned in the Potomac River, except Mary Surratt who had be secured in a female prison. With John W. Booth dead, all eight were awaiting trial for the assassination of Abraham Lincoln. The trial date had been set!

On page six of the Washington Daily was an article titled "Freeman's Bureau." The elderly black man sitting beside me looked over my shoulder as the train chugged along heading southerly into what I considered welcome territory. The article was educational, as the Freeman's Bureau had been established in March of 65 to enforce the rights of freed blacks so I turned and asked Mr. Charles Henry Moses if he had any information about the organization when he responded, "Hell no son, we blacks need jobs. Mr. Harpeth, ours leader say we need learnin. Mr. Harpeth leader say we need to vote. He'ed live in Washington and goin' to Charleston to help ours people. Mr. Harpeth, a preacher say he wants to raise monies for poor and sick."

I looked at Mr. Moses and asked where he was going when he replied, "To Fredericksburg and den to Charleston." "Is Fredericksburg where you call home, " I asked. "Yes sir, but weed not stayin long. Charleston, " he said. Was he really going back to his former home, I thought and for what? Mr. Moses quickly informed me he knew very little about the Bureau and trusted the preacher as I returned to the paper and continued reading. "Tell me about you son," he said.

We talked as the car bumped along and he refreshed my memories of the battle in his hometown in late 62. I told him I was defending his town when the Yankees crossed the river and invaded causing massive destruction accompanied by stealing before they retreated. I mentioned Marye's Heights when he told me his grandpa was a slave in the area working on a tobacco farm. He proudly referred to his grandpa as Father Moses. He described him well over six feet, arms as big as a mule's ass, and was repeatedly beaten for minor things like not saying 'sir' or 'massa' to the mean overseer. Mr. Moses said his grandpa died as the result of beating and starving when the master put him in a shed with no food. "Tat happened years before the war," he finished.

The loud talking in the train certainly didn't help the noise level as soldiers yelled about their most recent military adventures. Some discussion centered on the assassination, while other topics earmarked future plans and women. Swearing and vulgar comments quickly brought back memories of camp life where bragging and loud verbal exchanges controlled the night. Some things never change, I thought.

As I was preparing another question, Mr. Moses described his pa's escape when he was very young and how his grandpa and an older brother were beaten as a result. He commented, "We'ed hate massa Hainsworth! Fifty lashes and no food for days! Ma sent to the big house to work! Sister raped by whitie!" Completely understanding his feelings when my mind reflected back to Jonas's pa, I changed the subject and asked Mr. Moses what he planned to do when he got back home from his work in Charleston.

He said his two sisters and two brothers were still in the countryside living in shelters with many young offspring. "My sisters and brothers livin on the old Prichard farm and are ok. Ten other slave families work to build de farm. I get work when I come back, but first I help my cousins in the Charleston get their life back," he responded.

Mr. Moses was not married and had escaped about eight years ago. He mentioned a former tobacco plantation near Fredericksburg, named "Hatfield Haven", was planning on hiring workers and his brothers wanted work. Even though Mr. Moses looked considerably older than me, he informed me he was only about 35 years old. He said he couldn't remember his exact age and no one ever told him when he was born.

I really had trouble believing he was returning to such a brutal destructive area. Why? He must have some horrible memories of his younger years! Why not go elsewhere? Why not go north and find a job. Why return? What's there? The land is destroyed. The farms and plantations no longer resemble the past! Will he be comfortable trusting white people, who are already invading the south in large numbers? Can he truly believe the preacher? Will he be able to rebuild? Too many questions!

We continued to talk. We talked about farming, his brothers and sister's kids, his love for his family, and the future. He said one of his sister's children was half black and half white. Maybe the rape! He commented he was worried about many blacks and whites that are not happy about Mr. Lincoln being killed. He said he had heard about angry northerners who faulted rebels for the killing. He also mentioned his brothers had warned him about some former rebel soldiers forming gangs to punish blacks for not following orders. "Whose order," I asked. "Theirs," he answered. He finally said, "I just want to be left alone." I could not have agreed more!

With a few short stops behind us, the train was approaching Fredericksburg our final stop before Richmond when I complimented Mr. Moses about his future plans and wished him well. I gave him a hard peace of bread I had from my stuffed pack along with some ham from Sammy's saloon. "Good luck, Moses," I said as I looked out at the desolate landscape.

Richmond 1865

The train arrived in Richmond, the destroyed Confederate capital around 6pm. I looked out the train window! Streets were covered with blacks looking for help of any kind. Six or seven pigs ran by my window followed by a small group of teen-agers hollering and slopping through the four-inch deep mud! Former union and rebel opponents mingled around discussing wartime experiences while consuming recently discovered whiskey and smoking disgusting foul smelling cigars. Weather beaten women crying and carrying naked babies approached the train asking for any assistance. "Starvin," they hollered. Food, clothing, medicine, or money! Hundreds of citizens wearing nothing but rags struggled along asking for anything and everything. In the distance I could hear music from a military band that was obviously missing any organization. It was just noise!

I de-boarded the train, walked a few steps, and was immediately overcome with the massive destruction. My shoulders dropped. My lips froze! My eyes swelled wide open. My rubber legs collapsed. I had no idea the degree to which the once beautiful city was now nothing compared to the past. She was, but shambles! Life for many was at a standstill and for hundreds more retreating backwards.

A small child approached me and asked if I knew where her mother was when I told her I had no idea. Emerging from the corner of the building, her brother pleaded, "Please help us, we have not eaten in two days and are lost. We have been looking for our parents for over two weeks and have been living in the warehouse next to the river. I killed a couple of rats three days ago and that was our last food."

I tried to get away, but the two followed me toward the center of the city.

It started to rain as the 7 year-old, her 15 year old brother and I rested on

44

a cement slab inside a small building where a sign identified the dilapidated structure as the 'First Bank of Richmond.' Jessica and Samuel introduced themselves as we looked toward the James River that was overflowing from repeated upriver spring rains. "JT," I said as the two kids looked in my baggage for something to eat. We talked for thirty minutes as they detailed their passed few weeks. I felt bad and hopeless while listening to their descriptions but felt I needed to move on. "Here is some ham and bread," I said as I stuck out my hand.

The stars and stripes were flying on the capitol dome, and all remaining buildings close by were nothing but a thin skeleton. Bricks and mud covered the landscape. Chimneys stood isolated. A tall black man struggling along with his head down passed by whipping two mules pulling what looked liked some form of a carriage. The broken back seat had a woman and two small children inside. He never stopped or looked in our direction as the unrecognizable horrible music continued in the distance.

Across the street, about twenty men from a Massachusetts unit were wandering around attempting to look busy and not far away, an angry group of citizens did the same when someone hollered, "Where is old Jeff Davis when you need him?" No one answered! On a hill close to the capitol was another gathering of blacks listening to a preacher apparently informing them that help from the north was coming. Cheers were frequently expressed as arms pointed to heaven!

Jessica pointed to a building that was a former foundry and mentioned her pa had worked there and helped make weapons for the rebel army. I wondered if she really understood anything about manufacturing or the needs of the army. Samuel said, "Tredegar Works." 'Ok,' I murmured. Jessica proudly said her pa was a 'good man.' She kept talking about her parents and one older brother who had been killed in the war when Sam spoke up and said both parents had left them one night and never returned. "They just left," I questioned? "Just left," said Jessica. Her tone changed a little. "Just left," she sadly said again looking at the ground!

Samuel had talked with other kids in Richmond looking for his parents, but had no luck. The kids had found some shelter and food in the newly established kids home, known as Christian Landmarks, located in a section of the local hospital, but the facility did not have any sleeping space available. Samuel said they slept in the hallway for about a week, but were told food was in short supply and the northern government was sending help. Samuel said they decided to continue their search without any success and wanted to return to the hospital, but when they climbed the steps and asked for help, they were turned away. "We have been on the streets for days," commented Jessica.

"They just turned you away," I asked? There was no response. I began to wonder if they were actually telling me the truth.

I looked around with deep sadness! The city was a mess! Once beautiful homes, banks, factories, government buildings, and businesses were now nothing but a front wall with three missing sides. The destruction was widespread. The entire city had been destroyed when the Confederate government burned its documents, set fire to many government structures, and left in early April. What the rebel forces didn't destroy, the Yankees did. "Lets go back to the hospital," I said.

Eventually, I found the kids shelter at Christian Landmarks and I asked for help for the two kids. After two days of asking accompanied by a plea from the local preacher, the two children were accepted into the home and I started looking for a train to Roanoke. I felt better about the kid's safety. Plus, I had had enough of Richmond. But the speedy journey south encountered more unexplained delays.

It was May when the train rolled into Roanoke as I paid twenty cents for the newspaper and began to read. On May 10th, the former Confederacy President Jefferson Davis, outfitted in a dress, had been captured by Yankee soldiers in the small town of Irwinsville, Georgia located in the southern part of the state. The former president was tortured for two weeks by Union soldiers. Without any trial, Jefferson Davis was sent to Fort Monroe in northern Virginia and according to the paper, he would spend a long time in prison.

I grabbed my journal and made more entries. I was sitting in a train station waiting the next train to Knoxville when I started to write.

May 19, 1865

I might address my comments to Mary, but it makes no difference who reads my story as unforeseen events have unfolded over the last few weeks. My mind reverts to disbelief. I have expressed a desire to marry and am committed to Mary. I have had thoughts about grandpa. I have to keep reminding myself that I am young and still years away from maturity. I still feel like a kid who has seen considerable but at times I feel grown up. Confused, yes! Questions.

As the past few weeks have swiftly passed away, I find it hard to believe the sad situation in our land. Talking with Mr. Moses, seeing the kids in Richmond with no parents, and viewing the destructive city and parched landscape of the south, leads me to question whether the south can be rebuilt. Even the railroad tracks from Richmond to

Roanoke were destroyed and on two occasions the train was sidelined to allow workers the opportunity to rebuild. How long will it take to rebuild? Who will guide, instruct, provide, or even participate in the rebuilding plans for the south?

The once agricultural rich south now is home to desolate hills and valleys. On my ride from Richmond to Roanoke over and thru the mountains of once beautiful Virginia, I became quite discouraged. It was extremely depressing to view vacant farms and fields. It was horrible to sit and watch mile after mile of nothing that came close to normal farming conditions. Barns and farmhouses were memories. Broken wagons and carriages sat very, very still!

There were no animals roaming. They had starved! Dead animals could still be seen but the war was over! Was fighting still going on in the mountains of central Virginia? There was nothing growing. Even in the Shenandoah Valley, the once productive fields that provided the food supply for the rebel army now rested beside forest that were blackened from war torn fires. Broken caissons, silent cannons, idol old rifles, even torn and ragged clothing was scattered throughout the desolate land. Tobacco, corn, greens, and former cotton fields grew nothing. The planting season meant nothing. Men and women were not to be seen.

It's hard to see any good coming. As I read comments from editors who proclaim that there is a bright future, I ask them to travel to the interior of the south and witness the war results. I ask them to talk with young rebel soldiers and get first hand comments about war. I ask this because I have over the past few years had horrible dreams that resurface periodically that remind me of where I have been the last three years. I relive battles. I relive camp life. I relive long marches. I relive the personal wounds. I relive the horrors of hospital stays. In my dreams I rewrite letters to my brother who died in a Confederate prison.

I like to think I will be ok. I told the captain I was ok, but do I really believe that comment? I have about twelve federal dollars in my pocket and hope it will get me home. Am I ok?

May 22,1865

I'm still in Roanoke. Train tracks south of the city have not been repaired and the word here is that it may take another week. I thought my return to Clinton would be made by now, but maybe tomorrow will bring some positive results.

For the past few days I have been helping out in a livery stable and have earned enough money to feed me and pay for my trip south. Two days ago a band of ex-rebel soldiers came into town and beat three blacks who were working in a barn. The rebels explained to the blacks, they couldn't work as that work was reserved for whites. After the beating the gang resurfaced and hung the three the next night. Two white workers in the station found the three yesterday in a tree and buried them. About a dozen Yankee soldiers are in town, but they have done nothing regarding the incident. They are no better than the rebels! Every time a story like that appears I fear for Jonas.

The local paper is saying that the trial of the conspiracy criminals in DC will put a rope around those eight. Prentiss Heflin, the editor, says they all should be shot. Mr. Heflin says they all were the cause of this mess, even Mary Surratt, the owner of the boarding house where the gang met and planned. Shoot Doctor Mudd too, he wrote. I said to myself, 'How could Mudd know what happened, he lived miles from DC?' Anyway, it does not look good for those crazy stupid criminals.

I'll write more later as Mr. Fleming just came by to announce a train would be ready for the ride to Knoxville on the 24th. "The 24th of May, I asked?

May 30,1865 – 10pm

As you can guess, I finally arrived in Knoxville a little later than expected, but safe and sound as I wait. I will get a horse tomorrow morning and make the ride to Clinton. I can't wait much longer to see Mary and Samantha and explain to them my experiences over the last few months. I had plans to get married in early May, but Mary and me will have to plan for another date. I grabbed an old Knoxville paper and turned to the back page. Plus, I need to talk with Jonas.

The headline at the top of the page said, "CAPITOL TO WHITE HOUSE." I had read enough of the brutality of war, the assassination of Lincoln, the anti-black feelings that were common in the north as well as the south, and was looking for something different. Even though the article was about Union victories and the celebration that followed, I needed something positive to carry me home. O hell, I'll read it anyway! A celebration parade had been scheduled.

The article was dated May 22, 1865. It described the three-mile march in DC. The newspaper described General Meade's Army of the Potomac, well dressed in military uniforms with shinning boots and brass as they passed the reviewing stands near the White House. Following Meade's forces were the soldier's of General Sherman who had marched hundreds of miles through mud, swamps, and rain. Their tattered uniforms draped the malnourished white bearded old men carrying worn out rifles as they paraded by the reviewing stand and thousands of loyal citizens. Truly the two units differed greatly!

The editor of the Knoxville continued the story by stating that the northern Secretary of War, some guy named Stanton, had always been constantly at odds with Union General Sherman. The disagreement centered specifically on the Sherman-Johnston Treaty that basically ended the fighting in the east. Well, when Sherman broke ranks at the end of the parade he walked by Stanton positioned in the reviewing stands and did not shake his hand. He simply walked by saying nothing. Certainly, a show of disrespect for the secretary!

The final comment at the bottom of the page was anything but encouraging as it focused on differences and problems between the two sections of the country. Uncertainty prevailed!

Clinton has got to be a welcome sight!

JT

Six

TENNESSEE

My worn out horse and I arrived in Clinton to the open arms of Mary. The spring passed and summer of 1865 welcomed me home, when Samantha questioned, "When are you two getting married? I had spent enough time in the north for a while and was glad to be in familiar surroundings. Mary and I quickly got married and reside in Clinton as I work at the hardware store with a little help from my buddy Jonas and Mary's brother Cecil. I had reconnected with Jonas and our respect and trust in one another continued. He even mentioned schooling and maybe college as he had heard people talking about some newly organized blacks only state colleges forming in the south. That comment about 'blacks only schooling' led to many discussions over the days and weeks that followed.

I settled in, but the war years invaded my emotional landscape with frequent reflections of the past. I continued to have bouts fighting pneumonia with coughing spells spitting up blood as my lungs struggled with pain. Nightmares of battles and my experience as a prison guard never seemed to leave and I was constantly reminded of the war as Union soldiers occasionally presented themselves in our town. From the middle years of the war till its end, federal troops had been scattered throughout the northeastern corner of Tennessee where local union loyalists continued to make their presence known by welcoming union forces dressed in blue. And similar to war years, Yankee presence was everywhere!

1865 ended with a small unit of thirty Yankees roaming the area living in tents positioned about two miles from the middle of Clinton. Many were peaceful and kind except for one little corporal who thought he was the next

George Washington. Thankfully, he only came to town around payday while drinking himself toward insanity and swearing the south needed former slaves as he said, 'keep your blacks, we don't want them in the north'. I confronted him one day asking if he believed in slavery. He responded, "Hell no, but I don't want them up north either." I could never understand his position. When I asked him where are they to go? He simply told me to go to hell and take them too.

1870

Clinton had seen enough turmoil in the last ten years. Yankee occupation, declining population when many locals headed west or north, and businessmen, like Mary's pa, suffered through hard times. But, with the onset of a new decade I was looking forward to better times. The years following the silencing of the guns were trying and challenging for all! Changes were taking place quickly! The country was experiencing growing pains and everyone was involved.

However, when the war ended and I returned south, different events that transformed the nation seemed to emerge from nowhere. There were local and state events. There were northern events. There were strictly southern issues. I made entries and referred to my journal regularly.

Mary and I got married in July of 65 and immediately wanted to start a family. She never let me forget my war years comment about having a dozen children, but as sometimes happens in life things don't always work out as planned. Looking back, just before Christmas Mary had pregnancy problems and bled for sometime losing a lot of blood. Doctor Capp came to the farm. After the bleeding stopped the doctor said that a baby boy had passed during the bleeding, but Mary would be fine after weeks of rest.

Within the next four years Mary would successfully deliver two children, one boy named Thomas Trenton and a girl named Samantha Maryanne. I had mentioned schooling in my journal. Mary agreed. Not now, she insisted!

We had started a small farm with about fifty acres near the base of the mountains and by the new decade things were looking somewhat ok. Mr. Hershel Izard sold us the land and house for two hundred and ten dollars and said we could pay him as we went. Jonas and his family were close by. Both the McMurtrees and the Manfords raised hogs, chickens, goats that were a constant pain in my side, and cows. Betsy was my favorite white face! For beef Jonas had a prize bull and I bought six breeding cows. We shared the annual offspring and made a few dollars selling what we did not need. Along with four mules to help with farm work, I bought a horse from a former livery stable owner who had decided to head west across the mountains where he planned to raise tobacco in the Blue Grass State. "Prime fertile land," he had said.

Across the way Jonas had his own horse and was growing a small patch of tobacco while caring for his farm animals including a huge collection of honeybees. We got together every day at the hardware store and on slow days we would ride down to the bottom and race remembering those good ole days. His horse was always faster than my fat old mare. From childhood to adults our relationship only improved as the days went by!

Over the days and weeks Mary, me and Jonas and his wife got together and discussed where we had been over the previous twenty years and on many occasions I referred to my journal entries specifically, the events of the 60's. One Sunday evening in December just before Christmas we gathered our kids and sat around the roaring fireplace. Checking my notes I discovered the following. And by the way, my spelling greatly improved. I read the following entry dated:

July 30, 1865

By the end of June of 65 the eight conspirators associated with the Lincoln assassination had been put on trial by a military commission, and found guilty of a plot to kill the president. Since Booth had been killed in a barn in late April and David Herold was captured at the sight, those found guilty were hanged or imprisoned. During the trial, Boston Corbett, a former prisoner of war at Fort Sumter, (Andersonville) explained how he killed Booth that April night. At a prison in DC heads were covered with bags on the quickly built staging platform where Louis Paine (Powell), David Herold, George Azterodt, and Mary Surratt awaited execution. Four others involved in the assassination were sent to prison, including Dr. Mudd who had administered medical help to Booth. Mudd went to Fort Jefferson off the coast of Florida. Neither the newspapers nor government were completely convinced of his involvement!

I am amazed justice was completed in such a short time. Capture, trial, verdict, sentencing, hanging, prison, all were accomplished within a couple of months of the assassination. The country was ready to punish those involved in this terrible murder. Their hero and idol had been killed. The man who was trusted with reconstruction was killed in the open that dreadful night while some opposing forces were still fighting in the deep-south! Americans from both sides of the conflict wanted answers! Black, whites, north, south, it made no difference! Something had to happen now! Someone had to pay the price!

They wanted justice and wanted it quick. Comments in the news-papers were saying Secretary Stanton wanted swift punishment and loud statements to be made. Even as controversial as he was with the fallen leader, when Lincoln died that Friday night, Stanton reportedly had made the comment about Lincoln by saying "Now He Belongs To The Ages". A captain in the room at the same time said, what Stanton really said was, "Now he belongs to the Angels". What difference does it really make, Ages or Angels? Lincoln is dead. Anyway, its obvious to me, Stanton got his revenge wish! Someone had to pay and he didn't care whether Mary Surratt was part of the conspiracy or not, she would hang. She owned the boarding house where the killers met. According to Stanton, she was part of the conspiracy. But Doctor Mudd?

I wrote Captain Steele a letter expressing my views on the trial and punishment. Haven't heard from him since we said goodbye in DC. Sent one to grandpa too! I wonder what they thought. I had thoughts of Stanton and the new President. What would they do, now?

September 29, 1865

Not a good start at the farm. High winds and heavy rain destroyed the small patch of corn and Jonas said much of his tobacco went down and is ruined.

Haven't heard from Captain Steele or grandpa. Mary's pregnant with our first baby expected in the late winter or early spring. Mary's been sick a lot and in bed. I am working at the hardware store with Cecil. Jonas too. Have a meeting on the 20th of October with about a dozen war veterans. Some resided here before the war and others decided to settle in the area after treaties were signed. Cecil is part of our group with many stories of his war experiences. Plan a BBQ. I'm supplying the hog.

October 17, 1865

Broken window in the house when a rock came through! A note attached said, "Nigger lover". Don't know what it means as many people close by know, Jonas is my friend. What now? Need to talk with Jonas!

October 22, 1865

It is Sunday. Jonas and I took a ride to the mountain gap and talked at length about the note I found. He said over the last few months he had received many threats from some locals and a few Yankees when I said, "How come you didn't tell me?" "JT," he said, "I can't run to you

*every time someone does something to me. I need to stand up for myself
and protect my family with my own means. The Barnes family who
live in the valley said they have received many threats and those people
who don't like blacks want us to leave the area and go south. Benny
Barnes and his wife were slaves before the war living in Louisiana. He
told me he did not want to return to the swamps of the God-awful state
plus he reminded me of what you had told me about Lincoln freeing
the blacks."*

*I listened for a few more minutes then said, "We need to find ways
to combat these whites who hate blacks. I need to be more careful and
you need to continue to be my friend by telling me when you receive
any threats. We need to stick together. Remind the Barnes to tell the
authorities." Jonas laughed saying, "JT, Benny and I have told Mr.
Westerly, the constable, but he tells us he can't do much unless we can
identify who is harming us. He told us to let him know the next time he
is threatened. JT, I have told him twice that the Brown boys who live
in the mountains were the ones who stole my horses and pigs, but Mr.
Westerly just asked if the Browns hurt us. I told Westerly, they left a
note in the barn to sell our tobacco in North Carolina, not Knoxville.
The note also said to keep track of my kids."*

*Jonas showed me a note addressed to me. As he reached handing me
the peace of paper, he said he had gotten the note on Friday night after
we left the hardware store but couldn't find me. Mary told him I was
visiting with a banker about some business.*

*I took the note. On the outside it said 'Give this to your friend
JOHN!' Inside it simply said, 'Stay away from Jonas and Benny!'*

*"Where did you find this," I asked? He answered with, "It was
stuck on my kitchen door. I had put my horse away and was headed in-
doors but could not avoid the paper. And I didn't open it. I was afraid
of what I would find."*

    JT

We decided that was enough for one night so I closed my journal and
Jonas and his family went home. A light snow fell and covered the ground
as the Manfords rounded the bend. I put another log on the fire, told Mary I
would be to bed shortly, and sat thinking about what I had just read.

Over the next month Jonas, Benny, and I met on a regular basis trying
to remain somewhat calm and vigilant as we continued our daily work re-
quirements and obligations. We were observant to stay away from characters we deemed questionable. We stuck to our families and required that all
members let each other know where they were going, who they were in the

company of, and how long they were expected to be away. We became overly protective at times following family members to shop or to visit the local preacher. Things were changing and none of us were happy and comfortable. Basically, we were angry! Me specifically! I needed to do something, but what?

My last entry in my journal for 65 was made on the 31st.

December 31,1865

The last few months of the year have been trying and terrifying. Jonas, Benny, and their families are worried every minute of the day and night. Had a meeting with Jonas the day after Christmas and discussed some beatings of blacks over in Knoxville. Jonas said a gang of crazy whites dressed in butternut britches and rebel hats beat two blacks because the blacks refused to say ' master' when the whites asked them a question. Jonas had responded with, " I thought we were through with that!" Jonas told me to be careful and we both questioned whether we should be seen together. I told him about a rock and another broken window at the farm. Jonas said he would be ok. Don't worry about me. I'm fine!

I'm not so sure!

Mary and I got over the loss of our first baby and I'm thankful she is not injured and is doing better. Dr. Capp comes by every few days and reports good progress.

Got a letter from grandpa, dated May 1, 1865, saying he is not feeling well and that Yankee soldiers are everywhere in the Carolinas. Said he would try to get to Clinton in the summer after the snow in the mountains melts. That letter was seven months old! Reminded me of my army days where letters were lost for months and many that were written but never delivered.

Happy New Year!

It was months since the war had ended and I was looking at the New Year with anticipation of better things to come. The war was still hanging close as I had another bout of pneumonia reminding me of camp life and driving me to bed with plenty of chest pain and coughing. From Mary came constant reminders of what the doctor had said about drinking large amounts of water and bed rest. While resting one day in late winter, Cecil stopped by during a lull in the activity at the hardware store and said he wanted to talk. I had forgotten his full name was Cecil Alexander Gant and he loved to tell stories. People simply called him, CA.

CA had worked at the store before the war but enlisted in the Confederate

Army just after first Manassas in 61. Presently, he was living above the store by himself and reported things in the business were 'ok' but feared for other happenings in the region. He had read newspaper stories of abusive activities against blacks and stated he was concerned about my friends. I said 'I agreed with him' but neither of us had any specific immediate plans. Before he started complaining about the experiences he had in the army, he said, "Take care of my sister."

CA took out his pocketknife and picked his teeth saying he had heard of strange happenings that might be the cause of some of the current social unrest. I wondered where he had discovered these tales so I listened.

Apparently, what had taken place in other parts of the south during the war had not left the confederacy and had spread over the years to eastern Tennessee and North Carolina. CA said that murders, rapes, house burnings, farm crops destruction, animals killed for no reason, businessmen threatened for favors, local mayors hanged, blacks burned at the stakes, preachers dragged through town then covered with hot tar, and more abuses were daily happenings and were spreading rapidly. "The south is a mess," CA said.

I asked, "Where do you hear this?"

He responded, "Everywhere John. People talk and the papers are full of stories."

Tension was high. People were scared. Blacks as well as whites feared for their life. Businessmen, bankers, politicians, men of the cross, women, children, and veterans questioned everyone. No one could be trusted. People died. CA said, "Become more vigilant. JT, this is just the tip of the iceberg." He was right!

I had remembered some of CA's past but had very little information about his past few years. He had shared some of his war experiences with the veteran's group at the October meeting and BBQ but was a little reluctant to detail specific events as he really didn't know many ex-soldiers and wanted to become familiar with others before 'sounding off'. Those were his words, sounding off.' But, he was an avid reader.

CA was 21 when he left Clinton. He was wounded twice and is missing one half of his third and fourth fingers on his right hand. He carries a limp and drags his left leg as a result of injuries he sustained at Cold Harbor. He wanted to say something. So I let him talk! He wanted to talk war!

He started, "JT, I just returned from a visit with a former buddy who now lives over in Stickle County near the North Carolina line. He grew up in Alabama and decided to live in Carolina after the war. He wanted me to know that during the late stages of the war that Ball County in his home state was controlled by a group of men known as the, Milton Mapes Marauders'. Their total number was somewhere between 65-75 men who created havoc for the confederacy. They were a group of former Confederate soldiers who had joined the army, deserted, and decided to actively conduct hit and run tactics against their former buddies and leaders. They turned union sympathizers and wanted rebel forces harassed, punished, or killed. They caused extensive damage to plantations, small farms owned by southerners, railroads, bridges, factories, rebel sympathizers, and clergy."

The story was getting my attention, so I let CA continue. He followed with, "Milton, their leader, was constantly on the run. He conducted business at night. He and his gang moved extensively evading rebels when outnumbered. When challenged he fought with vengeance! On one expedition, his men captured 20 rebels tried them and then hanged them in the swamps of Ball County. On another mission, his men destroyed an ammunition factory in the small town of Evans and escaped when a rebel cavalry drove them back into their camp in the swamps. The next day the former rebels returned and destroyed the local newspaper.

Milton's men never gave up until he was captured, tried by a rebel Major and hanged. Shortly, activities of guerilla warfare re-invented itself in other parts of the south. Groups like the Marauders are everywhere.

By the way, how is Jonas?"

"OK," I said and left it at that!

Cecil said his friend up on the state border is really nervous as similar activities have developed in Tennessee and wanted locals to be aware.

After some ham, greens, cornbread, and apple pie flushed southward with apple brandy, I specifically asked Cecil about his final years in the army. He had heard my story. I wanted to hear his!

The first thing he did was start complaining about army life. Much of what he said, I had heard many times! Indecisions of leaders, stupid night marches, never any food worth eating, cooking my own food, never any warm clothes during the winter and uncomfortable summer clothes started his list. He continued with frozen feet caused by no boots or footwear that resembled torn and shredded socks. He informed me on two occasions he used cardboard to wrap his frozen feet and continue his march to another battlefield. Eventually, I discovered that movement from one location to another he described was from one bunker to another while he was positioned near Petersburg during the siege in the winter of 64-65. "Water was a foot deep," he ended.

He complained he never received any mail from home or anywhere and had to ride in uncomfortable noisy dirty trains next to smelly vomiting sick soldiers. As he was reporting on his impressions of untrained worthless doctors I asked about his final days of the war as I knew he had been near Appomattox.

He described the events saying, "You know, John, the final days of the Confederacy were just as devastating as the previous three years. More tragedies among our starving troops who fought to the end! When we left the Petersburg area, we burned and destroyed buildings, bridges, railroad tracks, and workshops in the area, including water tanks. Billy Yank was not going to get anything! Up the road a little in Richmond, soldiers destroyed almost 1,000 buildings before retreating. Even though men had not eaten in days, dressed in ragged clothes, hundreds with facial burns, bruises, and scars, they walked barefoot and died while fighting Yankees in close quarters. Those final days of the confederacy were hell! Skirmishes and fighting continued from the time I left Petersburg until the proud Generals decided to stop the slaughter."

I had read some of this before but hearing from someone who witnessed it first hand was always better!

Cecil stopped for a minute as tears welled in his eyes describing his friends and superiors suffering through the week. Thousands died that last week! Horses and mules pulling wagons with supplies, artillery, and men dropped and died as their tired bodies succumbed to the exhausting travel. General Lee's 30,000 forces was drastically reduced by the time the fighting stopped and the food train that southerners were expecting had been captured by Yankee forces.

Cecil continued, "John, when the indiscriminate shooting stopped, we sat down and realized we had been defeated. Some wanted to continue fighting, but I was tired of fighting and so was the General. Plus Yankees had captured over 10,000 of our men that final week. After it was all over, I read many accounts of the final days as some reported the happenings clearly while other reports exaggerate the events. It doesn't matter anymore. The war is over. We did our best!"

As the days passed and I recovered from pneumonia, Cecil and I reflected on the war. We really didn't have much more to offer. I wanted to move on with my life and so did he. But, the issues of the war, state's rights and slavery would not vanish. I continually asked myself if the federal or state government was more instrumental in my daily life. And working beside Jonas in the hardware store, I continued to fear for my life as well as his.

By the summer Mary and I had settled some questions about children and we were expecting a baby in the winter. I continued to meet with a few veterans, including CA, on a monthly schedule and Jonas and his wife and baby continued to receive threats. Some whites wanted Jonas dead! Jonas mentioned he and his wife had discussed a move further north into West Virginia, but said they had not decided yet. Again, Jonas mentioned a Blacks Only School.

Sadly, I had received information that Alton James Phennesey, grandpa, had died in the late spring and Mary and I had made the trip after the funeral. We arrived at the farm in western North Carolina, paid our respects, talked with Aunt Julia and family and headed back to Clinton. Grandpa had been a great inspiration in my life and I certainly will miss him. Grandpa filled in the blanks with letters and visits. Everything from the explanation of the Constitution to his work on the Underground Railroad had been covered. For someone who had emigrated from Ireland in 1818, he had truly demonstrated his dedication to this country. He understood what American freedom was and could explain it in a simple way. 'Thank you so much, Papa A.'

I grabbed my journal and made extensive entries about grandpa. They covered fourteen pages. I had a lot to say about a very important man.

Following our trip to Carolina, we found the train station and bordered a car to Knoxville when we met a very interesting fellow with warnings about the ride back. Mary and I sat down with some hard candy and I brought out some apple brandy as we got underway.

I offered some candy to the man sitting across from us when he said his name was Booker something. Forgot his last name! Immediately, he asked where we called home and wanted to know how we had gotten from Clinton to Carolina. After a brief explanation of our trip and purpose, he informed us of some strange events taking place close by. He got our attention real quick when he discovered we did not have any guns or knives to protect us.

I didn't need any guns, the war was over!

The stranger was a former Confederate Major who fought with General Joe Johnston during the final conflicts against General Sherman in NC. He was with Johnston when he and Sherman met to end their fighting and sign the treaty in 65, but his greatest fear now was the violence spread by former armed men and women who live in the mountains of NC and Eastern TN creating fear by conducting raids killing innocent civilians and destroying farms and small towns. The major said, "These people are just mad." He didn't have any reasons or could he identify their issues. Just mad! He called some of them bushwhackers. I had never heard that term before.

He described the mountains were controlled by full bands of a variety of people. They comprise former confederate state militiamen, Yankee guerillas, and angry deserters. The violent cutthroat angry thieves were comprised of former prisoners of war, both Yankee and Rebel, and occasionally a group of roaming blacks joined forces. The major said the local paper in Olden, North Carolina, identified some as outliers, local union sympathizers who simply lived in the mountains to escape fighting for the confederacy.

He continued by identifying names and towns, but as I listened, I did not record much information. He said his cousins were attacked last week, but the only destruction that occurred was the burning of two small barns and warnings to not get caught hiding former slaves. Immediately, I thought of Jonas.

We were given a list of towns to avoid on our travels as the bands of men could resurface anywhere. Stay away from Castle Way, Warden, Indent, Franklin, and Moseley. I had never heard of these places except Warden, but we took the advice and avoided any confrontations. Plus, our train was headed for Knoxville with no stops along the way.

Hours passed as we listened to Bookers' description and warnings of the eastern side of Tennessee and western border of North Carolina. He was certainly interesting, but Mary and I arrived safely back in Clinton. Now I understand what Cecil was referring to with that story he had passed my way back in the winter.

The three weeks away from the farm and the hardware store proved to be disturbing as we fell behind with the farm responsibilities. Betsy, my prize white face cow died, as did one of the goats, plus the corn crop needed attention. CA and Jonas had secured the store, but personal matters got worse when we opened the door to the farmhouse. The inside had been destroyed with notes of 'Nigger Lover' attached throughout. Two of my 'Springfield Rifles' were missing and Mary's favorite pictures of her family lay shredded in the living room. After placing our furniture back and taking care of the animals, we made some quick decisions.

Immediately overcome with fear, Mary and I made the trip to find Jonas. We all began to fear for our lives. We checked with Cecil at the hardware store. "Not here," he said. We passed two of Jonas' black friends on the street and asked. They had not seen him in a week. I ran into the bank and asked Ms. Whitehead, the clerk if she had seen Jonas. She said she had seen him two weeks ago when he came by but has not seen him since. We went to his farm. Nothing! On the wall next to the front door was a sign that simply said, 'NIGGER' and beside it was a drawing of a tree and a person hanging. The search continued.

Just before sundown we found Jonas and family in the woods secured in a cave where he and I used to play. He said he was ok but he sounded really worried. We started talking. I asked how he was doing. "I can't go back to the farm, JT," he said, "I'm scared. My wife is scared! They will kill us next time. I talked with Benny and he is scared. He wants to move away, but where will he go? Benny said he wanted to move north into Kentucky. Is that any safer? Did you see the Baptist church? Those hoodlums did everything except burn the building. Even the preachers getting threatening notes plastered on the outside of the church and his home."

I interrupted Jonas to ask about other blacks in town. I asked, "What do they mean the next time?" He said he had heard about notes and threats, but no one had been killed. Just warnings!

Jonas replied, "JT, three whites from Baldwin came into the store just before I closed it two weeks ago and told me not to come to work anymore. I had never seen them before when they said their friends in Baldwin would be over to visit me if they heard I was working with you and Cecil. First I told them I needed the work, when they insisted that my presence was not welcomed. Some fellow by the name of Jefferson said us blacks need not work in Clinton as more work is needed on big tobacco and cotton farms in Alabama, Louisiana, and Mississippi. Jefferson said, get out of Clinton. Head south! Don't look back."

Mary started crying as she listened to what Jonas was describing.

I asked Jonas if he and family wanted to come and live with us. Even with all the threats and abuse in my family, I decided my closest friend was not going to face the threatening anti-blacks in my town by himself. Somehow, I had to address the problem! But how!

Jonas said he would discuss the offer with his wife and that he would be ok in the cave for a while. Mary talked to his wife before we departed and Jonas told me he would be to work the next day. "Good, I'll see you tomorrow," I said as Mary and I left. Good on his statement, Jonas came to work 10 hours later!

Cecil, Jonas and me continued to work in the store being more vigilant with every passing hour. No more threats came. Benny and family were ok as he constantly mentioned moving away. Jonas had decided to move back to his farm and was ok. He ventured to Knoxville and purchased another rifle. Much to the displeasure of Mary, I did the same the next day. I even bought an extra repeater rifle and placed it in the barn.

BUT!

Seven

REVIEWING THE 60'S

Days went by with fear surrounding our every move. Jonas, Cecil, and me discussed disturbing abusive events every day! Even Benny came to the store and reported very unsettling conditions. Some store business slowed when outsiders came to town causing Jonas to question his position inside. Locals were talking of abuse to blacks that had taken place in neighboring towns like Knoxville, Baldwin, and Jonesboro. Northern invaders to our town who came for whatever financial reason complained of abuse and tactics used against blacks. The local Clinton Gazette had a few stories of torture, but when I picked up the Knoxville paper, I read heart-wrenching stories that were spreading across the south.

That's when Jonas told me of readings conducted at the local library about his particular interest in local, state, and federal laws regarding the issue of civil rights. I had no idea his interest had sparked! "Civil rights," he said! Where did that comment come from? Maybe, my friend is not telling me everything about his life! Eventually, I asked Mary if she had had talks with his wife regarding his most recent weekend trips to Knoxville. Maybe he was seeing others in the big city when he ventured south to purchase our hardware supplies! I began to wonder if he had fellow blacks, including Benny, to discuss his findings. Jonas mentioned the newly passed Enforcement Act in Washington that was earmarked to ease the violence against blacks, when he responded with, "But who really cares, JT? Politicians don't really care about us folks."

Every week local reporters continued to describe abusive tactics taking place in Columbia, South Carolina, New Orleans, Louisiana, as well as the local scene in Knoxville. Blacks were being threatened! Blacks were being tortured! Blacks were being hanged! Secret organizations were being formed designed by former rebel soldiers who decided that blacks were not white's equals. Groups had formed in Cain, Needles, and Oakmont Tennessee, not far from the capital of Nashville, and wished to torture and abuse blacks every way possible. Their identity was hidden with the cover of white sheets over their entire body including white hoods over their heads and to remain more secret and obscure, they operated at night. Scare tactics and threats spread as Slinger's Tavern in Knoxville, a local gathering hole for blacks, had been burned to the ground with about a dozen blacks inside. On certain occasions whites became victims when the white owner of the tavern, Mr. Torrington was taken out back, beaten and than hanged.

Seemed like the entire state was involved! Small towns, large cities, former plantations, small farms, everywhere fear was the daily topic at work and in homes. How big were these organizations anyway? Were locals from my veterans group involved, I asked myself!

Shortly, a local group known as the KKK was identified and many local blacks faced more beatings and torture. Elisa Mae Brown, Jessie Walker Brown, and twelve-year old Lincoln Homer Brown had been found hanging from an oak tree two nights ago behind the Brown's shed about four miles from Clinton. Christmas was no respite as beatings, burnings, and lynching's continued through the holiday season. Mary and I put away our holiday decorations, and spent hours talking about what was next. Southerners, northerners, blacks, whites, former soldiers, businessmen, preachers, farmers, and politicians studied recent events in state capitals and Washington DC while contemplating America's future.

Numerous newspaper editorials reported support for the KKK while its members continued their rampages. Charleston, Columbia, and Atlanta papers supported placing blacks back on plantations or sending them to California, Africa, or some island off the coast of Panama. Up north in small towns and big cities surrounding the northern capital of Washington, many spectators supported the KKK while holding true to their beliefs that blacks have a certain place in society. Many times while reading and discussing the northern views I had to remind myself that all Americans have not accepted the end of slavery. Laws don't mean anything if citizens don't abide by them. Can feelings and dominance of heritage views be legislated? "I guess not," I said to Mary.

Some northern newspapers contained articles describing situations and indentifying locations where blacks were not welcome, specifically northern farms, northern factories, and northern homes. They proclaimed blacks were not equal to whites! Boston, Chicago, Detroit, and Canton were mentioned in some of the stories.

In Washington, politics had gotten into the act in the late 60's when President Andrew Johnson suggested giving considerable power to any white southerner who had more than $20,000 in property allowing the wealthy to again control the south. I asked myself if the President was referring to blacks as property? Sounded like slavery all over!

In Indiana, where many whites and blacks settled close to one another, violence broke out on a regular bases when interracial issues were argued. Black children, who had white fathers as a result of rape before or during the war, were unwelcomed and taken from homes and factories. If a child was even 1/8th black he/she was considered black! Hundreds of black children were raped, beaten, and in many cases hanged. Before and during the war plantation owners, and in many cases overseers raped black house workers resulting in mixed raced children who now covered the countryside. Their life was in jeopardy and facing daily abuse.

It seemed like the past proved more powerful than the present. Social and cultural change was not taking place! Are citizens willing to work together as Lincoln wanted? Is the color of a person's skin the determining factor when evaluating someone? Again, I asked myself if these issues are answered by federal or state laws or by individuals who willingly examine their personal beliefs and values. I don't know! If the War Between the States was fought to end slavery were victorious northerners supplying damaging fuel to the expanding fire?

Benny had asked what the country would have been like if Lincoln had not been shot. That night while we four sat in the store discussing the question with guesses that proved worthless, Jonas and Benny feared for their lives and Cecil and me tried to assure them they would be safe. That's when Benny spoke saying, "Words are just hot air, JT. We need action. I'll defend myself. If I go down, I will be fighting. If I see any white sheets around my home, I will shoot first and talk later." What next, I thought?

Lives are being taken for what? Will peace ever be restored? The battlefield is no longer Gettysburg, Pennsylvania, Petersburg, Virginia, Chattanooga, Tennessee, Columbia, South Carolina, or Andersonville, Georgia. The battlefield is America! The political, social, and cultural landscape IS the battlefield! How could the new generation prosper with such turmoil while the older generation is acting with minds from ago? I said to myself, JT think! Would life have been any different if Abe was alive? I'll never know.

A visit to the preacher produced many questions and comments. Mary and I stayed for about an hour before we left and continued our own examination. Nothing was really accomplished that night, except our complaining.

Childhood values and ideas hang on! Good times and bad times surface in people's mind! The past does not hide! Sometimes beliefs and opinions contradict! Value systems don't change quickly! Old well-oiled feelings are hard to separate from the past. "It's hard to block out heritage," Mary said.

I remember reading that some northern states did not abolish slavery until just before the War Between the States, as did New Hampshire in 1857. I remember saying to myself at that time, "Did that northern state have any slaves or plantations?" As a young twenty something, I had no idea. Besides, I knew very little about slavery except what I had learned from Jonas's pa, my grandpa and they were gone.

As I sat and talked with Mary I looked forward to stability in my life. I looked forward to the birth of our new child. That's when more fear entered my head! During a midwinter snowstorm the roof on the barn collapsed that ruined stored crops and killed a few animals. Following that, a group of angry former rebels from somewhere near Jonesboro made a visit by torching the fallen barn and reminding me that I had no need to be socializing with my black friend. And my extra rifle was destroyed!

The next evening they approached me again. Only this was more physically damaging!

As I was closing the hardware store for the day and heading to the livery stable, I was grabbed from behind, knocked down and beaten by four individuals who were covered with white sheets. They ripped off my shirt and whipped my back! They continued to holler and scream while they inflicted bruises and cuts. As a result of the attack, my face was covered with blood. Blood poured down my back all the way to my ass. My arms were beaten severely. My legs ached! They kicked me where it really hurts. At one point I fought back to no avail. My pocketknife was useless!

I screamed but no one heard. They threatened my wife, and even threatened Jonas with severe punishment and hanging. "Find other friends," they hollered. "Stay away from Blackie," they yelled. Stop selling to Niggers they insisted or more will come your way and we'll destroy your store. As they rode away into the night, one guy hollered, "I'll send Forest next time."

I lay there in the new fallen white snow bleeding for some time licking my wounds! My new woolen jacket Mary had given me for Christmas was colored bright red. Forest, I asked myself. The wounds of this war were severe, but this wasn't Gettysburg or Fredericksburg. I surely hurt! I was reminded of my wounds after Pickett's Charge. I was a mess then. I was a mess now! But, this was Clinton, Tennessee! The War Between the States has passed!

I discovered the comment about Forest was referring to Nathan B. Forest the former rebel cavalry soldier, a noted black hater who possessed a violent temper! Forest commented back along that blacks belonged on plantations with no freedoms. He believed blacks were inferior to whites and blacks should respect the superior race.

Eventually, I climbed aboard the old mule as the bleeding continued. I had been beaten severely! My head hurt! My arms hurt! My shoulders hurt! My legs hurt! My knees hurt. I hurt all over! The beating lasted but 20 minutes! I headed home!

Eventually, I got home, got cleaned up while Mary and I discussed the possibility of moving, but I insisted we cannot run away from the problem. She showed me another sign that someone placed on the reconstructed barn. The sign said, "Listen Nigger Lover, Mary could be next. Mr. Gant's Store Too."

We went to bed that night with newly purchased rifles close by. Not only was Jonas in trouble, so were we. Eventually, I purchased another rifle for the barn.

I found Cecil the next day and together we discussed Jonas and his friend Benny. Cecil wanted to know about the facial wounds and why I was limping so I took a few minutes to explain the previous night's attack. I told him about the barn messages, but Mary was ok. Things were getting real personal and extremely dangerous. Since Jonas had been away from work for a few days, Cecil and I expressed concerns, people who might be helpful, and strategies to deal with our dilemma. Cecil warned that some locals in town are not who they say they are. "Some hate blacks just like those rebel mountain men," he commented and I put my pistol in my front pocket before going home that night.

"Lets get Jonas and make sure he's ok," I said as we struggled to get out of bed the next morning. With the reflecting sunshine coming off the new snow, Mary and I headed to Narrow Passage Creek and tried to find Jonas. We search for hours! We had no luck. We looked everywhere with no positive results. I checked the cave. I checked the log cabin shed Jonas and I had build as kids. We asked two farmers in the valley! Nothing! I feared the worse! Finally, I told Mary to get back to the farm and get the rifles. I'll be home soon! Maybe, Jonas had gone to Knoxville to talk with some of his friends there!

I went to Boxford Forge and found no one. I continued on to Mattle, Rancort, Bear Mountains, and finally back to Clinton before I finished my search. Nothing! Where was my friend? No one had seen or heard from Jonas or Benny in days.

Mary and her brother Cecil were in the hardware store and I told them of my recent search. Cecil said, "Jonas and wife may be near Benny's place. He likes the area. More mountainous, more caves and hiding places."

Then more startling news!

Cecil said he had been to Knoxville for supplies on Saturday and said he was refused supplies because we were selling to blacks. What next, I thought! When I asked him about travelling elsewhere to get our supplies, he mentioned other warehouses and factories were doing the same, not selling to stores who were dealing or selling to blacks. "How widespread is this, I asked? Can Echols over at the livery stable get his supplies? And what about Doc Lister who runs the apothecary, can he get his medicines? What about Stickles food market, can they get their foodstuffs? Are the paper companies selling supplies to the Gazette?"

Needless to say, I was extremely angry! Questioning I said, "Is Clinton going to survive this or are we going to step forward and address these brutes? Do we have to carry guns to protect ourselves? If so, I will arm myself everyday."

Cecil said he had looked at supply possibilities in Kentucky just a few miles north of Clinton, but he had heard conditions there were not much better. He thought the small community of Reed's Forge in Kentucky could supply many farming tools if the prices are not too high. Cecil mentioned the train through the Cumberland Gap can get us to supply houses in Kentucky and it leaves Knoxville tomorrow morning and stops here around 8:30. "Let's think about that," I said.

I complained, "This isn't fair! That's not right! Why do we have to travel so far to make a living? And where is that northern help anyway? Where are those men sent south to assist us? What are they doing? Where will blacks get supplies or other needs if we don't carry them? They need supplies just like me and you!" Cecil returned to his bare shelves as I said goodbye, returned to my horse, and headed back to the farm. I was mad! Damn it, I will not let these abusive measures ruin my town or family. I will find a way! And where is help from those Yankee soldiers living on the outskirts of Clinton?

Days went by as I went to work and Cecil and I tried our best to answer as many requests as we could. Cecil made numerous trips to Reed's Forge. We explained to everyone the supply shortage. We even limited the amount we sold to any one person. Some people got upset explaining they would go to Knoxville or elsewhere, but they all understood the problem was not of our making.

Finally, Jonas and Benny returned.

Each carrying a rifle and pistol, Jonas and Benny appeared one night about closing time and expressed their continued anxiety about situations in the area. They had spent two days in an old dilapidated barn about four miles from Bear Mountain and had gotten a few supplies from a local white man who they did not identify for fear he would be exposed and punished. I said ok. Glad you are safe. I didn't asked any more! Jonas and his friend returned to their homes.

We survived the long cold winter. A new baby boy, named Thomas Trenton, was born in late winter and the summer of 69 brought some new hope. Jonas had returned from hiding. He never identified the exact location where he had hidden and I didn't press the issue. Maybe, if I didn't know, I would not be lying if I said I had no idea when asked about his whereabouts. Northern and southern newspapers continued to publish stories of KKK dealings as the destruction of black lives spread. Congress in Washington, DC even got in the act by discussing the problem. But that was IT. They talked and talked and talked!

Jonas and I decided to head down to the bottom one Sunday afternoon and race. I lost again. That's when Jonas said he wanted to talk about the black-white issue. "Ok," I said. We strolled to the river's edge and sat!

Jonas spoke, "You know JT, I am married to a beautiful black person. I have started a family. I have one daughter and my wife is with another. I live close by and have you as a great friend. We both know the KKK is close and we both fear for our families. We know the Klan is abusing blacks and we are almost helpless. When the war ended, I felt I could go to church and sit wherever I wanted while listening to God's word. Isn't that my right? If I go on Sunday, I sit in the back or go to the all black church over the mountain in the valley. I thought I could go to any store or building in Clinton without any problem. I thought I could walk wherever I wanted to in Clinton. I can't. I get looked at as if I was growing horns on my head. But with what is happening now, I am feeling nothing has changed. My pa would be furious if he were alive," Jonas continued.

"JT, I wasn't a slave. I haven't been living on a plantation in South Carolina. I shouldn't have to beg for my food like my pa did. Yes, my pa escaped from a Georgia plantation before the war, but he became free and chose a peaceful life before he was brutally murdered when you were up north fighting for the Confederacy. JT, I ask you, when will this change? How long do I have to fear for my family? When? Will it be soon? Will my daughter ever live free of fear? Will I ever be able to question anyone, black or white about being mistreated? And when trouble surfaces again, do I have to revert to hiding?"

He was on a roll so I let him continue. "JT, I have been reading a lot about new laws that were passed in DC, have a friend in Knoxville who got his law education in Memphis, and he says getting an education will be helpful. Go to school, now! He stresses that lawyers will be asked to work defending the state and federal laws. He has given me many articles and a few books on laws that are in effect in western Tennessee. But, with all of that said, I still fear for my family."

I sat, leaned back against a tree, crossed my arms and began to feel I was going to lose my friend.

I wish I had answers and I wish I had them now! I thought about as many issues as my mind could hold. But, in the long run, I was not very helpful, except to agree that education was the answer. The questions were overwhelming. The topic was simple, but the answers involved more than I could handle.

I began wondering if laws would make a difference as the Emancipation Proclamation did little. Then the 13th and 14th Amendments; were they truly going to give blacks some relief? If all the laws passed were going to make a difference, why did the current conditions in America prevail? I asked myself, what good are laws without adherence?

The other issue I contemplated was the social conditions. Finally I said to Jonas, "Can blacks and whites live together? You and I know what we expect of one another. You and I know how to treat each other. You and I know what each likes and dislikes, values, and we respect each other as equals. I'm not sure others, especially many whites, are ready to say the same thing. Jonas, I don't see you as an object of any particular color, black, red, or brown. I see you as a person. Is that right or wrong. I value you as a human being, not as a piece of property. Am I wrong or just dreaming?" My childhood buddy looked dejected as he settled backward.

"Jonas, remember when we were kids, roaming the mountains and playing in caves catching rattlesnakes and fishing for catfish, did we care about the color of our skin? Did we argue over any issue based on the color of our cheeks? Did we even think about color? Hell no, we wanted to share our growing pains with fun times and friendly people. I helped you. You helped me. What more could two young innocent boys want?" Jonas just sat and listened.

"If you remember, we both cried and laughed a lot. We suffered together. When one hurt, so did the other. When one rallied with victory, the friendly handshakes and congratulations were expressed. I think that sounds like a team! Well, it is Jonas, and I will be by your side to support you."

We tried to ease the fear and verbal pain we both felt that afternoon and we finally climbed aboard our horses. It made me feel good to hear Jonas say something because I knew he was scared. I don't think we solved anything. I don't even know if we answered each other's questions, but we did have an opportunity to express our concerns. I think it felt good that both of us said what was on our minds. We slapped our horses and again, he beat me to the fork in the road.

More brutality

A month later as the sun was setting, I walked out of the hardware store to get on my mare when I heard "Help." I went around the side of the livery stable and there on the ground was my close friend, Jonas. Damn, I mumbled. He was bleeding from his mouth. His shirt had been ripped from his back and blood was oozing out of wide-open wounds. When I tried to pull him up to stand, he said one of his legs was broken. One hand had three broken fingers and he was wearing no pants. His legs were covered with a black concoction and his feet were swollen. He was a mess! Again, I was speechless! Enough is enough! Jonas had been beaten to a bloody pulp.

Eventually, I loaded Jonas into the livery stable wagon and we made our way to the doctor's house. Dr. Capp worked on Jonas for over two hours as I guessed who were the attackers. Jonas said the hooded group of eight came to his farm early in the day and found him in the tobacco patch and beat him. Jonas said they took him to a tree and threatened to hang him, but thought otherwise when the leader said, "Let's let JT see what we mean." The hooded group brought him to the back of the stable and dumped him on the ground. Jonas said they warned him about saying much as they understood he had a daughter and wife. The more Jonas talked, the madder I got! They can't do this to my friend. He could have died! I will fight back! I thought, where's my pistol. Get my rifle!

The wounds were taken care of by the doctor and the lacerations were covered. Doc told Jonas to stay off the leg for a while. It really wasn't broken! I thanked the doctor and we left. On the way to his farm I asked Jonas if moving might be an option. His only response was, "JT, where will I go? I will not run," he said. "I will help," I said.

However, two weeks passed before Jonas came to the store to report he had taken his family and moved to Bear Mountain near the cave. Living in the old barn for the summer would be just fine, he explained. Jonas mentioned he would no longer be working at the store and finally said, "JT, I'll be fine. Go!" He told no one but me!

Eventually, I rode the old mare to Benny's home and told him about Jonas. Benny assured me he would tell no one explaining that he was contemplating a move out of the state, but had not chosen any particular location. He said his mother's folks lived about sixty miles away, near Bristol and that was an option. He wasn't sure about his future either as he likewise feared for his family.

Following some work at the store and discussions with Cecil about our black friends, I decided to spend more time working at the farm. After three hours of working in the hot Tennessee sun in the tobacco patch and attending to the ever-starving hogs, I worked four hours with farming tools repairing wagon wheels, mule harnesses, and redesigned a horse stall. It was an exhausting day of farm work and I fell asleep that night with little help from Mary or the screaming kid.

The next morning I grabbed my journal and made a few comments. I recently read a Charleston newspaper article that truly disturbed me. I though about the country and where it was headed! When would the violence end? My entry:

September 20,1869

Just read the following quote from an ex confederate soldier who had owned a plantation outside of Charleston before the war. He said, "I will raise my southern children so they will always hate every northerner, every hour and every day for as long as I shall live, so help me God. The northern Civil War was a Nigger War and arming blacks was social dynamite." I reckon he hates northerners as much as he hates blacks. He probably wants his plantation back and making thousands. Maybe he's just a hateful person?

Maybe staying here in Clinton isn't so healthy! Mary and I have to talk. I wonder if all northerners still feel the same way about southerners. I need to talk with Jonas.

September 24,1869

I found Jonas and family in the Bear Mountain area and asked him about his farm. He said he was ok. Food was ok! Cool at night he commented. He said he went to the farm after he recovered from his injuries and there was nothing left. The house, shed, barn, and all animals were destroyed. His favorite bull was no longer around and his vegetable patch had been burned along with his tobacco field. A sign stuck in the ground simply said, "YOU NEXT BOY." Lying beside the sign was a white sheet covered with blood.

I mentioned to Jonas I was leaving the area for a short time, but would be back with some good news. He said he would check on my animals while we were away. I was actually trying to paint a positive picture, but wasn't really sure he believed me. Anyway, I told my friend that I would find him when I returned and we could start re-

building his small farm. I went to his former farm. There was nothing there, not even that sign.

Later

As I tried to make sense out of the late 60s, I had to believe that there were other things taking place that were more positive. I wanted to check on my sister at school and see if her experience in the north brought any new ideas about educating the young. I hoped she was ok as her letters from normal school were sparse. She had mentioned she liked school and occasionally saw some disruptions when people rallied or small riots broke out regarding black and white issues. Was the KKK nearby? I wondered where Captain Steele had settled and maybe I could find him. I had not heard from him in some time! And I really didn't know what had taken place north of Clinton. I was curious! I had always been! Now is the time to go!

I asked Cecil for some time away and he said fine as business was slow. Supplies in the store had dwindled leaving shelves vacant. Cecil said he might not even have the hardware store when I returned. "Times are tough," he said. The livery stable would have a horse for me when I resurfaced, but I told Mr. Philip I didn't know how long I would be gone or when I would be back. "No problem," he informed me.

The North

As I prepared to leave my farm and work, I mounted my horse and returned to Bear Mountain to see Jonas and family. I explained that Mary and I had discussed a trip north to visit Samantha, my younger sister, but would return shortly. As the cold temperatures from an approaching late fall storm drew near, Jonas and I reassured each other we were ok. We convinced one another we would be diligent with watchful eyes and we would continue our work to find answers to the dangerous problems in the area. He assured me he would keep tabs on Benny and visit Cecil in Clinton. He had heard of work opportunities in Kentucky but he wasn't very clear so I basically ignored the subject. He showed me a lawyer's book he received from a friend in Knoxville. "Interesting stuff," he said.

We said our goodbyes as I reassured Jonas I would return. Really, I had no idea what lay ahead!

After another two nights of talking with Cecil about the store operations and planning our trip, Mary and I decided that a brief trip to northern Virginia might be very informative. I had been to Virginia during the war and wanted to return to see for myself if conditions and people had changed. But before the three of us boarded the Knoxville train to Winchester, Mary informed me she was with child. I had been wondering why she was having those morning sickness spells. Now I know! The doctor had mentioned the week before the train-ride would not hurt her.

It quickly became very obvious that economic conditions in the south had not drastically changed since the end of the war. Northeastern Tennessee was not much different from other southern areas. People were struggling everywhere. The city of Knoxville, once a thriving southern community, was suffering with bank and store closures, vacant factories, and wooden planks covering churches windows and former wealthy homes. In the area near the train station poor whites in rags roamed the streets scrounging for food. Seemed like everyone was looking for a handout. Many civilians still lived in the woods surviving on whatever they could muster. Emotional damage covered the town as a young lady walked by carrying a baby and cried, "I wish I had died." I think she was referring to surviving the war. She looked about twenty-five years old!

Mary, Thomas, and I walked around as groups of young and old mingled in muddy streets. People were talking about many issues including moving west to the Rocky Mountains or California. Some mentioned that former President Johnson was from Greeneville in eastern Tennessee and should have paid more attention to "our needs." Northern troops were in town supposedly to enforce laws and a sign hanging on the local Southern Lord's Baptist Church simply said, "GOD WILL SAVE US." With the newly elected Grant, people continued to ask the same questions.

Eliot Wade, the local saloonkeeper was recruiting people for a rally scheduled for the weekend. He was bragging about his guest, Nathan Bedford Forest. Three northern soldiers were positioned outside his front door as I questioned what they were doing? I got no response!

As I approached the train depot to secure tickets, the sales person informed me that hatred of the north was widespread here in the south. I looked around and saw another group of union soldiers near the awaiting train. The sales person informed me union soldiers were scattered throughout the city and they were not the friendliest group this side of the Mason-Dixon Line. He continued by saying many soldiers acted like generals directing people around while others spent their time in the saloons close to the brothels. "Be careful," he warned.

Eventually, he asked where we were headed. I answered "Winchester, Virginia." He said tracks had been destroyed by some mountain-men over the weekend and getting to Winchester may take some time. He identified an angry gang of former confederate soldiers hiding in the hills of Virginia near Roanoke who stopped every train going through to check for blacks or black sympathizers. "No tellin when ya'll get to Winchester," he finished. "Thanks," I said and boarded the northbound train as Mary looked at me with a puzzled stare. "Do we truly need this trip north," she asked. "We should be taking care of business here in Tennessee," she finished. Maybe she was right! But, I wanted to see Samantha.

Eventually, we arrived in Winchester after constant delays due to track reconstruction and angry former rebel soldiers who boarded the cars to check for blacks, we located the closest church for some safety. The trip north through the Shenandoah Valley had taken over two days. Mary was sick most of the ride and the baby cried constantly. I was just glad to get off the train!

Confusion seemed to describe the town! Winchester resembled the scene in Knoxville with civilians looking for work, beggars on the street looking for a handout, and former soldiers with "C's" or "D's" imprinted on their cheeks representative of cowards or deserters. Locals asked questions about our status. They wanted to know what we wanted, who we were looking for, and why we were in their town. Stupidly, I asked if anyone knew a person by the name of Edwin Steele. Not to my surprise, not a person or animal had ever heard of the captain.

What struck me as unusual was that I had remembered very little of the area. As a soldier, I did not remember going through Winchester. Reports had described the town as having changed hands at least ten times during the war and the wartime destruction was still evident! The rebuilding was taking longer than expected as very little reconstruction had taken place. Looking eastward I could see the beautiful colorful mountains, but the local area still exposed viewers to dilapidated houses, barns, and destroyed businesses. Locals looked at us with strange stares. They could really use some rebuilding materials and a workforce to get their city up and running.

Our first night in town was no bargain! The local preacher had provided us with something to eat, but informed us very little food and supplies were available. He said, "Tomorrow a rally in the square is set. Our purpose is to gather support for a trip south to help relatives and friends who survived the war." I asked the preacher why head south? Winchester seems to be suffering just as bad as southerners. That's when he mentioned a new law that came from Washington identifying wartime torn towns who could get federal dollars. I had no idea what he was talking about!

"Will the southern states get some of that money," I asked? Preacher Chandler said, "Hell ya, young fella! But the north has to be built before money is sent south." I didn't know what he was trying to say so Mary, me, and the baby left to find a resting place.

After a night of tossing and turning in a room provided by the church, I decided to see what the rally was all about. Led by the local town leader who called himself Felix Roy, the rally produced some interesting characters. Many businessmen, bankers, politicians, and hundreds of the general population seemed ready to move south. Mr. Roy spoke of the need to bring the south under control. Control, I thought, he has enough to deal with right here.

Roy said, "They need northerners to help! They are desperate. They are poor! The south is a mess! They have no leadership! They have no farmers to work the fields. Blacks are coming north by the hundreds. Women are asking for help! Here is your opportunity to make money. The south has none!"

I thought his town WAS in the south! Winchester IS in Virginia! Man, how things have changed in such a short time! Virginia IS the south! Virginia fought for the south! How much further south was he talking about? Clinton? Atlanta? Jacksonville? What was he really saying and asking? Why is he saying he is a northerner? Was he serious? Plus the south doesn't need any more 'so called' northerners who think they know it all.

The more he talked the madder I got. I had been here less than one full day and did not like what I was hearing. These people are crazy! He sounded like he was invading the south and proclaimed the north had the 'know how'! Seemed like he and the listeners were angry at the south.

Was he a true southerner or a transplanted northerner looking to profit off starving and helpless rebels?

Did he want northerners to control the south? Did he and other northerners have answers to southern problems?

Was HIS north ready to save MY south? What was he truly saying? What did he mean by "you can make money?" Mr. Roy sounded REALLY strange!

I looked at Mary and said, "But this was and is the South, as I know it!" Mr. Roy continued to talk saying a train headed to Atlanta with stops in Clinton, Knoxville, and Chattanooga would be leaving within the week. I'll be on that train, I said to myself. I leaned into Mary saying, "He's scaring the shit out of me." "Me too," she responded.

Later that afternoon I left the square, secured Mary and Thomas and tried to find the preacher who was next to the train depot buying a ticket for Atlanta. I told him what I had heard at the rally when he said he was positioned close enough to hear everything. We talked for a few minutes when I said, "Sounds like all the northerners, including Mr. Roy here in Winchester, want to do is continue deeper into Dixie to make money at the expense of the depressed southerners. Do northerners feel we southerners can't rebuild if given the chance? Do northerners feel the same way Mr. Roy feels that all southerners are stupid, have no smarts, and can't learn if given the chance?

Do northerners believe they have all the answers to our problems?"

I asked the preacher about many local blacks who were living on the out-skirts when he responded that they had been in the Winchester area since 64 when the Yankees controlled everything within fifty miles. "Bout four hundred," he replied.

The preacher looked at me than said, "Oh, I forgot to mention last night when we spoke that congressmen in DC are discussing a law to stop the KKK from abusing and hanging blacks." Angrily, I responded, "Laws won't make any difference if the people conducting these abusive acts don't change their ways. Laws won't change those minds! Laws are not going to help. Laws will not stop the violence. Those white hooded hoodlums could care less what Washington passes. The members of the KKK are so fond of their tradition of controlling blacks they don't and won't listen to anyone, let alone some lawmaker far away from where they operate. What will that law do? Will the federals send more military to the south? Will they hunt down those hoodlums? I don't think so! Laws are made for reasonable people, not criminals!" I was mad! Obviously, the preacher was not very convincing!

While Mr. Roy and the preacher talked about the south, I turned my thoughts to Clinton and remembered the local Yankee soldiers who were positioned around our town. I remembered watching as many business-men, bankers, and very shady looking fellows had wandered into town a few years ago, but mainly had been reasonable. No real issues from the transplants, but the angry locals living in the mountains were another story. And as we waited for transportation south, Jonas and Benny came to mind!

Let's get a couple of tickets to Clinton! I had had enough of Winchester and the north. I was truly frustrated! I had been here less than a week! I had not been to see Samantha at normal school. She was some miles away, so Mary and I decided to wait till next summer. In the meantime, Mary and I had to find some answers.

As luck would have it, the train got stalled near the normal school that Samantha attended so we had a chance to spend two nights with her before heading back south to Clinton. She enjoyed school and I was happy for her. At least for the time being!

Eight

JONAS

By the end of the 60's Mary and I had two kids, I was still working at the hardware store in Clinton along side Cecil and Jonas. Our
second child Samantha Maryanne was named after my sister. Mr.
Gant had passed away in late 69, and my sister, Samantha was doing
fine at normal school in Virginia. In other news, rebuilding the national economy and construction of railroads were of great concern
in Washington. Southern newspapers had reported massacres of
large numbers of blacks had taken place in cities like New Orleans,
Atlanta, and Pulaski, but as a new decade got under way anti-black
abuse in the local area had slowed somewhat. All southern states
were under military control identified by a plan politicians and businessmen identified as 'Reconstruction' and all former confederate
states had re-entered the union. Tennessee had outlawed interracial
marriages, President Andrew Johnson had been impeached and escaped by one vote, and General U.S. Grant was occupying the White
House on Pennsylvania Avenue. And if war broke out again and men
were needed, questions would require quick answers as the size of
the United States Army had been reduced to 25,000! It was late November when I made entries in my journal.

November 22,1870
Lexington, Virginia
   I hate to start on a depressing bit of news but one of my favorite
men of the war had made headlines over the previous year. On a very
sad note, Confederate General Robert E. Lee just passed away on the

12th of October. Following the treaty signing and the subsequent se-
cession of fighting, he was named President of Washington College in
Lexington, Virginia. With a school fighting reduced enrollment and
limited curricula options, over the years as its leader, he increased
both, placing greater emphasis on math and science while expand-
ing opportunities for women. Dedicated to his religious beliefs, he at-
tended prayer services at church on the campus every morning before
circulating through the grounds to say hello to students and faculty.
Mr. Lee intermingled with students on any and every opportunity. He
even got to the stage where he could name all students by their first
name and where they called home. When he was not talking with stu-
dents or faculty, he mounted his famous horse Traveller for a ride to
the countryside.

During his years as president, he had been asked to go to Washing-
ton and testify on the War Between the States in front of congress. Re-
luctantly, he made the trip north. Even when some congressmen paid
great respect to the former general, they continually asked trying and
challenging questions. On a daily occasion, he was grilled about seces-
sion, state's rights, conduct of generals, southern expectation after the
war, responsibilities of leaders, and more, but he never blamed one
side or the other for the conflict.

While the congressmen tried to get Lee to admit southern wrong do-
ing, he never showed anger and remained calm as he claimed both sides
were dedicated to respective beliefs and objectives. He never wavered!
He was truly the gentleman in front of congress that he had maintained
throughout his life, including the war. He never blamed generals on ei-
ther side. He placed no blame on northern or southern governmental
leaders, officers, volunteers, or enlisted soldiers in either army. While
testifying, he placed no blame on the politics, businesses, or civilians.
At times he confused the congressmen with responses as he insisted on
finding no fault with either group and believing both sides were equally
responsible for the war and the outcome. He returned to Lexington and
continued his responsibilities as president of the college.

I never met the general and only know what I read in the papers
and magazines. He died a peaceful man at the age of 63 and is buried
in the school chapel.

I discovered many interesting articles specifically from the New
York Times, that endorsed trying the general for treason, but it never
took place. Some congressmen, business leaders, and hateful aspiring
political candidates wanted someone to take blame for the destruction

and Lee was their scapegoat.

An old article dated June 8, 1865 from Norfolk stated that Lee, Johnston, Longstreet, and others were indicted by a grand jury. Opposition quickly surfaced when General Grant emerged supporting his promise made at Appomattox that Lee would not be put on trial as the southern general had been paroled at their meeting. Grant was livid!

During that particular exchange, President Johnson wanted the former southern commander and others placed on trial. Grant told Johnson he would resign before he arrested Lee. Arguments between Grant and Johnson were brutal. Like Lincoln, Grant wanted peaceful measures for reconstruction. Johnson was ready to place blame even after he had confided in his cabinet that he would support the Lincoln plan. Both men stood their ground. Eventually, President Johnson agreed with Grant's position and charges were dropped.

Later

With the help of Cecil, local church members, a local family of Amish who were passing through the area, and Mary and I, we helped Jonas build a house and barn near his former farm. He and family were doing fine. Threats and notes had been reduced and weekly violent attacks from the mountain men had died down. At least for a while! That's when Jonas and I started talking about our kid's education!

And ever since my days in the army, pneumonia always welcomed winter. I had pneumonia every January! My battle wounds resurfaced with aches and pains. Scars on my legs and face reminded me every time I jumped in the river or looked in a mirror. And reminders of the war awakened me many nights with horrible dreams of recurring brutal slaughter of friends or enemy. The war was always close by!

Monthly Meetings

Last week I attended another veterans meeting in the barn close to St. Michael's Presbyterian Church. All attendees had different looks. Since the war ended local veterans had been attending monthly gatherings to refresh commitments to the southern cause, rehash old stories, and basically get support from each other. Someone brought Tennessee's finest, another supplied the tobacco, and everyone wore unit caps or hats. Many brought their Springfield rifles, as trust of the occupation northern troops was not widespread among all participants. Northern soldiers were everywhere and may appear at our meeting at any time. We were vigilant! Occasionally, we would BBQ a hog! Monthly meetings were healthy!

The Potts twins, Raymond and Randy, came with patches on their old butternut pants. Ray still had the scars across his forehead and Randy walked with a considerable limp from a hip wound taken at Chickamauga. The 22 year-old brothers were from Georgia but settled near Clinton after the war.

Cecil Alexander Gant (CA for short) had joined the group following his return. He was 22 when he entered, had fought at first and second Manassas, was wounded in Fredericksburg where he lost two fingers on his left hand, and was wounded at Chancellorsville, but it was only a scratch. I never knew he was so close. We were fighting for the same cause! One night he told everyone about his recovery from a broken leg at Cold Harbor. He mentioned the leg took ten weeks to really recover while he fought infection, pneumonia, diarrhea, and dehydration. Later, I discovered the break was not that bad! His final battle site was Petersburg where he described the charge of 13,000 Yankees that led to many deaths. All in one hour, he said. On another night, Cecil mentioned Appomattox and the return home of thousands of rebel soldiers.

And new veterans surfaced monthly as numbers grew!

David Ripple rode in on his old mule carrying some sausage from a recent hog slaughter. He informed the group his newspaper just reported that one half a million KKK members are now circulating in the south. David is black! David was recruited in North Carolina and fought for the 2nd Carolina Confederate Infantry. He said he never fired a shot, just hauled manure. "I could sling it with the best," he proudly said.

As meetings continued, we all talked about old battle wounds and how the war changed our lives. Donald Fletcher mentioned his constant battle with horrible dreams as Manassas and Sharpsburg recur every night. Donald said he woke up one night and ran to the barn with his rifle looking for Yankees. Then he started shooting in the air at no particular target. His wife came to rescue him and she almost got killed. "Sometimes I think I'm going crazy," he said. Donald also mentioned he got a letter from his brother who fought for the Union and now lives in Cleveland, Ohio. He works for the railroad but he too has battle scars and fights every day with emotional issues. His brother spent two years in a mental asylum after he tried to kill himself. Donald finished by saying that his buddies from Alabama had a favorite rebel saying: 'We will fight to the last man, we will die in the last ditch.' David Ripple responded, "That didn't work."

Barney Fisher, Lester Gross, Charles Cotton, and Philip Whelan all fought in the same southern Virginia unit. Most of their buddies were killed at Ball's Bluff when the Yanks overran their position. They returned to their little town of Tyler with only sixteen from a unit of two hundred and twenty. Lester and Charles made sergeant, but the others only showed corporal stripes. Barney said he liked northern Virginia as women were everywhere and visiting the local brothels was great fun. That's when Philip hollered, "Ya, did you love that scratchin' that followed!"

We passed around the sausage and whiskey as some grabbed chewin' tobacco, while the rest of us relaxed close to the squealing hogs located next to the church. Dennis and Gary Turner bragged about their most recent tobacco sale to a northerner as they had returned from Charlotte with new farming equipment, a nine hundred pound bull, and money to venture west. Veterans of battles in Arkansas, Tennessee, Kentucky, and northern Alabama mentioned a trip to Arkansas where land was cheap and plenty of it. Neither of the brothers could hear very well as a result of cannon blast and I wondered if they had not been sold a bill of goods about the west. A new bull and the west!

Late one night as we were about to say good byes Chuck Olsen described his most recent encounter with Yankee soldiers. Apparently, Chuck had been to the local bank in Knoxville to get a loan for a new corn crop next year and was coming out of the bank when four Yankee soldiers approached him and wanted to know where he was going. Because his grandfather was black and he was darker than the rest, they wanted to know why he did not have papers to identify himself. He argued he didn't need any particular papers. They exchanged words when the sergeant said, "We need to see the mayor." Chuck said he struggled a little before they grabbed him and away they went to see Mayor Palmer.

After a heated exchange between the six, Palmer told Chuck he needed to pay a two-dollar fine for not having the correct paperwork. Chuck continued to argue. The mayor said he could pay or go to jail. Chuck argued, "For what?" I'm a white person. My grandpa was black. My parents are white. I fought for the Confederacy. Eventually, Chuck discovered that Palmer had just arrived from Providence, Rhode Island and was a real hater of blacks when the mayor hollered, "Blackie, pay up."

Fearing the worse, Chuck reached in his pocket and gave the mayor the two bucks. If Chuck was confused, so were the rest of us. Who knows what we can expect and who knows whom to trust? Damn Yankees are everywhere!

We went our separate ways committed to return next month for another 'bull session.' Our group, the Confederate Veterans Society that started with four, now was increasing monthly. Who knows what we will discuss next. It could be New Year's resolutions. Maybe, something else!

After work and on rides to the bottom, Jonas and I discussed many issues, education for black kids, problems with farming, demands placed on locals from newly arrived northerners, and trouble with those former rebel soldiers who hated blacks. The KKK was still performing its brutal attacks on blacks throughout the south, but not to the same degree it operated in the earlier years. Newspapers reported comments from N. B. Forest claiming he could muster as many as 1,000 KKK men on a moments notice. I did not need that reminder! Jonas and I still did not trust northern strangers including Yankee soldiers in uniform or some new comers from New York City, Boston, or Cleveland. And there were many! Coal miners from Scranton, Pennsylvania came, as did factory workers from Lewiston, Maine.

In 1869 just before Mary's pa passed away a number of northern men approached Mr. Gant and wanted to buy his hardware store. Mr. Gant still owned the store but did no work as his physical condition had deteriorated from back and legs problems.

Thanks, but no thanks Mr. Gant said to the strangers that day and discovered they had invaded the town to buy and operate as many businesses as possible. They had purchased the local saloon and prices skyrocketed as quickly as they opened their doors. Luther McDowell and his buddy, Spencer Kane, bought the local tobacco warehouse and started buying tobacco from local farmers at ridiculously low prices and selling it to northern buyers at inflated prices. The twosome bought five bundles from Jonas at real low prices then shipped their products to northern Ohio. Mr. Kane said he could get a higher price in the north. Jonas took his goods elsewhere as trust of northerners dwindled.

Northern Invasion

I recalled the late 60's and situations that occurred when three men from New York came to town with ideas of controlling our town by promising more jobs and reduced land taxes. They promised everyone could vote, including blacks. The 14th Amendment, opposed by President Johnson, had been passed in the summer of 68 giving blacks citizenship and in February of 69 the 15th Amendment was passed giving them the right to vote. However, consistent with his early administrative ideas, Johnson wanted white man rule in the south. And in the former confederacy democrats did not favor blacks voting.

My yearly farm taxes were $18 and transplanted northerners said they knew ways of reducing that figure. They spent about two months talking with citizens before they were successful. Webber Handlemen is now the town mayor, but in a recent meeting with local citizens, he mentioned it could be a while before any reduction in taxes took place. Mr. Handlemen also owns a local bank and says he should have money to loan in a few months. As of today, there is no money in the bank except for the small amount placed there by Mr. Kane and Major Cookson who own a huge hog farm just outside of Clinton. The men now have over three hundred hogs they would sell in the fall. Slaughter time is just around the corner! Matter of fact, Jonas and I are preparing for our hog slaughter soon!

As I look back on the past few months, the people coming here from the north have very few belongings when they arrive, but seem to imply they have the knowledge and money to help us southerners. Some seem educated while others look like nothing more than braggers. Kane, McDowell, and Handlemen all have a convincing talk! When Mr. Gant died Cecil and I took over the hardware store and decided to stay away from any northern businessman or any person from up country. Mr. Gant had referred to them as carpetbaggers. Local newspapers editorials had placed the same identity on them and warned people to be careful whom they associated with. They can't be trusted! Cecil, Mary and I diligently watched the store business. And I hardly venture anywhere without my pistol.

The life in the hardware business was challenging. Jonas worked for a short time until he became threatened again and we agreed to limit his involvement that was reduced to helping when I requested special assistance. On special supply runs through Cumberland Gap to Kentucky, Jonas would take the train to purchase specific items. Only one time did he encounter any trouble and was fortunate to talk his way out. Hidden in his oversize coat is his pistol.

Supply purchases were always questionable. Problems mounted! Sales to citizens were always threatened by price increases, demands, and the weather always had an impact on quantity. Trains headed to Knoxville from the north got delayed and food supplies rotted. Plus train accidents were frequent! Steel, iron, clothing, and factory supplies for farming were lost or destroyed by broken or sabotaged tracks and on many occasions shipments that made it south were sold at ridiculously high prices. Thankfully, Knoxville is now rebuilding many of its steel and clothing factories and the dependence on northern shipments could cease in the near future. Jonas said, "Lets hope so." Prices rose. Supplies dwindled.

Occasionally, shipments were stolen by crooks and sold to unscrupulous individuals such as businessmen or political figures from other states. When business was slow I would close the store early and venture back to my small farm and finish the day without much to show for it.

Thanksgiving was approaching and reminders of Lincoln were everywhere in newspapers. It had been five years since he was assassinated, but his impact on Americans never seemed to vanish. He was an icon. He was a hero. He was the answer and thousands wished to honor him. Despised southerners continued their hatred while some northerners did the same. Those who idolized him continued their support. In death his love affair with the nation increased!

Like millions in the country, it was during my military service that I became familiar with Lincoln and his ideas. People across the country were overwhelmed by his life. Americans could never get enough of their fallen leader. The more I read, the more fascinated I became. I liked what he said. I agreed with many of his ideas about life. He was a character of many talents as described in an article in the Washington DC paper on the anniversary of the Gettysburg Address. Dated November 19, 1870:

Reflections of Abraham Lincoln
A Soldier's President

It seems almost like ancient history as we start a new decade and reflect on the life of one of the great men of the past. Today is the anniversary of the Gettysburg Address and comments you and I have remembered and memorized. We remember the sight of the event on one of the unfortunate landscapes in our country. Many remember the rainy cool November day and were present when Mr. Lincoln spoke but just a few words that today ring with hope for our great nation. As a writer for the paper who recently returned from Gettysburg where the townspeople are still recovering from the war, I would like to share with you some of my recollections of the former President.

Besides all the hilarious cartoons that criticized our former leader's walk or facial structure, besides all the political disagreements he had with his cabinet or congress, besides all the emotional or physical ailments, besides his difficult and complicated wife and the fact that he lost two sons early in their life, and besides the fact that he entered the presidency at the onset of the Civil War, he managed to keep this country together in what now is named The United States. It is a miracle he survived his first term as angry individuals were always within reach. His popularity was always threatened! Today, his impact on America is greater than when he resided in the White House.

From an obscure background far from the political scene in Washington, Lincoln rose to achieve the highest office in the land. He carried with him a personality that touched everyone, specifically the common soldier during the war. He was a soldier's friend. He visited campsites to talk about food, shoes, and earmuffs. He even attended fund raising events to help secure dollars for supplies. At one event in New York, he signed a copy of the Gettysburg Address to be auctioned off. He took pictures of himself (taken by Alexander Gardner) to be sold at auction.

He rode to northern Virginia battlefields to see for himself the volunteer soldiers and on many occasions had to be rescued from the direct line of fire. Lincoln believed volunteers were truly dedicated to the military life where conscripted soldiers were reluctant to follow orders and disrespected superiors. By 1864 Lincoln complained that draftees were less motivated and were more likely to disrespect authority and challenge rules. Records demonstrated that they deserted on a greater scale. Plus, he recognized that draftees and many seasoned veterans did not get along! Lincoln gave considerable credit to the young. Remembering his early years when referring to the Mexican War he said, "the young did not make the war, they only answered their country's call." On a personal note I remember writing that throughout the war, it was the generals who gave Lincoln the most trouble!

He walked and talked with injured soldiers in field hospitals and did the same with hospitals in the DC area. President Lincoln always believed in the common soldier and their dedication to the cause. President Lincoln was concerned about their pay. He spent time convincing chaplains to visit battlefields and hospitals without any pay. Eventually, Lincoln was able to get some funding for men of the cloth.

When black regiments began to fight, Lincoln rallied soldiers with assurance he would get them a respectable pay as upon entry into the army they had been paid significantly lower than white soldiers. With his constant move to abolish slavery, specifically passage of the 13th Amendment, Lincoln believed that if soldiers could die for the cause, they should also have the right to vote. He worked on legislation to that goal but unfortunately was struck down before his ideas came to fruition.

Thousands of family members, friends, or politicians visited the White House on a regular basis as the doors were always open where the president held daily meetings with the public. Topics centered on food, supplies, feed for animals, and pay, but on many occasions the topic was pardon or parole. During the war, at least 5% of union soldiers were court marshaled for something with the outcome being a firing squad or some form of embarrassment in front of their peers. Killing more soldiers was not the answer! Citizens asked for help! Since the president believed soldiers were not needed elsewhere, meaning above the clouds, he pardoned or paroled thousands during the war sending them back to their units or home when the situation warranted it.

It is no wonder that for thousands of white or black soldiers the

president became known as "Father Abraham." Have a Happy Thanksgiving!
   Editor in chief
   Samuel Abraham Maxwell

The former president was an icon. Common soldiers from above the Mason-Dixon Line continued to honor their fallen president with not only celebrations when individuals gathered memorabilia like Lincoln pictures, cards, stamps, newspaper articles, but with paper money with his face on the bills. People saved documents like the Gettysburg Address, his famous speech before the war at Cooper Union, and his most important Second Inaugural Address. Citizens and veterans built monuments, statues, named parks, streets, businesses, and many states named counties after the 16th president. Parents named their children after him! His birthday became a time for celebration! Lincoln was everywhere!

The more I read about Abraham Lincoln the more I considered where I had been over the course of the war and my recovery. The south did not have any monuments, streets, building named after its former leaders. Oh, maybe Robert E. Lee who had risen to President of Washington College.

The Confederate government was no more! Ex-president Jefferson Davis had spent two years in prison and was released after some prominent northerners like Horace Greely and Cornelius Vanderbilt posted his bond. But, by 1870, I wondered what the south had to show for itself. Veterans, civilians, businesses, cities, towns, and states were just a little bit better off than before the war. Or were they?

A few days went by and I picked up a magazine from Knoxville that described some of the Union Soldier's benefits. It made me think of what rebels received when they returned from the war. Rebels got nothing from the southern Confederate Government while up north Yankees were receiving money and aid for medical injuries and more as medical facilities were built in almost every state in the north.

Since the confederacy government did not exist no medical or mental facilities were ever built by any southern government! There was no widespread southern national government. To assist Yankee veterans when they were released from hospitals, soldier's homes were constructed to care for them! The south had no such organization or government. Transformation from soldier to civilian was made easier when Father Abraham's government provided pension for thousands of northern soldiers. Rebels got nothing. No rebel soldier received anything from the Confederacy. And I discovered from Cecil that stories of rebel soldiers receiving money at Appomattox were that, stories! A few got pennies, most got nothing but some rations for a few days. I sat the magazine down and went to the barn.

I was busy in the barn helping one of the cows with a newborn. Mary and the children had gone to town for some candy as the youngsters were celebrating. You know kids they can find any excuse to celebrate! Mary said they needed some smiles on their faces and hard candy was the answer. There was no holiday or birthday but Mary had a way of making everyone smile. When she returned and handed me the mail, another surprise.

The letter was from Captain Steele.

December 1970
John Trenton McMurtree,

JT I don't write many letters. Matter of fact, I haven't written to anyone in a long time. You probably wondered what happened to me after we separated in 65.

With the start of a family in the late 60's my wife and I decided to settle in southern Virginia and I started taking finance classes at The University of Virginia. Every day I went to school I was reminded of Thomas Jefferson as his house sits atop a mountain overlooking the town. After two years I stopped and started farming but life has many ups and downs.

As you remember, my entire family was lost in the war. My grandparents are no longer around. My life has been a wreck over the last few months as my business has taken a slide down. The damn northern soldiers are always causing problem with outrageous demands, plus they steal anything not tied down. My farmhouse got hit with high winds last summer and my roof came off. The wind also destroyed my cornfield. But that's only a small part of the tragedy I have witnessed recently.

It seems like everywhere I turn here in southern Virginia abuse of some kind is controlling my life. I went to church last weekend and the only topic of discussion after the sermon was the beatings and torture of Moses Lincoln True. His pa was a former slave on a plantation in Mississippi. He escaped before the War Between the States. He and his family live on the outskirts of the town in a small home. Following a prayer meeting at the black church last Wednesday night, Moses was severely beaten by an angry mob from the Klan. I never met Moses only know the name.

Many people in our church mentioned riots taking place in Charlottesville, Roanoke, and Richmond. Blacks are being mistreated all around. Seems like the state of Virginia just turns its back. No authority is around to help. The Yankees are worthless. They just stand by

*and watch. When I asked about the incident one dumb sergeant just
smiled and said, "Take care of it yourself, smarty." He's useless!*

*Businessmen from Philadelphia invaded our little town! They stole
everything. Money that was supposed to be used to help our town rebuild was never received. They cheated us out of our farming supplies.
One fellow promised me one price for my corn, than changed his mind
when I brought the produce to his warehouse. Three men who claimed
they were from the Freedman's Bureau came to town proclaiming they
would help all blacks only to discover they were not from Washington
but were former cavalry soldiers from the south turned robbers. JT, I
trust no one any more! I'm beginning to hate anyone from the north.
Many southerners resort to crime. I agree with the preacher. People
from the north have a new name-Damn Yankee!*

*For no other reason than sadness I have decided a move from the
south. I am a little reluctant to go into a lot of details but I need to let
you know that dramatic changes in my life have taken on new meaning. I hate to repeat but summer last my wife died while delivering a
baby. The baby boy also died. Dr. Woodstock said she had lost a lot
of blood and the baby had no chance of living. It was, what they call,
stillborn. The doctor told me it was not unusual for women to have
a hard time during deliveries but new medical findings are helping
patients survive the traumatic event. She and the baby are buried together near Pugh's Run.*

*Sunday next John Edwin, my three year old son and I are headed
west. I sold my farm for three hundred dollars last Friday to Tanner
Treadwell. He also owns another farm right next door. He raises corn
and tobacco and a wacky plant that he dries and smokes. Its not tobacco! He said it makes you feel happy! Made me think of some of those
rebel soldiers during long winter camp nights. Anyway!*

*Locals are saying there is land available out west. Jobs are avail-
able in mines, local businesses, and maybe I can get a job in a bank. I
still remember a lot of what was taught by the professors at college. I
talked to many close friends. I told the preacher of my intensions but he
just looked questioning my plans and said, "Stay and fight." I told Mr.
Thomas at the warehouse. He immediately questioned my move. I told
the doctor of my intentions when he responded with, "Captain, you
may have to learn Chinese." I asked him what he meant when he informed me that the Chinese had helped build the new railroad way out
west and they were looking for new people to work in small towns as
their construction on the RR was over and people were heading west.*

"And watch out for the buffalo herds and those wild Indians that are killing whites," the doctor finished. I promised I would!

We will make a few train stops before we get to St. Louis but after a change there, we will board the new train that goes all the way to the coast of California. I don't know if we will stop in the Rockies or continue on to the west coast, but we are leaving for sure. Can you believe that JT, we can go all the way from one coast to the other on a train? No longer will it take many weeks for supplies and goods to reach their destination. And no one has to walk any more!

As I close this letter, it may sound like I'm running away from the problems here in the south but, you know JT, I have had enough sadness in my life. I need a complete change. I need to start over and bring up my son in a place that is without violence and angry people. Seems like I need to get as far away as possible for our safety. Besides I understand thousands are doing the same thing, headed west. Former Union and Confederate officers and volunteer soldiers are making the trek. Some are going to help with the Indian problems while others are settling in Iowa, Nebraska, and Colorado. Many want to farm while others want to become ranchers.

Goodbye. Good luck. I'll write sometime soon. Take care of Mary. Do you have any children? By the way, how is your friend, Jonas?

Captain Edwin Steele

I grabbed a stick of candy, reread the letter, and placed it beside my journal. The problems and violence that had penetrated my surroundings over the long days and nights were not only invading my territory but the life of my friends. First Jonas now the captain! Captain Steele had and will always be a true friend and I had no idea he was so close. Charlottesville was few hours away by train! I wondered if he had already left. It was mid-February when I received the letter! Truly violence had spread throughout the south and was widespread in the northern part of America.

Then my mind returned to Clinton.

Yes, the south was a mess! The dreadful days of reconstruction continued with abuse from northern carpetbaggers and southerners who performed similarly. Rumors had circulated that those throughout the south who became rootless to their own neighbors took the unusual strange name of 'Scalawags'. Carpetbaggers or scalawags, it made no difference, southerners were vulnerable! Who were these scalawags anyway?

Scalawags, poor white southern trash were out for adventure at the expense of any black or white gullible to listened. Scalawags betrayed everyone including thousands of whites who wanted to keep blacks from polls.

Profit was their motive at any cost. Color of a person's skin made no difference! The further south one traveled the more abusive the stories.

Stories circulated that most scalawags were middle class planters or businessmen who used intimidation, violence, and discrimination to reach their goals. Mental and physical abuse raged. The poor white southern trash looked and sounded just like carpetbaggers! Southern newspapers couldn't get enough of their abusive ways!

I complained to Mary, citizens read weekly disruptive and damaging stories preventing economic, social, and political recovery while bank loans for rebuilding were not available from scrupulous northern loan officials. Mary and I read daily reports of damage and destruction. Local churches began screening new members with extensive questionnaires and over in Rebald County politicians were passing ordinances prohibiting blacks from even walking around without personal documents identifying themselves and where they lived. Many towns in Louisiana, Mississippi, Alabama, and South Carolina prevented blacks from walking on certain sidewalks or prevented them from entering any public building. In the eastern Tennessee Mountains and along the North Carolina border controlled by former confederate soldiers, blacks were prevented from voting or entering town halls. But, strange as it seems, some small towns here in the south had black mayors.

It certainly seemed as though thievery and misaligned principles would last forever, as no answers were forthcoming! No government in Washington, Albany, Richmond, Nashville, or Montgomery could address the problems. Who really wanted to I thought? Seemed like, no one cared! I continued to complain!

The former great General Grant, now the country leader, is without answers. What about those handsomely dressed legislators in Washington and state capitals across the south? Can't they see what is happening to America? With no forthcoming answers the abusive measures continued and got worse.

Weeks went by as I made entries in my journal mentioning the captain and described some of the comments he made about the west. After pages of my complaining about current situations and stories, I grabbed newspapers and magazines from Charleston to continue my search for answers. None surfaced!

Three years later-few changes

Selfish carpetbaggers, who cheated, lied, threatened, or used fraud tactics continuously spread. Larger population centers such as Richmond and New Orleans, home to more prosperous southern whites responded with pleas for protection against rioting and rampaging blacks. Supported by carpetbaggers and scalawags alike, bribery in local elections helped place politicians in offices and in great power. In some cities such as Montville and Coldwater blacks were elected to political office with unsuspecting influence from conniving whites. Trickery and false promises was commonplace! In states like South Carolina, Alabama, and Louisiana where no political parties existed to challenge any competition, corruption ran state legislatures as they continued to write abusive laws against blacks. Black Reconstruction stalled! Blacks became the laughing stock of northern carpetbaggers and southern scalawags.

Eventually, blacks who were lost with nowhere to go or could not find a job went back to newly redeveloped plantations or farms and worked as sharecroppers. Thousands of former slaves had not gone more than a few miles or maybe a few hundred miles from their original home. They simply returned to the same grounds they had known throughout their earlier years only this time they worked for food, living quarters, and very little money. On many former plantations blacks signed individual contracts for employment receiving no money only food, clothing, or shelter while other plantation owners had blanket contracts written for all blacks that worked the property. Former plantations became sharecropper farms!

And money hungry scoundrels were elsewhere!

When enough abuse had taken place in one town or community, carpetbaggers and scalawags picked up their small sacks containing all they owned, and moved to another unsuspecting location. Small towns and large cities all were exposed to the money hungry swindlers. Different population, similar results!

In some isolated communities circumstances and results differed slightly. Locals questioned everyone. Businessmen and preachers became more vigilant. Bankers started scrutinizing strangers! Trusting unknown new arrivals from the north was not recommended! Law enforcement provided little or no protection while hundreds of Yankee soldiers positioned to maintain peace or restore order were basically noncommittal! Enforcing the law belonged to someone else!

'JT,' I said, 'If God was so powerful, why is he not helping us southerners? The war has ended and I'm no better off now than I was when Lee and Grant met at Appomattox. People throughout the south are suffering, starving, and many roam the countryside looking for answers. A good example is my friend Jonas.' I am reminded of his personal fight daily! And I worry about those in my veterans group!

America was into the new decade. Mary had delivered another baby girl in 73 who we named Roxie Marie. Cecil and I still ran the hardware store and Jonas was always close while keeping an eye on Benny. Mary and I talked every night about the veteran's group I had organized. Education and Captain Steele were topics we discussed and I even mentioned my long lost big sister who had left the farm with her boy friend before the war. But the topic many nights was our safety and Jonas as we had heard rumblings of more threats to the blacks in the area.

We tried to understand the cultural traditions and how they impacted reconstruction. Was the old culture of the south prohibiting any progress? Really, how strong was the belief of white control? A book written by a former tobacco planter was circulating and on evenings after the children had been secured in their sleeping quarters, Mary and I discussed the book. We had borrowed the book from the local library and both had read the complete four -hundred page book titled, "White Supremacy-Negro Inferiority". Truly a disturbing book! We were curious.

Contents in every chapters identified blacks as incompetent illiterates. Whites were superior. Whites were intelligent blacks were not! Whites had money. Whites belong in power blacks do not! There were chapters with abusive comments about black women where prejudice was described in detail. Black women were not worthy as people. Even when black women were raped by a northern or southern whites nothing was done but, when a black man attacked and raped a white women and tried, blacks were lynched or castrated.

Eventually, I took the book to the local preacher. He said, "I'll find a good place for it." I didn't know what happened to the book and at that point in my life, I didn't care. I don't think he returned it to the library. Besides, was THAT the culture southerners really wanted to keep? Could the south progress with THAT past history stalled? With three children I was thinking of the future and what kind of life they would face. Southern state governments were a mess, congress in DC was still controlled by radical republicans and thousands of blacks were back on plantations as slaves. Only now, former slaves carried a different tag, sharecropper!

When I entered the Confederate Army I carried values of hard work, loyalty to the southern cause, and individual responsibility. What little I knew of local or national government rested peacefully in a secured place in my little brain. But I quickly discovered that loyalty to state control government was more important than what was taking place in Richmond or Washington. The more I had read during the war the more I realized the Confederacy was not as powerful as the Federal lawmakers in Washington. Southern governors could not get along with President Davis and his weak administration. Local control meant states would provide for them selves.

Or that was the perception! That idea completely vanished with the domination of the northern victory, but the south continues to honor tradition. How long will it last?

I continued my monthly veteran meetings as the small group enlarged with almost fifteen attendees. I continued to fight nightmares, pneumonia, and violent dreams of former battles. Tension between blacks and whites continued in and around Clinton and the local black preacher left town for places unknown and no one has taken his place. The local black church gets renewed threats now on a regular basis and Jonas and I talk every week.

Even with all the scare tactics, uncertainty with the hardware business, lack of support from northerners and Washington, and lack of a financial help from any lending institution, Jonas and I have decided to build a black school in the future and more work on that project will take place shortly. Jonas even mentioned he was interested in some type of college schooling for himself. I wondered how serious he really was when he surprised me with a pamphlet from some small college in West Virginia.

And those monthly meetings with my group brought discussions of wartime heroes to another light. In towns and cities like Warrenton, Durham, Richmond, Savannah, Memphis, Marshall, Cheraw, and hundreds more, Confederate war heroes had started reappearing. But not in person! Statues and monuments were being erected in town squares! Ideas of honoring war heroes had spread throughout the south! Eventually, Robert E. Lee, Stonewall Jackson, James Longstreet, Jefferson Davis, Nathan B. Forest, George Pickett, Joe Johnston, and Jeb Stuart were only a few of the former leaders that now occupy valuable space in the middle of town squares. In a way of embarrassing and demonstrating opposition to northerners, many statues are positioned facing south. They simply turned their backs on the north!

Last Sunday, Mary and I watched, as a statue of a common rebel soldier was placed in the town square celebrating April 9th as the treaty signing in 65. That evening the sun set on the right shoulder of THAT southern soldier as a way of turning away from the north! Other social events continued as southerners became more involved in honoring their individual state or special people!

In Lexington, Virginia, Robert Edward Lee got special recognition when Washington College became Washington & Lee. The college chapel is now Lee Chapel. And in 1871 the school became a University.

Throughout the former confederacy citizens are now beginning to save pictures and old confederate money as souvenirs. Even the battle flag of the Confederacy is being displayed everywhere and fights are breaking out when opposition to the flag is demonstrated. An editorial blasted the destruction of the battle flag by saying that people who are burning the flag or destroying it are trying to erase cherished southern tradition. Attacks on Confederate symbols are attacks on southern history, our heritage! I made extensive entries in my journal.

Future Plans

I grabbed my family and headed to find Jonas and his family. It was a beautiful southern sunshiny day. It was midsummer! The wagon, pulled by two mules, was loaded with early summer goods from the garden. Mary had fried some chicken and made her delicious corncakes. She said she had gotten the recipe from a drunken rebel soldier who had stumbled into the hardware store during the war looking for a barrel of corn. I didn't ask how a rebel soldier showed up in Clinton at her pa's store! The soldier simply dropped his small booklet as he was leaving the store empty handed. The children loaded a few melons, early tomatoes, and greens. Like a good wife, Mary made me some hardtack for old time sake! We headed to the bottom reminiscent of years gone by as I loaded my mouth with 'goober peas.'

As we rode along my mind reflected back to army days where camp food, such as potato soup, corn chowder, black-eyed peas, corn cakes, hardtack, or "what have you stew" made chow time very adventurous followed by sprints to the latrine.

Food and preparation itself reminded me of sowbelly and roasting ears meals followed by upset stomach cramps that lasted for days, sometimes continuing when long boring marches took longer than anticipated. And when we needed a break from what was being served by the cooks, we ventured into the countryside shot and prepared whatever wildlife we encountered. Needless to say, food was always on a soldier's mind!

The hardware store was closed on Sunday as Jonas, Cecil, and I had planned to discuss the black school construction as preparations were in their final stages. Cecil skipped the trip to the bottom telling Mary he had other plans and a friend in Knoxville!

Jonas had mentioned he had talked with others who were interested in helping with the project. Some had been bricklayers and a few had worked to build cabins before the war. Jarrell Randall had been asked to help with his knowledge of roofing and an Amish group who visited the store occasionally from North Carolina had showed interest in helping. That was reference to the same Amish family who had help with his home. Prospects looked good as the Sunday discussion approached. I had recruited some members of the veteran's group and we felt progress was being made.

We arrived at Johnson Creek and settled in for the afternoon when Jonas and his family came riding down the hollow. Kids gathered and started swimming in the shallow creek while we grownups gathered spreading out food and taking care of the mules. Jonas and I decided the mule race we had talked about might be cancelled due to the ages of the animals. He suggested we might bring the horses next time, as he wanted his dominance of winning every race. Besides my old mule was having a difficult time just getting me back and forth from Clinton on workdays.

Thomas, the oldest of all children, came running up from the creek claiming he had seen a big black snake in the water. Jonas hollered for everyone to get out as we ran to the creek's edge to investigate. It certainly was a water moccasin and the young rascals decided to play in the bottom rather than swim. Thomas located a ball and started throwing it when I asked where he had found it. Mr. Wilson Montgomery had given it to him. Mr. Montgomery was the director of the local Pioneer Lodge that helps young homeless kids who have no parents or family. He was a minister from New England before he ventured south in 69. The kids acted like kids and threw the ball around leading to competition to see who could throw it the furthest.

Our discussion got off to a questionable start when Jonas mentioned he had talks with Mr. Anderson a businessman from Frederick who runs the local bank. Jonas said he also claims he owns about 60 acres of forest and some of his timber can be cut to use in the project. He qualified his comment with, "For the right price!" Jonas also informed Mary and me that Mr. Anderson refuses to lend any money to him because he is black and it would look bad for him and other white businessmen.

I said to myself, 'That issue won't go away!' I started questioning where we would get the money for the wood. Maybe, Mary and I could use our trees. We would have to carry the material some distance to build, but it could be done!

On with the discussion as we talked about the necessary wood cutting, helpers, and arranged to get started a soon as possible. We talked about black families now numbering over 35 living in the area without any place to get an education. Kids wanted to learn. According to the most recent comments made by black leaders, the only way to get ahead is through learning. A few black youngsters were attending a white school in Knoxville, but constant fear was expressed regularly and some teachers paid very little attention to black children's needs.

Jonas explained, "The more education a kid has, the better opportunity he will have in the future." I shook my head yes. My friend mentioned he had been spending many nights reading the Bible and other books to his children, but Jonas Junior, his oldest, said he wanted more. He had told Jonas, "I want to read Uncle Tom's Cabin." Jonas had replied that it made him feel proud!

Many of the new black arrivals to Clinton from Georgia, South Carolina, and Alabama were living in very small homes. Jonas mentioned some of the older men applied for work in the newly rebuilt small wood mill near Greenville Creek, but were immediately turned away. Now they resort to small gardens and work for very little wherever they can find work. Some drive wagons for the Atlanta-Roanoke Railroad Company, as the train owners always need new supplies and material. A new livery stable opened up in Adamsville about six miles away. Three adults are now working there building manure piles. They make about ten dollars a week. But, there is no real educational facility for blacks! Kids spend their days roaming streets, working on their small parcels, or bored with nothing to do. Plus the black church could use a new preacher!

A teacher, books, benches, and a wood stove were on our short list of supplies for our new one room school. I told everyone I would contact my sister, Samantha, and see if she was interested. Privately, I had my doubts! We all agreed on a name, 'Freeman Manford School,' in honor of Jonas's pa. Sounded just fine! We picked a spot at the edge of town to build the school near the mountains. "I'll see how much it cost for the land," I said. Everyone agreed. I'll let the group of Amish and the veterans know when we decide to start. We had been discussing the school for months. Preparations had been finalized. Now we were ready!

We had spent a busy afternoon. The food was delicious. The children had fun in the water until the snake was spotted, but managed to play ball and entertained themselves without any more interruption. Privately, Jonas mentioned the local Baptist Church had gotten another threatening note attached to the back door, but as of late July nothing had transpired.

"Lets make our contacts and set a day to begin work. I'll check on the land," I said, as we reloaded the wagon, hitched up the mules and watched the sun settled behind Watchful Knot.

But life can change on a Confederate Dime!

Nine

TRAGEDY—TOO CLOSE

Cecil and I were unloading farm supplies when Jonas came flying into the store hollering. He was crying and could hardly speak. He screamed, "JT, she's dead." I had no idea what he was talking about. Apparently something was really wrong. "Hold your horses," I said. "What do you mean?"

That's when he continued explaining, "JT, my little girl is dead. Elsie is gone! Just gone, JT! Just a minute ago!" He continued crying and wiping tears from his cheeks. "What do you mean she's dead," I asked?

Jonas said his oldest daughter who had suffered typhoid fever the year before, had recently broken her ankle from a fall at the creek, and had for two years survived winter bouts of pneumonia had now died from a freak accident.

"Why, JT?" he asked. She had just finished playing with her favorite rabbit and wanted to go for a ride on Charger. Charger was a 20 year-old horse that Jonas had won during our racing competition days but was aging and Jonas had spent very little time riding him. "That horse is old, he said. He can hardly move."

Cecil asked him to tell us what happened. Elsie had been for a ride up Rocky Mound Gap and had returned to the barnyard. As she was riding the horse around the backside of the barn and ducking under a tree a low branch hit her head and she fell to the ground hitting a rock. Jonas said she died instantly. He continued saying his wife found her within minutes but she was gone. At the time, Jonas said he was in the woods looking for lumber for the school when the accident occurred. He went to find the doctor and preacher, but no one was home. With no help from either, he came to the store.

'Jesus,' I said to myself, he doesn't need any more brutal emotional attacks!

Tears welled in my eyes as he finished the story by saying she would be buried in a private family plot next to his ma and pa. While Cecil closed the store I went home, grabbed Mary and the children as we headed to Jonas' home.

With very little to do except be close to my buddies side, we spent the early evening with Jonas' family before the new preacher finally arrived. I could not imagine going through burying one of my children!

The next day we buried little nine-year old Elsie right beside her grandparents as Jonas wished. The preacher said a few words, read three passages from his Bible, and gave a closing prayer. Samantha Maryanne hugged me tightly as Mary held little Roxie. My kids were overcome with disbelief and sadness as one of their childhood friends was laid to rest. Benny and his family stood silently watching with tears pouring. As everyone was leaving the area, Thomas, my son, came to me and asked, "Pa, why her?" I had no answer except to say, "She is now resting peacefully with God."

Months went by as Jonas and I prepared for the school construction. With money raised from the sales of homemade blankets Mary and Jonas's wife had made, the sale of Charger, dollars raised by Thomas from sales of his prize hogs, and the sale of three of Jonas's favorite rifles from his pa's collection, we prepared. Jonas and I had conducted a day of horse racing at the bottom and charged two dollars to enter. The grand prize for the event was a cane whittled by Jonas's pa when he was a slave in Georgia. Local blacks came in support of our adventure and offered their assistance when construction commenced.

With constant reminders from Jonas about the loss of his daughter, we completed each day with a short visit to her grave. Emotionally, times were tough as we struggled along while, piece by piece we gathered material for the new black school and looked forward to its completion in the near future. Then more surprises!

I opened my mail to discover Captain Edwin Steele never made it to the Colorado Mountains or the west coast. The letter described his venture west was interrupted by delays as train schedules changed with sunup and eventually, he and his son decided to rest and settle in the Chicago, Illinois area. After many months looking for work, the captain found a job with the Pullman Railroad Car Company working in the office handling the finances. He was living in a small three-room apartment in the middle of the city overlooking some big lake and true to form his letter described his job!

Apparently, the company builds sleeping cars that are attached to box cars. Sleeping cars provide comfortable accommodations for passengers and the captain looked forward to coming east for visits. But, there were problems with the train business as accidents were taking place frequently.

Captain Steele described a recent accident occurred when a big train pileup took place with hundreds of passengers killed, including the conductor and many recently hired workers.

Mr. Pullman, the company president, blamed sabotage on the accident and called on workers to report anyone they thought were guilty. Without any proof and anger spreading resulting from no positive results, Mr. Pullman fired many workers. Former workers rebelled as hundreds gathered to support the fired employees. A riot ensued! Twelve people died and many more were injured followed by destruction of sleeping cars, boxcars, tracks, and engines. During all the turmoil the captain had stayed secluded in his upstairs small office. "I was not hurt," the captain wrote.

I was extremely glad to hear from the captain and within days sent off a short letter. I mentioned the tension in the area, the project Jonas and I were attempting and the constant presence of Yankee soldiers who were truly not worthy of the occupation. They're lazy. They do nothing but walk the streets. They're supposed to help keep the peace, but hide when danger approaches. They're really worthless! 'They need to go back north,' I wrote. I even mentioned the untimely and unfortunate death of Jonas' daughter.

I refused to detail the Clinton riot last month where an angry mob of citizens burned the sawmill then the drunkards continued into town and started a fire at the bank after attempting to obtain a loan and were refused. The small fire was put out as the disturbance spread. Four soldiers didn't know who started anything and started firing, killing two youths and two innocent blacks who were trying to avoid the confusion. My son Thomas, Cecil, and I stayed inside the hardware store as we locked the doors and grabbed rifles. Thomas hid behind flour barrels with his rifle when bullets came through a window shattering glass throughout.

The bank was saved from total destruction, but Sammy's Sawmill was gone. When the bullets stopped flying and peace was restored Mary and the two girls came to town to report more sad news. I did not include Mary's story in the letter to the captain. He had enough!

Mary mentioned Jonas had come to the farm earlier that day and reported his friend Benny and family had not been seen in over a week. He was worried. On a trip to Benny's the previous night, Jonas discovered no one was home and it looked as if the farm had been vacant for some time. Jonas reported Benny had no relatives in the area as his parents died years ago and his older brother lived in Georgia, but Jonas didn't know specifically where. Jonas went to see the new preacher and he had no idea where the family was or any indication of any problems he was having with the boys from the mountain. I grabbed my pistol and Springfield rifle and proceeded to find my friend!

Jonas had gone back to Benny's at sunup searched the area and discovered no farm animals in or around the barn area, no guns in the house, and no wagons in the fields. He did find an old brown piece of paper in the barn that simply said, 'DO NOT VOTE.' Jonas ventured to our old hiding place in the mountain caves and found nothing. He asked Mr. Wilkin, Benny's closest neighbor, if he had seen the family and got a flat 'No' for an answer. Mr. Wilkin did mention a group of mountain boys had been seen about a month ago, but nothing from them in a while. We both had worry covering our faces as we began to discuss the disturbing events!

After Jonas had finished describing his findings, I complained saying, "You know Jonas, that Enforcement Act passed in Washington years ago doesn't mean a thing. I'm mad like you. Those men who voted to outlaw fraud, intimidations, and specifically violence did so to protect you, not prevent you and Benny from voting. That work the congressmen conducted didn't mean a damn thing! Those mountain men and a few others from the outskirts of Knoxville continue to harass not only you but us white folks who support blacks. Those damn Yankee soldiers are useless. They should go back north! They just turn their smiling white cheeks and strut away! Violence is still here and Benny could be dead." I was not finished!

"Plus it's been almost ten years of northern so called help. Northerners invaded our town after the war with promises of helping us recover from those horrible four years of southern destruction. Progress has been slow. Politicians are crooked. Even the new doctor in town says unless you're white don't come for help. He's from Montgomery, Alabama. And my property taxes are too high, loans are still hard to get, and the KKK just recently made another appearance about twenty miles north of Clinton in Sweeter, Kentucky. I hope Benny wasn't headed that way!"

For the next three months Jonas, Cecil and me searched the area. Every day after we closed the store, we headed to the telegraph office and wired friends, relatives and local authorities asking about Benny and family. We finally contacted Benny's brother who now lives in northern Florida, but he had no information about the whereabouts of his brother.

In late summer on our way over the mountains we were approached and surrounded by men who wanted to know what we were doing in THEIR mountains. We mentioned we were looking for a friend while never mentioning the color of his skin. A few heated exchanges took place! No one raised any weapons! We never dismounted and finally they let us return down the mountain.

Following the tobacco harvest, Jonas mentioned he and his family were going to take a short trip up to Bristol to see one of Benny's childhood buddies and would return in a few days. I told him to stay away from those mountain men. "Don't worry," he replied. "I've had enough of them."

As October rolled in another black preacher appeared in Clinton. His name was Simpson Sharpe from Franklin, Tennessee. He bragged he had attended Peabody College in Nashville and wanted to reside in our town. I thought it was strange for a preacher to find us as many blacks were refusing to move anywhere fearful of local governmental restrictions, as blacks understood they could not move anywhere unless they carried proof of a new job identifying their position. Preacher Sharpe quickly learned conditions in our little corner of northeastern Tennessee were identical to other small towns in the south where blacks remained unequal. After discussions with many people in town including members of the local black church, Mary, Jonas, the local white preacher, and me, Preacher Sharpe felt he was truly welcome. The short-term preacher relocated over the mountain in Dustin.

'Peabody,' I murmured. How can he expect to change the cultural and social problems in eastern Tennessee? What were his plans to help blacks? Did he have some new innovative ideas? I'll wait and see!

Mr. Sharpe seemed like a friendly fellow and on many days ventured into the hardware store just to chat. Many times discussions centered on the slavery issue and specifically the Nashville area. One afternoon before Cecil stocked the selves with new supplies from Knoxville, the preacher complained about the days of the war and described problems defending Nashville in the early stages. He described problems locals had securing food and supplies as the Confederate army was more important than the citizens. Feeding the local population came second to the rebel army as he complained local small time farmers were having difficulty getting a fair price for their produce.

Preacher Sharpe continued by mentioning problems freed blacks were having with shelter as many were simply living in shacks or on the street. Even with the threat of abuse and uncertainty, some travelled west and north looking for jobs and/or adventure, but most stayed in the area!

Then he mentioned the planters! During the war he described opposition coming from most big time planters who refused the mayor's request for help. Specifically, the mayor asked planters to supply their slaves or former slaves to assist in constructing defensive structures, as the union armies were about to descend on the major supply city in the state. Planters refused the request. Needless to say Mr. Sharpe finished with, "The Yankees just waltzed in and took over Nashville in 62. Eventually, they controlled all supply warehouses, government offices, major businesses, and train routes in and around the city."

One week later looking for farming supplies Mr. Sharpe came in with his wife and seven children. While the kids grabbed some hard candy and talked with Mary, he said, "You do know Yankee soldiers have left the Nashville area?" "When was that," I asked? "Back along," came his reply. "Are all Yankees headed back north," I asked. The preacher just hunched his shoulders. He really didn't know what was happening but assured us things would be better. He was the first black I had ever seen with a college education!

The preacher and I discussed the black school Jonas and I were preparing to build. I mentioned we were gathering material, had a work force, and were anxious to begin construction shortly. Many local blacks have volunteered to help along with a contingent of Amish workers. He was a complete supporter and looked forward to construction saying he would even volunteer to teach English and Math.

Yankee soldiers leaving Nashville, I thought when the preacher said, "We're having a revival meeting next Thursday evening. Come on over and see for yourself what we are planning. The meeting starts at 7pm. Brother Abraham from over Charleston, West Virginia way is our guest speaker. He's bringing some good news."

I missed the preacher's revival as monthly veteran meetings continued while I became more discouraged with some members who could not get over their physical or mental injuries from the war. It appeared that every time we gathered the discussion always centered on war stories and most of them unpleasant. Maybe, that's the healing process, I said to myself. I know, because I still have nightmares! But, I too, still recall too much of THAT war!

Jonas returned from his Bristol visit with no mention of Benny and his family. Benny's aunt and uncle never saw him. "Haven't seen him since 56 when he left as a kid," said uncle Blackman. Former friends had no idea. Benny's childhood friend, Rascal Redface, had not seen Benny as he described a beating by the white hoods he had witnessed the previous year. Jonas said he just listened and left. But Jonas described his return had been delayed when the train stopped in a small town with more damaging news that continued spreading throughout the region.

Yacknot

Jonas had stopped at Yacknot Junction located about eight miles from Bristol in the hills of southern Virginia. The town of less than three hundred residents where almost everyone was black interestingly had a black mayor! "A black Mayor," Jonas said. "How about that?"

Jonas learned a lot about the mayor in a short time!

I had heard of some towns in the south with black leaders but not as a mayor. His story was close to home!

The mayor's name was Cyrus Ben Brown who had grown up in the town and lost some of his family before the war. He lived in West Virginia as a boy free from any slavery. Both parents died before the war and mentioned his older brother, Sanders, fought for the Union Army and imprisoned at Salisbury. Following his release from prison brother Sanders returned for a short time but decided to venture back to West Virginia where he found work in coalmines.

The mayor mentioned his family had been coal miners in the new state of West Virginia and had moved to Yacknot Junction in late 63 after the Emancipation. His small town nestled in the peaceful mountains of southern Virginia was a great place to live, but things changed when the fighting stopped in 65.

Mr. Brown talked about Abe Lincoln and was saddened when he heard the president had been killed. Following the war northerners invaded his town with promises of a better tomorrow. After years in the small community, Mr. Brown concluded, "They all came to the area just to make money and that was years ago. Life is not improving." While he complained of the unfortunate events of the last ten years, he continued describing disturbing situations.

Mr. Pringle, who runs the feed store, and Mr. Franklin the town banker came to Yacknot Junction from up north; some place called New Haven. Jonas reported he thought the mayor said New Haven, New York, but wasn't sure. Mr. Ellsworth from Oakmont, New York who runs the saloon and a little reluctant to let blacks enter his establishment also raises hogs on his small farm and sells them to blacks at ridiculously high prices. Some get in for a drink, many don't. Depends on who you are! One hundred dollars for a hog that doesn't even weigh two hundred pounds! "Neither Franklin, Pringle, nor Ellsworth give a 'shit' about blacks," complained the mayor, "and those eleven Yankee soldiers who walked around town to keep the peace were useless." That was in the late 60s!

Brown continued with other stories.

Now most black families have small farms and raise just enough to get by, but they all need help as kids run around in the same clothes for days and weeks! Clothes that are never washed turn to rags! Families are lucky to have one good meal a day. Some smaller children starve to death. And when an epidemic surfaces, many die quickly. Mr. Brown complained Washington had promised help. Nothing yet! He questioned Jonas, "Isn't this an election year"? Jonas said he just looked away saying, "Ya, but who knows what the 'hell' that will bring?"

Jonas continued with more details of his stop. Another new banker who had slipped into town almost unnoticed refuses to loan any money to blacks and even refuses to let them into his establishment. His name is Theodore Bannon from Mansfield, Connecticut. Jonas said Mayor Brown complained about Mr. Bannon saying he thinks he runs the town. Plus, he came to America from Ireland in 55. Go to Bristol is his response.

The local hardware store is now owned and operated by a big man over six feet tall who weighs three hundred plus pounds named Luther Yeager who raises his prices anytime he sees a black enter. And while blacks are struggling to stay alive, the 250 whites in town who support northerners like Yeager, attend their own white church on Sunday wondering when blacks will move away heading further south. Mayor Brown asked the white preacher if blacks were allowed in his church, but true to form, the answer was, "No blacks are allowed in my church or any other white church." And the whites in town own many of the small businesses.

Over the last few years, the town has lost one black church to arson, locals watched as feed, tobacco, and food prices have gone excessively high, and cried as their only hope of education vanished when the only black school within miles was destroyed by the KKK in 73. The local black preacher who remained nameless wants to build a new school and the mayor is fighting with businessmen and the banker to get money for the project. Most of the adult blacks in the town can't read or write and there is little chance their children would get any education unless some formal schooling was provided. The local white school that holds only 48 kids refuses black children participation. The mayor said he had tried to convince the white teacher, Samuel White to let blacks in, but when push came to shove, blacks just turned away and went home. Numerous black leaders have been more demanding in the last few years but no real movement towards 'mixing the colors' have materialized. That's how northerners referred to the problem, 'mixing colors'.

Blacks have expressed disappointment with the mayor's inability to successfully address black needs including voting issues. Blacks want to vote in local, state, and federal elections. Brown argued, "They want a voice and representation. Washington DC had sent a man to Yacknot Junction to educate blacks about voting but, blacks still do not vote! The white man from Washington said, blacks need to get educated and learn to read and write while he insisted the south marches to a different number, alone with specific rules for colored."

While discussing the voting issue, blacks claimed they are intimidated with threats of physical harm and therefore refuse to attend the voting booths. Mayor Brown wants it to stop, but no local supporter is ready to lend a hand.

When Jonas asked Mr. Brown how he became mayor, he responded by saying elections were controlled by northern businessmen and politicians.

"In small towns like Yacknot Junction, northerners felt by electing a black person they could control former slaves. Elected black Mayor's become spokespersons for blacks. Blacks listen to blacks! Northerners encouraged blacks to vote 'the right way' and since most of the town was black and I had lived here for some time, it was easy to get elected," claimed the mayor. Most whites rested at home while blacks were escorted to the polls. Local whites knew when to vote and when to remain away from the polls. Yankees knew when, how, and why local elections required their assistance and provided the means.

Yankees controlled voting with threats, intimidation, or bribery and recruited locals who supported Yankee ideas. During specific elections, signs saying 'Blacks Not Needed, Don't Vote' and if that didn't work, a local hanging might convince voters of the proper results. For those few blacks who went to the polls, 'Vote the right way!' Someone close by always had something to say. The proper election results in Yacknot Junction were guaranteed!

Other then voting the right way the mayor had more problems!

Mr. Brown explained before the war hundreds of former slaves from the Cassamore Plantation in South Carolina moved to the area. Their former home had over five hundred slaves. Most of the residents of Yacknot Junction had escaped riding the Underground Railroad hiding and travelling through the mountains at night while trying to outrun the angry rebels during the day. Now most of the blacks work for Mr. Howard Haywood Honeywell who owns a huge tobacco farm on the outskirts of the town and all workers get paid about five dollars a week while living in sheds at the edge of the fields. Mr. Honeywell has two business partners from Baltimore, Maryland and Fredericksburg, Virginia who 'take care of business' visiting Yacknot Junction in the fall. Mayor Brown calls the farm, sharecroppers!

The mayor explained following his election he attempted to talk with the white teacher about education. No luck! He approached white church leaders and parents of white students just to talk. Again, no luck! He talked to the banker the feed and hardware store owners about prices blacks were forced to pay. "Go somewhere else," they shouted. Mayor Brown visited with the DC administrator about taxes, prices, and threats. The Washingtonian listened. Nothing happened. For many years the mayor got nowhere with the white public, was rejected by small contingents of vocal blacks, and was extremely frustrated with the lack of any support. And he got very little satisfaction from the sharecroppers.

The mayor reported the future of the town did not look good. Quietly he complained to Jonas. Prices still climb. Taxes are too high. Threats occur periodically. Washington is no help. Get rid of Grant! Mayor Brown claimed, "Corruption is everywhere!"

The mayor continued, "Even a black mayor can't get anything done to help his own! Look around! A black mayor in Young County was killed by another black when the killer claimed the mayor was too friendly with the local whites. Fear and tension is throughout! I might have to take my family and move as many blacks are losing confidence in what I say or try to do for them. Seems like my efforts are no good any more. While some talk to me about their support others claim I ain't getting' anything done. Jonas they forget, I live in just a small house here in town and everything I have is from my own hard work. My wife and me work our own little farm and raise hogs. That's it! And I don't want to get elected again. Not this coming fall or ever."

Two months later

I was glad he returned safely, but sad his friend was still not found! Jonas and I feared the worse as discussions centered on possible outcomes. We continued our boring job at the store.

On weekends during the winter, Jonas and I had started to cut wood from my property and take it to the newly rebuilt sawmill run by Sammy. Weekends went fast as we built our inventory. Planks and many large beams were cut and hand sawed. With a little help from me, Thomas became an expert driving the loaded wagon to the sawmill and construction site. He would be eleven years old before the new-year got too far along! Plus winter brought my way another bout with pneumonia!

Mary and the girls always supplied plenty of food. We could vision the construction of the new school that would begin shortly. Anticipation of completion of our project increased. Helpers were notified! Veterans were ready. Amish families were notified. Jonas's friends were contacted and the project was moving in the right direction. We had done a lot of the cutting and sawing during the winter and spring was approaching. After the spring floods receded clearing the bottom and surrounding hillsides and the area was clear of any mudslides, we decided to begin construction in late March or early April. Even the preacher was contacted!

My old cow pasture was ready, but Jonas and I had changed the site of the school to be located at the edge of what little land Jonas owned. Throughout the winter and early spring we had stacked a goodly portion of the wood needed for the project and I had even recruited two new rebel veterans to help with construction! We were ready! I asked Jonas if anything had surfaced regarding Benny, as he responded with a sad 'no.'

I said goodnight to Jonas and Cecil, located my son Thomas who was lost in a farming magazine, grabbed the hardware store keys, locked the door, and ventured to the post office to collect any mail. My sister didn't disappoint me. Finally, I had a letter from normal school. I quickly discovered the name had been changed to Owensville College. That was fine. I knew where she was!

The letter was full of information about Samantha as Mary and I read and reread the letter a number of times before we went to sleep that night. Sam mentioned her classes at school were very exciting and she loved the religious subjects. Her teachers all from the north taught with authority. Sam said, "They have excellent knowledge of the subject area." I wondered why she felt that way! Were northern instructors better than southern teachers? She said her favorite class was Theology Theory. What is that, I asked myself? Then she said one of her close friends suggested she take a class in Teaching Dynamics. Rhetoric sounded like a course that was truly confusing, but my little sister said she really enjoyed the class and the discussions that followed. 'Rhetoric,' I said to myself! What?

In her spare time Samantha was working with disadvantaged homeless kids, and in many cases simply kids with no parents. She gave details of a young boy named Raymond who had been living on the streets for weeks without food or proper clothing. He told her he came all the way from North Hampton by way of train. He had spent days living in an old shed and begging for food. He lost his ma when she went to the local food warehouse and never returned and his pa was beaten to death in a brawl. His three brothers and two sisters were in orphanages and he refused to be taken when the federals came to their farm.

That sounded like a complete plate! I needed to write and ask if she had any time by herself for fun. Seems like she was working 25 hours a day. I recall she had not been home since she left for college and now I see why.

Three pages into her letter Samantha mentioned she had met a fellow from Maine. She identified the town as Waterville. She had met Wallace Libby the second year of schooling and they had taken many classes together. He had two older brothers and five sisters. His pa had been a major in the Union Army, fought at Gettysburg and died at Petersburg in late 64. His ma still lives in a nursing home in Waterville, but is not well. Samantha mentioned Wallace had returned home the previous Christmas to find the farm suffering from severe shortages of food as diseases had ruined fall harvest. The local paper mill was suffering losing workers as many citizens had decided to either go south or west looking for new opportunities. The letter continued by saying that living conditions in Maine were not much different than other parts of the north. But she really liked Wallace.

Samantha broke the news that she and Wallace had become really close and were considering getting married when school was completed. They even talked about opportunities for work in Morgantown, West Virginia!

Even with all she wrote about her life, the work she was doing, and the future she was planning, I still feared for her safety. Maybe that's the big brother in me. With reports of riots, gangs, angry whites and blacks, and newspaper reports of corruption in local, state, and federal governments, I was extremely concerned. On one hand my mind said she is grown up while the reverse said, she is still my little sister. I will write soon!

The New Black School

It was early spring when Jonas and I gathered our work tools and rode to the school construction site to begin work. Mary and Jonas's wife packed food for everyone. The Amish, my veteran buddies, the lively blacks, and other workers had been notified. It was a beautiful sunny day as we rounded Rattlesnake Mountain in our wagons. The mood was joyous. Everyone was excited! We were ready to build! But, that was not to be!

The gray smoke billowing above could be seen for miles. Smoke covered the tops of the mountains. I could smell smoke coming from the construction site. The smell of burnt wood spread throughout the valley. My heartbeat accelerated as if rebels were wildly screaming and running forward approaching the Yankees at Gettysburg! Anxiety accompanied by fear set in! Again, thoughts of threats! Thoughts of turmoil and thoughts of intimidations! Again, mental and physical abuses that were circulating throughout the southern culture were driven home by what lay in the distance. If looks could kill, we all would all be dead. The thoughtful rude awakening of what was truly happening in our little community was now visible to my front angering everyone as we approached. I turned to Mary asking why?

Our construction site was nothing but a huge mound of destruction and burnt rubble. The boards, planks, beams, and other supplies we had assembled were nothing but ashes. Metal works lay scattered about! Windows, we had purchased from a new factory in Knoxville, were demolished with glass everywhere. Two wagons full of small supplies were tipped over scattering the material. Fire had destroyed our tool shed. And draped over the newly dug well were three large white sheets covered with bullet holes.

The smoldering remains simmered as everyone looked on! The devastation was widespread. Nothing was left! Anger overcame everyone! Standing in disbelief, we all wondered why! Even the kids inquired why and started crying? Thomas and Samantha questioned who was responsible for the devastation. All that preparation gone! All that work planning, organizing help, and labor, now gone!

Outrage and revenge entered the minds of many! Jonas and his wife started crying, asking why! His kids cried! Hopelessness set in with questions of the future school. Perspective builders stood motionless! Jonas screamed, "Hours spent planning and organizing lost! Why us? Why me? Why now?" Blacks fell to their knees crying while screaming asking God for help. Not a soul could believe what lay to our front!

Now the dream of any education for young blacks looked very, very bleak! We walked around with stupefied looks until Jonas spotted another reminder of the violence that still circulated within southern communities. Attached to a tree nearby was a cartoon of a white hooded person on a horse carrying a sign with three K's in big bold lettering! In his right hand was a rifle raised to the heavens. Jonas took it down and threw it into the rubble.

I retrieved the sheets from the well completing that dreadful task! The preacher approached gathering the workers and responded with reassurance that better days ARE ahead. He followed with a closing prayer. What tools and supplies were worth saving were gathered, placed in our wagons, and the mass of dejection left the devastated remains. Disbelief, anger, and questions covered sad faces!

Three months later

After weeks of discussing the loss and unlikely prospects for another school in the immediate future, Jonas went to Knoxville to inquire about printed information regarding homesteads on federal lands. Apparently the government was providing land out west for settlements and Jonas wanted information from government officials. Jonas mentioned prospects of moving.

Jonas discovered the application process took hours. He waited, waited, and waited to talk with someone! Finally after sleeping in an old railroad car for one night, he was able to contact a government spokesperson from up north. Jonas described 'up north' as being, Richmond, Virginia.

However, no one had any real information regarding available land nearby. Jonas mentioned land was available out west and some small parcels of 40 acres were being offered close by in West Virginia. Jonas returned with information regarding the newly completed railroad running through the Cumberland Gap saying with connections in Charleston, West Virginia he could ride the rails all the way to Chicago. Made me think of a trip to see Captain Steele! Jonas handed me a copy of the Knoxville Gazette and said, "JT, that was a waste of my time. That smarty pants government official was useless." I had to agree!

Headlines from the Knoxville paper:
>*Register Now for Fall Presidential Election*
>*Federal Troops Needed in Pennsylvania Coalmines*
>*Rockefeller Needs Workers*
>*Confederate Money Auction at Philbey's*
>*Federal Land-Homestead*
>*Three KKK Members Arrested*
>*Editorial from Tenor-'Grant a Waste'*
>*History of 'Caster Thunder' (Richmond Prison)*
>*Biography-Civil War Veteran Running for President*

After a day of working our tobacco fields Jonas found time to describe some of the comments made by the uneducated smarty northerner!

When the over weight cigar smoking government official talked about Jonas's application, the man explained the process while asking for written proof Jonas was working. Jonas told the man he had none and I hadn't supplied him with any written work contracts from the hardware store! Jonas complained the process required the applicant to currently be employed, have been offered a job and approved plus have papers identifying and describing the job and location. The agent wanted proof like a written contract. Jonas argued the government agent explained that notice of a job offer was 'a must' to acquire any federal land.

Jonas argued, "I didn't have any contract! I didn't have anything except me and my family and interest in moving away from this dangerous place to a more peaceful area. I need to leave this damn place." The west he was referring to was West Virginia.

Jonas described a heated discussion ensued and eventually a decision was made. Jonas was refused any land. He was upset. He was angry and hollered at 'skinny' as he left the office. He mulled over his next move before he said, "JT, I need work. I'm leaving." As he was complaining he reached into his belongings and secured a college handbook! "What is that," I asked?

With the loss of the school, the disappearance of his close friend Benny, fear of personal safety for himself and family, devastation from crop diseases, no work in the area for the foreseeable future and no job in site associated with the homestead application process, Jonas informed me he was headed to the coal mining area of central West Virginia. His part time job at the hardware store was history. I sarcastically asked, "Are you serious?" "Damn right!" he responded. "They have a college there," he finished.

I understood what he was saying! I believed his frustration regarding family safety issues were real. I continued to ask customers for answers regarding the burning of the school materials. No one knew anything. That's not surprising. And I knew we were not doing well at the store and Cecil and I could handle all the work, but I did not want to see my closest friend leave.

I had some future plans that could involve him. Concern regarding the health of formers rebel soldiers, was beginning to surface. And his mention of the college interested me! Was he seriously planning on college for himself?

Jonas and I continued discussions that lasted for weeks, me trying to convince him to stay while he insisted he would be ok. And he continued to mention his interest in getting some college! It could be a short trip he said during one conversation. Referring to the coal mining possibilities, he said, "Trains need coal to run. I'll go there." I briefly mention my interest in my veteran's group that got no response.

We talked about the move. He knew no one in the area but was confident, he could find help from many blacks who had settled near Gabriel. I remembered what grandpa had said about the Underground Railroad describing the many trails of the escape route and emphasizing many had gone through West Virginia continuing on to Indiana and Illinois. "Coal mining is dangerous work," I said. I had read stories in the Gazette regarding coalmining accidents where men were killed deep inside the caves. I relayed those stories to Jonas while saying I had some plans for the near future, but I didn't detail them at the present moment.

Cecil and I spent the days working in the store when I left early many afternoons, went to talk with Jonas, then ventured on home. Mary and I had to talk. She was just as worried about Jonas' move as I was, plus she was pregnant with another child due in three or four months. Business was slow. Cecil had been thrown from his horse and was recovering from a broken shoulder. We were barely getting by. Prices kept rising and we were working harder I complained to Mary.

Coinciding with Jonas, work, and my family there were too many other disruptions in town. Four hooded men robbed the bank a few weeks ago, took all the cash, and a small amount of silver. The little rebuilt black church was fired again. They now hold services in the open air beside the ashes while the new preacher continues his uplifting positive approach to social and cultural unrest.

Captain Steele had mentioned job opportunities in Chicago, but I didn't want that far west. I didn't know if I wanted to venture too far north and I knew I didn't want to travel any further south to live. This whole entire Reconstruction Act from DC was not moving forward very quickly. And I needed to check on my little sister Samantha and meet her new friend, Wallace. Decision time was approaching for my family! Jonas! The Captain! Benny! Mary! Me! My Kids! My mind was spinning out of control!

Jonas said his goodbyes as he and the family departed for central West Virginia. Mining coal in the dangerous mountains was his next stop and all our discussions proved fruitless, at least from my standpoint, as my childhood buddy had made his decision. We had spent the last Sunday together at the bottom watching the kids play as us parents talked. He said he would be ok. I reckon he would be! His leaving touched every emotional inch in my body. I had spent my entire life with him and I felt alone for some time! But, I still feared for his life and family.

Weeks passed. Mary continued with morning sickness. Our bedroom was a mess! We visited with the doctor for help. He was useless and a waste of time! Two new calves were born and the kids were spending more time with math and reading. Mary decided to teach the children herself and I could assist. The hardware store shelves were pretty bare and the backdoor livery stable was getting a rebuilding job under the watchful eyes of Brother Babcock and his Amish family. And throughout the country people were discussing the new elections set for the fall.

Newspapers from Richmond, Charleston, and nearby Knoxville were covering many interesting stories. Some depressing headlines got attention followed by sad stories of corruption and editorial comments that always carried varied viewpoints.

Headlines from Richmond

Federal Supervision of Southern Schools Questioned
Yankee Soldiers on trial for cheating Local Authorities
Military Reconstruction Act Gone
Ammunition Factory Completed
Civil War Veteran Running for President
Blacks Demanding More Rights
Flesher Railroad Company Looking for Workers
Libby Prison-No More

I read the story by Henry about President Grant saying the former Union General had no idea about rebuilding the south. Henry complained about the president being drunk as the liquor consumption was greater than his mental consumption. And when he wasn't overcome by the bottle while attempting to make intelligent decisions his former generals were bombarding the white house looking for favors or handouts from the federal government. Many wanted government jobs and greater pensions. Soldiers complained to Grant about feeling abandoned by their government. They complained about the lack of jobs available. Some needed help from war wounds and required medical attention and wanted Grant to provide for them. Hammer carried on for a full page before I stopped reading.

After reading the article, I asked Mary, "I wonder how former Rebel generals are surviving? They had no government to rely on and support them!"

But, I had read other stories of President Grant. When he was elected in 68 he was not in complete agreement with President Johnson about reconstruction. Grant remembered that on the day Lincoln was shot, he met Johnson in the White House with Lincoln's cabinet and they discussed the Appomattox Treaty. Johnson opposed many aspects of the treaty and wanted southern generals and the Confederate President tried for treason. Punish the south, Johnson demanded! Grant disagreed.

Grant wanted a friendly transfer to recovery similar to Lincoln's plan. Grant wanted everyone in jobs. He wanted businesses and industry rebuilt. Grant wanted protection for blacks. Midway through his first administration, he got congress to pass an act outlawing the KKK. The Ohioan felt that when Lincoln was assassinated the reconstruction plans would be set back and that congress would be severely challenged.

I reckon he was right! The ten years following the war have been a mess!

Ten

LEAVING

While Mary and I tried to decide what was best for our family, I continued to work and read more articles. Our fourth baby, another girl who we named Frances Leighanne, was born in the middle of July during a blast of excessive heat. Mary had a little trouble with the delivery, as the baby weighed almost eleven pounds. Recovery was a little difficult, but with a few weeks of bed rest and me spending more time in the kitchen and school lessons we survived. When the doctor left he had commented, "She's going to be a big kid. Look at those feet!" One boy, three girls, what more could I want? That's when Mary said, "How about a move?"

During the weeks of rest, Mary and I talked at length about when, why, and if we moved from our childhood location. We discussed possibilities and problems. We discussed where to relocate. I returned to thinking about further education for me. I had no formal schooling and considered my future without an education. And my comments about safety for my family always came to mind. But Tennessee will always be my home! Plus those veterans needed help!

A real turning point came when I went to the monthly veterans meeting and was reminded of the horrors of war, its immediate aftereffects, and what the future held for millions of men and women, specifically southerners. The monthly meeting was about to begin! And I worried about veterans! Many had nothing! Like many of them, I could never get away from the war!

Many of the veterans were relatively young when they went off to fight. Now, most were in their thirties except a few older fellows and twenty six year old Bubba Hays who said he was just fourteen when he left home. Five bottles of the newly produced Jack Daniel's Tennessee Whiskey was passed around as we circulated for a few minutes introducing new attendees. It was twelve years after the war ended and the scene at the Baptist church was depressing. Everyone had bruises from the war. Bubba was missing an eye! Scars, unhealed wounds, missing limbs, and emotional damage defined the gathered soldiers. Johnnie Crump yelled, "Drink up boys, I have plenty in the wagon."

Preacher Sharpe grabbed a swig, said a few words, a prayer, and then one of the older veterans spoke about a gathering he had attended in Knoxville where a new hospital was under construction. "Should be finished in about a year," he said. Someone in the back of the room hollered, "I can't wait that long. I need help!"

Everyone had a chance to talk when I asked the group that had expanded to over twenty what were the most pressing issues. They all responded with jobs and health issues! Comments of medical problems surfaced. "Home loans for building anything are not to be found," complained Jack Thomas. Since the previous meeting last month five members had travelled to Washington to talk with Congressmen that proved fruitless. Eddie Mitchell shot back, "Hell, all those good for nothings guys in Washington do is talk about getting re-elected. They don't give a shit about us or even know we exist. F__'um all."

I asked if anyone had gotten any financial or medical help at all since the war ended. Not a single soul responded until Jacob Snowden smartly said, "I don't even know where to go to get any damn help. Where do I go? Everyone tells me, it's a waste of my God Damn time. Banks are f__'n useless! There's that crook at the bank with his vault locked that said I needed to have a God Damn job to get any of his f__'n money." When I asked him about money from Washington, fifty-five year old Booker simply laughed and said, "Sonny, are you crazy?"

The preacher resurfaced asking if there was any interest in education as a new college was under construction over the mountains in North Carolina. No one said a word! Coal mining jobs in West Virginia was mentioned with no interest in 'that' business. And there was very little approval from anyone about northern jobs. Former confederate soldiers wanted help in their hometown. "I don't want to go anywhere. Any kind of good job would do," complained Jimmy Campbell. James Catlin hollered, "I'm going crazy and my ma is dying. I lost my job at the blacksmith shop because I can't sit for a long time and drive the wagons to Knoxville and tonight I'll be sleeping in the barn with the cows. My ass hurts from the wounds I suffered at Fort Donaldson when that f__'n Grant almost killed me."

After two hours of complaining and six bottles of whiskey, the group dispersed as I watch James limp to his carriage swearing and cussing about his sore ass.

I went home thinking about tough life changing decisions that demanded attention. I worried about my family! I was concerned about Jonas' safety. I thought about him everyday! What happened to Benny? I was consumed by unhealthy mental and physical conditions veterans witnessed every day. I was anxious about conditions in Clinton and the rest of the reconstructed south. Would there ever be a black school in Clinton? My sister Samantha's schooling and her future surfaced! I couldn't save the world, but could I make a difference somehow? Is education really the answer?

"Yes," I said. "I will make a difference!"

JT, I said to myself, life is full of decisions. The future is not guaranteed, but making a quick decision is not smart. I love the south. I love my family tradition. My children! My wife! And running away is not the answer. Make a decision!

Decisions

As the administration of President Grant was drawing to a close with little success rebuilding the south or any positive prospects for the future in the Volunteer state, a decision was made. Following many long days and sleepless nights of discussing varied topics, Mary and I decided we would pick up our family and head north. Destination, Virginia! Education was my focus!

Mary and I discussed education, jobs opportunities, and the safety of our family, plus we had reviewed the horrible post war conditions of local veterans. I truly felt former rebel soldiers were not getting any relief from local businesses, the federal government, and their future certainly looked dim. But, I had some ideas! My head swirled with thoughts of the future as Mary and I informed the children!

The move would be a joint effort. We investigated conditions and employment, some located in the west, others in Ohio and Indiana, and some just north in Virginia. Mary was a true southerner through and through, but commented that she felt we were not moving forward and more opportunities might be available. "Let's go," she said! And we would return to Clinton someday!

Mary convinced me the countryside had quieted down somewhat. But, violence continued! Disruptions included killings between blacks and whites. Some reduction in violence surfaced in tiny spots by adherence to local laws. Many blacks were reluctant to move north or anywhere. Fearful of unknown conditions and opportunities in new territory, thousands went nowhere.

But, I wasn't going anywhere because blacks were remaining in the south or any other black-white reason. I was thinking of family, my veteran friends as well as the future of my hometown! Hell, my best friend was black and I wanted to know more about his situation. Maybe a visit to West Virginia to see Jonas was needed. Color was not a deciding factor. My family took first place followed by my veteran's group

There were rumors spreading through the community that Yankee soldiers would be leaving Clinton after the presidential election in 76, but that was not certain. Even with promises from aspiring candidates, the results of the new presidential election gave no assurance things would be any better!

Mary and I visited with Preacher Luther Littlefield our new white preacher for two days discussing every issue we had reviewed. They were great visits. When I mentioned my interest in a new soldier's home for disabled veterans, Mr. Littlefield answered with complete surprise and approval. Matter of fact that announcement caught everyone by surprise! I had never shared that interest with anyone but Mary and Jonas.

Then we decided to venture over to the black church and see Mr. Sharpe.

Preacher Sharpe asked me if I was running away when I responded with, "NO, I'm moving forward for the betterment of my family and community. Plus, I have decided to get some schooling to work with disabled veterans and build a home for veterans. My buddies and me could use some help!" Likewise, he was caught off guard!

The monthly meetings with the veteran's group convinced me my ideas regarding the recovery of soldier's mental and physical wellbeing was equally significant as anything in their lives. We all had horrible war stories! They needed help! I needed to help! At the last meeting, I told Jimmy Ray I would return! I don't think he believed me as he raised the confederate battle flag saying save the south! Before leaving that night, I shared with all my plans for a soldier's home. But I was not convinced everyone believed I would return.

Mary and I decided to sell the farm and move in the fall, but we thought otherwise when Cecil offered to live and run the farm until we returned. Cows and other animals would not have to be sold. The house and barn were being repaired with the help of the Amish clan and Mr. Ayers, a bachelor from Clinton, said he would help with the hardware store. He had lost his wife to scarlet fever back along and his two boys and a daughter had moved to Illinois and North Carolina respectively. Sixty-four year old Mr. Ayers wanted to rent some of my farmland saying he could give me one hundred dollars a year, as he wanted to grow tobacco on my small spread. That sounded good. "Okay," we said. Cecil could simply run the store. Mr. Ayers could live upstairs!

A few quick months went by when I gathered my family, loaded a wagon pulled by four mules and headed north up the Shenandoah Valley. Mary and the children wanted to ride the train but I wanted more goods! We had prepared everything. Plus, I had a history lesson to present to my kids. We loaded clothes, some basics, and tools. We covered everything with former army tents we received from an old rebel warehouse, and I placed my trustee old Confederate rifle along side. Brother Elisha gave us some honey from his beehive, a side of ham from his father's farm, and off we went headed. We should be in Lexington in a few days. "Lexington?" questioned Thomas. And I wanted my kids to see the landscape I had walked after my enlistment in 62.

Roads were terrible. Heavy fall rains complicated our movement! Muddy conditions slowed progress. Frances cried continually. We stopped along the way in small towns and communities where locals helped with shelter and food. Everyone wanted to know where we were going! Roxie always hollered, "north!" Thomas assisted with the young girls plus the mules needed extra food and rest the further north we tracked. We passed groups of blacks headed somewhere, small groups of former soldiers gathered to say good luck as we moved along, and at one train depot where we inquired about tickets, we discussed job opportunities with some well dressed northerners headed in the opposite direction.

We stopped in Smokey for two days, another three days layover near Summersworth, before we arrived in Lexington, the home of Washington and Lee University. Along the way, I collected newspapers and magazines and any current material for my transition to my new life. And those dangerous mountain men, who caused anxiety between blacks and us whites, never were seen. Maybe they've dispersed. I told my children my trek north during the war was basically the same road they had just travelled when Thomas asked, "You walked the entire way?" "The entire way and more with my trusty rifle and dressed like a farmer's kid," I responded!

Washington and Lee

The travel wasn't easy. But we were in Virginia and the school had classes I would investigate. I had read about the school and wanted my college experience in a respectable university.

Adjusting to Lexington was quick and relatively easy. Kids found schooling, while I discovered college life and Mary became the 'jack of all trades'.

Before leaving Clinton, I had spent many nights reading about Washington and Lee University, its offerings and I was ready.

The school brochure described science, history, math, economics, astronomy, English, social dynamics, manuscript, politics, and rhetoric classes. I had some idea what I was getting into and I wanted to study classes that helped rebuild social conditions of veterans, especially my buddies in Clinton. My focus would be veterans, politics, and economics.

Newspapers and discussions with locals were helpful describing the immediate area, its education system, and the local church was instrumental in getting us started. Our plan was to join the church and attend regularly.

Eventually, I ventured to the college, enrolled, and got a part time job at the local hardware store making $25 a week. When I wasn't studying, helping with the kids, or working I read the papers and magazines. Classes started right after Christmas. And I befriended a Yankee who would prove to be a valuable resource.

Richard Patterson, a former union sergeant, and I became pretty good buddies during my schooling years. We discussed our respective war experiences, our concern about the reconstruction effort in the south, and he had great concerns about the explosion of moneymakers in the north who were employing workers who were paid very little. He mentioned coalmining, the railroad industry, and someone was discovering oil in the land just north of Virginia. We were in many classes together and he helped me with English correcting spelling problems and I assisted him with social classes, economics, as we discussed politics every Thursday night at the local saloon. He even went fishing with Thomas and me!

Richard was from eastern Ohio near the West Virginia line and had worked in a few factories but never fully explained details or conditions. He worked for three years in Turnersville Coal Mine located near Wheeling, West Virginia, and described the horrible scenes with danger around every turn. He complained his lungs hurt all the time and coughed himself to sleep many nights. Over a few beers one night at the local saloon, he described awaking nights spitting blood and described his years in the coalmines when he reported to work having had very little rest. He commented, "I put others in danger just by working with tired legs and shoulders. I passed out one day and had to be carried outside. Plus, it's hard to see in the mines."

Richard wasn't married and had a brother injured in the battle at Cold Harbor just before the war ended. His brother was in a veteran's home where he gets food, shelter, and occasionally medical help. "He can't think straight," Richard sadly said, "and I haven't seen him in months." Richard spent two years at school before he decided to leave and work on the railroad, but his comments about the home drew many unanswered questions to my plan. Before he left, I had asked him where the home was located and specifics about the facility.

He said it was located in the town of Sayersburg. The veteran's home had about twelve former soldiers as patients in various mental and physical conditions that required around the clock attention. The building was a former hospital before the war but the war took its workers and the building stood vacant for years. Now it lacked repairs! "It's ready to fall down," Richard complained. Frank Taylor and his son Randy, who run the local hotel, help with any repairs and the local mayor wants to expand the home but he has no funding. Richard said he had no idea who owned the building or who ran the home.

He continued saying there were no doctors in town and if a doctor was needed it usually took days before anyone arrived. Dr. Aubrey McDuff from Bullet comes by monthly to check on some of the patients. He's only thirty years old and is well liked but he needs help. Richard commented, "I don't know where he got his medical knowledge, but he does good when he arrives."

Workers at the home are paid peanuts. The staff is very small and the turnover rate resembles a waterfall. The last time Richard contacted anyone at the home he discovered less than five people worked the facility. He had visited the home the previous Christmas. It appears the cleaning ladies and the kitchen staff of two come and go monthly. It's hard to keep good help! "Plus, some of the patients are real obnoxious," he commented! Some employees get extra food from the kitchen rather than a decent wage and to make stories more interesting, some time ago two sisters were fired when they let a patient escape as all the doors and windows were supposed to be locked. "Jasper just threw the kitchen window open during a cold spell and left," Rich said. He continued describing the facility. Carefully, I listened!

The federal government is no help giving very little assistance. "Sayersburg is too small. Small towns get lost in the paper shuffle in Washington. Applications for assistance settle at the bottom of some pile in the corner of some congressman's office while the fat useless legislator is off speech making to get re-elected. Hell, no one even knows my brothers there," he complained! My interest in the home answered a few of my questions, but I needed to know more!

Many days after classes we spent hours in the library finally retiring to the local saloon where Richard continued. Rich mentioned local farmers helped with foodstuffs and some local stores provide basic tool supplies or wagons to transport medical goods from far away Pittsburg. That's when I asked Rich why supplies were not arriving by train when he responded,

"Hell, they don't have any good working tracks in Sayersburg. They're broken! Rebuilding train-tracks is out of the question!" Most discussions lasted longer than expected and my return home usually found everyone including Mary, sleeping.

With my friend gone and more time to research, I discovered medical journals in the newly refurbished library that contributed considerably and eventually asked one of my instructors if he had ever heard of the Taylor Lincoln Johnson Veterans Home located in Sayersburg, West Virginia. Mr. Bayers, my economics/political instructor, responded with a no. "Why do you ask," he inquired? "I need to go there and see for myself," I answered.

A medical journal, published the previous summer, detailed some of the organization and administration of most veteran's home. It described the structure and how floors and rooms were designed to better administer to the patients. It described staffing and necessary professionals needed while never mentioning the owner. The article mentioned federal funding available, but suggested applicants take notice that there were 'limited funds'. I didn't fully understand that section of the story, but I read on! The ten-page article had an application that I asked for at the library desk. The librarian had an extra copy of the journal so she let me take the application on the last page.

I returned to my little rent, played ball with Thomas and the girls, had dinner with my family, and grabbed the application. Mary and I talked well into the night before we went to sleep. I felt I was headed in the right direction! "Mary," I said, "I need to go to THAT home and see for myself what it looks like". She agreed.

For the next two years I spent every day after classes in the library reading federal funding, articles regarding local and state laws, stories related to veteran homes (north or south) contracts, and medical journals. Toward the end of my years at school, many stories simply could not be avoided! The Lexington Ledger was read daily!

Just before Christmas my final year I read stories of riots taking place in coalmines in northern West Virginia and immediately thought about Jonas. No one died, just lots of knife and shovel wounds. There were never any names of injured as I turned page after page. I read other stories of former army generals like Longstreet, Sherman, and Burnside. I thought about Richard and his stories of the veteran's home. Indian uprisings and beatings were stories covered by all papers. Washington DC always managed to get enough coverage as politics was always on the editors agenda!

On page seven of the Chicago Times, dated April 15, was a very interesting story I could not bypass! Lincoln stories appeared almost every month. It seemed as though the country could not get enough of the Lincoln family! I could not get enough of the former President! Stories were printed about every aspect of the former president's life, his childhood, his family, his lawyer days, his presidency, and famous speeches. There were stories of his constant fight with congress, his disgruntled cabinet always antagonized him, and the family issues kept the president up all night. Based on pictures and cartoons of a physically and mentally worn out president, he could use some rest!

At one point I began to think southern newspapers were increasingly fonder of the 16th president than northern writers, but this story was right out of the Midwest. I shared the story with Mary!

Mary Todd Lincoln committed to Sanitarium

Like millions, I couldn't avoid the article! Over the previous ten years there had been hundreds of articles about Lincoln in newspapers and magazines. But this story was specifically about Lincoln's troublesome deranged wife and his only surviving son, Robert.

Mary Todd Lincoln had been committed to a sanitarium in Illinois as she faced depression and had been under medical care following the death of her husband. Mary had spent many depressing years as she had seen her husband shot in 65 and had three of her four sons die before reaching twenty. Under the watchful eye of her oldest son Robert, she resided in Illinois. Following graduation from Harvard College, Robert became a practicing lawyer with an office in Chicago while administering his mother's affairs including money problems.

Eddie Lincoln died before she and her husband moved to Washington. Another son, Willie, had died while they lived in the White House and eighteen-year old Tad had died in 71. Following the death of Willie, she became extremely depressed even to the point of never entering the Green Room of the White House where he had been placed for review. When her husband died, depression mounted to a greater degree. Anger followed. She wore black! No other color, ever!

In 65 Mary's situation changed when Robert became her protector, advisor, and financial planner. They moved to Springfield, Illinois. Mary's depressing condition increased and her oppositional relationship with her son reached new heights.

Nothing seemed to go right for the former first lady. A husband, three boys, and now, only Robert! He scrutinized her finances. He provided assistance acquiring housing. But, no matter what Robert provided, it was never enough for his mother. She always wanted more. To make matter worse and increase her anxiety, she and Robert had never gotten along and relocating back in her hometown did nothing to please her. They argued over everything; food, medicine, housing quarters, travel, friends and neighbors, and eventually she refused any help from him. Any of his suggestions became nothing more than noise and wasted effort. Mary became extremely obstinate.

But, she had been a perfect child and always had an extensive 'want list.'

Mary came from a very wealthy Kentucky family where slaves worked the fields and money was no object. She was pampered! She could do no wrong. She was never scolded or reprimanded. She was perfect! Her childhood upbringing never escaped her. Coming from money, she wanted and expected more! During her years in Washington, she spent while the president worked endlessly! She was an overly aggressive anxious spender. Spending money was her answer to depression! The president could not control her money woes. While her husband was attempting to keep the union together, Mary took numerous trips to Baltimore, Philadelphia, and New York City to shop. Over the White House years, she mounted an extensive and expensive shoe collection, dresses were purchased in mounting numbers, and dinnerware from the orient was collected. The president's $25,000 annual salary was used up quickly! Not only did she spend the annual salary on personal and White House furnishings, she held dinners, parties, and functions in the presidential house, the cost of which came from Lincoln's salary. Mary spent!

She never had enough! Her enormous thriving continued. Eventually, congress approved a separate budget just for White House functions. And she continued her extravagant ways.

After leaving Washington in 1865 and for many years, Mary petitioned congress for more pension money. She felt the government owed her. She was alone and destitute! She badgered congressmen asking for assistance. She contacted former Lincoln cabinet members who rejected many of her requests for assistance while she became friends with local Springfield lawyers asking for their financial support. She was relentless, always wanting more. More was always better! When others could not or would not help, she continuously argued with Robert about her finances. Very little came her way. Never enough to satisfy her appetite! Depression continued and got worse!

The newspaper story continued as I read more!

When Robert decided she needed extensive medical help, Mary fought the move. She demanded to remain in her small accommodations. Tension between mother and son intensified! Mary continually argued with Robert with stories of White House years, his schooling, his need to become a solider, and his lack of passion for her condition. She argued that she had protected him during the war insisting he stay in school at Harvard. She argued she had saved his life. She expected his help! She was never satisfied!

He refused to listen and they continued fighting! Looking for sympathy, she got none. Robert insisted medical help was needed!

Looking back to the war years, papers reported Robert had entered the army, became a Captain, and was at the treaty signing just days before his pa was assassinated.

Robert had remained at Harvard until the last few months when his desire to be part of the war was answered as the president agreed to let him join the army. Captain Robert Lincoln was given a position with General Grant. When the war ended, so did his military commitment! His stay in the army was less than four months.

The story continued with specific details of more spending sprees, Mary's interest in travel, especially to Europe, her admission to the mental hospital, and her timely well planned escape. Her short visit to the facility lasted less than four months and Robert was not happy! As the story ended the final comment said it all, "They never settled their family disputes."

Eventually, I let my wife read the article. "What a mess," she responded!

Nightly, we talked about Sayersburg, Jonas, and our kids while I expressed my desire to help veterans. I fell asleep nightly dreaming of Sayersburg and what Richard had said. I needed to get there and see for myself what a Veteran's Home was like! If I could build a home for my buddies in Clinton, my adventure to Lexington would have been well worth the work!

After four long years, my college education came to an end with graduation and I packed my bags and headed north never once considering the degree of confusion or surprise I would encounter. Reflections of my younger years in northern Virginia as a confederate soldier overcame me as I boarded the train!

While my slow trek north was accompanied by frequent stops and reading interesting magazine articles answering my immediate needs, Mary remained in Lexington giving her time to review math and spelling with the children.

Arguments over the confederate battle flag surfaced. Magazine articles described the resurgence of former southern generals and their plight. My innocent eyes really got opened! I didn't need to take history classes as the newspapers did an outstanding job. I read everything!

There were extremely interesting stories on Harriet Tubman, Jesse and Frank James, oil and some guy named Rockefeller, the expansion of the railroad, and one extensive article on Andrew Jackson. Rockefeller and Carnegie were making millions while laborers were just surviving. One story even covered an accident of railroad cars in which over one hundred people were killed. Apparently, a bridge had collapsed and the railroad company was sued and lost millions in the court case.

As I was beginning to understand newspaper and journal coverage of the country, I came across a story on the impeachment of Andrew Johnson. The title of the story was 'Stevens and Sumner Put Down The Hammer.'

I had grabbed two extra medical journals on my way out the library before I boarded the train. One interesting story covered Doctor Olive Wendell Holmes and his experience in Europe, another covered the untimely arrival of a fourteen-pound baby to a ninety-pound mother, and the final story in the spring edition covered new improved treatment using cocaine. But the newspaper story about Johnson's Impeachment was more interesting.

Apparently Capitol Hill's hatred of Democrat President Andrew Johnson started long before he became President. Johnson and Lincoln had not fully agreed on reconstruction plans. Radical republicans, spearheaded by Pennsylvania Congressman Thaddeus Stevens and Senator Charles Sumner from Massachusetts, had befriended one of the most powerful men in the Lincoln administration. Edwin Stanton, Secretary of War and a political White House insider, had been having secret discussions with congressmen on reconstruction. The group opposed Lincoln's plan for Reconstruction as the radicals felt the president was too lenient.

The group believed southern whites should be punished for treason and the war, as they wanted blacks armed and put in control to hold local office and run businesses. Equality for blacks was needed, they claimed. They wanted southern whites stripped of their wealth and resources and should no longer be considered citizens. During the Johnson administration congress slowed progress with delaying tactics and overrode many of his vetoes. It was the Radical Republicans in Congress who established dominance by increasing taxes on real estate forcing small southern farmers and white planters to sell off land. Decisions in Washington convinced many southern whites along with blacks to leave their homes and become sharecroppers.

Tension built in congress as republicans opposed black codes that handcuffed the black southern population. Local laws that restricted blacks from owning firearms, or prevented them from obtaining jobs without permits, or disallowed citizens voting privileges continually angered house members. A representative from Florida was criticized in front of a congressional committee when his state was blamed for its misuse of federal money as the state's debt had risen over 900% in six years. Florida became the joke of congress as its representatives continually expressed displeasure complaining about reconstruction policies and unenforceable laws. But, the radicals had an ally!

Disliked by Johnson, Secretary of War Stanton fed the republicans all they needed and the president became aware of the secret meetings. Anger between the two bodies boiled. Johnson wanted an excuse to fire Stanton and when Johnson discovered the sabotage, he fired the Secretary leading Congress to bring impeachment charges.

Realizing that a fight was brewing, Radical Republicans had previously passed legislation that prohibited the president doing such. Court proceedings followed!

For a few months, the senate prepared for trial. Eventually, the trial commenced with The Supreme Court Chief Justice presiding and after delays and interruption a roll call vote was taken to begin. And, since the senate was the judge and jury, they had ultimate control as the house prosecuted the case. Senators argued over everything! They argued over procedure! They argued over seating arrangements! Every senator could not speak, so they argued over who would answer procedural issues! They argued over witnesses! The argued over whether Stanton would testify! They argued over whether the president could or would be called to testify! Senators agreed on little! Finally the trial commenced!

Whenever there was an objection, the senate had to vote on the motion and on many occasions the vote on the objection took days delaying the proceedings. Many witnesses were called. Delays and objections continued. Decisions took days because of constant 'in fighting' brought on by senator disagreements!

The president never visited the senate chamber and never testified. Testimony was long and drawn out! Arguments ensued in the senate chamber and hallways of the capitol. The chief justice sat and watched while trying to control the fighting senators. Plus it was hot in DC and tempers flared!

With a 2/3 vote needed for conviction and removal the senate readied to cast their ballots. Lobbying for conviction votes circulated among the senators! More in fighting surfaced with name-calling, spitting fights, and charges of treason. With many behind the scene tavern and private meetings and considerable pressure to convict, eventually the senate voted.

When the final tally was recorded, the radical republicans had failed by a mere one vote. Johnson survived! Stevens and Sumner would continue their respective fights to the end. That was short lived for Stevens died within a few months. His service to his country ended with a loss!

Quite a history lesson, I thought!

One story I read was about the war deaths. The last sentence in the article said, "Of the 300,00 rebel soldiers who died in the war, two thirds died of camp disease." I had had enough! I was ready to move forward.

I needed to get to Sayersburg! When I left Lexington and headed north with a college degree, I had my sights set on returning to my roots in Tennessee with visions of helping my buddies and raising a family. I was proud of my accomplishments and I was proud of my family for having survived the last few years away from Clinton. Virginia citizens always seemed polite and courteous! My family was welcomed in many local facilities and we basically felt at home. We had joined the local church, made friends with bankers and businessmen, and I had numerous opportunities to refresh former war experiences with many local veterans from both sides of the fight. Mary stayed busy with her sewing circle and the kids were growing fast occupying their parent's by keeping order.

Thomas Trenton, my oldest, continued his playful torture of his three sisters, Samantha Maryanne, Roxie Marie, and Frances Leighanne. My girls surely reminded me of my younger days in Boxford Forge with tussles in the barn or the kitchen, as those sisters of mine never gave up! Remembering, my responsibilities drastically changed when pa and brother Thomas left in 58! Back than, I was a young 14 year old with adult responsibilities! Since my son Thomas was the oldest and approaching adolescence, I understood and appreciated his dilemma. Nevertheless, he did fairly well. He kept his sisters in order and was basically kind. Well, most of the time! I even had reminders of my oldest sister Ruth Anne who ran away at 14!

During those years in Lexington, Thomas and I spent time fishing and hunting when I wasn't buried in some book. Deer meat, wild hogs, and an occasional possum always helped with food supply. I had a habit of always demonstrating my expertise at cleaning the feral animals before we returned home. Thomas was not impressed! Thomas was in his few remaining years in school and was interested in applying to some college in Roanoke. We talked at length about schooling and an education.

One night back along, he asked about the Civil War. I turned that around saying, "You mean the War Between the States?" "I guess so," he responded. "Later, ok," I asked? And Thomas always reminded me of my brother, Thomas, who always had a funny side.

We had purchased an old mare from a neighborhood blacksmith shop and Thomas enjoyed riding demonstrating his expertise aboard old Hazel. Mr. Stapleton told me the mare was about 25 years old. "That's fine," I said. On many days while I was in school listening to some boring instructor explain a confusing math concept or explaining the finer points of the Second or Fifth Amendment in my political science class, Thomas would take one of the older girls for a ride. But he never could get by without playing some kind of joke. With no saddle and the short end of the bridle in the hands of the rider, usually Sam, Thomas would slap slow moving Hazel and watch as Sam struggled to stay aboard. I would always hear about the afternoon ride when I got home! While explaining himself, Thomas just laughed!

Thomas got the end of Hazel's foot one day when he walked in back of her while trying to shovel manure. Dr. Aimsberry said he probably broke his shinbone and needed to stay off it for a week or two. That didn't happen! Thomas was back on his horse in three days. Kids will be kids!

Our kids squabbled all the time! Seemed like everything was a crisis! Simple arguments over who would sit in the middle or on the end of the table at dinner always caused some confusion. "She sat there last night," complained Frances! "Move over Roxie," Frances hollered. Someone was always needling someone! Kids argued about who would clean the stable where we boarded the mules and horse. She did this! He did that! I can't do that! One night during dinner, they fought over who placed the well bucket next to the manure pile. Roxie admitted she had worked hard during the day and said she forgot where she had placed the tool. Sam, hollered, "Pay attention, will ya?"

They disagreed over whose turn it was to gather clothes for Mary to wash. Then they argued who would hang out the wet clothing. Someone was always in some ones way! She's sitting to close! Move over! Since Samantha and Roxie shared the same bed, they constantly argued over who had the fluffiest pillow! On many nights before I said good night, I would have to take a walk to see Hazel just to clear my mind. At least, she didn't talk back!

Samantha, named after my sister, thought she was the boss always telling the young ones what was right and how to do it. "Get this. Get that", she would instruct. Roxie was the practical joker, usually with a frog or snake in her pocket as a result of spending her time at the river's edge. If a snake or frog didn't get any response from Frances, a hairy spider did the trick.

Frances liked her simple responsibilities in the kitchen while the older girls always wanted to be taken for a horse ride without Thomas and all three always pleaded for my attention. I used to think, 'How did ma and pa do it?' Frances Leighanne, the youngest always looked to Mary for attention or sympathy with a crying spell or a tantrum. Usually the childhood incident was meaningless that led to Frances spending the better part of her day in some secluded room away from the rest of the family. Mary complained, "Those terrible young children!" By the end of the day the flame on the candle couldn't get blown out quick enough! "Extinguish the lamp too," I hollered.

Whew!

Eleven

RUTH

Finally, I arrived in Sayersburg. The train made two stops after leaving Mary and the children. The crowded uneven platform beside the train was filled with anxious travelers. Groups of blacks congregated to one side. A small group of Amish in their black clothing waited. Three soldiers in uniform talked while smoking and drinking coffee. Men in suits, looking as if they were headed to a business meeting, stood at attention. And pacing back and forth on the wooden platform were average citizens waiting for the next train to Chicago. Richard had been mistaken about train service to Sayersburg. There were no destroyed tracks.

I left Mary with the intention of visiting the soldier's home where Richard Patterson's brother was a patient. I wanted to know more about veterans and their problems, how they adjusted to their injuries, and what services were available. I had visited two homes near Lexington but was not satisfied with either the medical treatment or the services.

The train ride was interesting to say the least. At a transfer stop in Martinsburg, a stranger named Alexander Tang talked at length about the railroads. He explained the importance of the new widely expanded transportation system as it provided work not only on the railroads, but in industries that supplied material to build the tracks and trains. I decided he must have been an expert when he emphasized the importance of getting the products to market quicker with more efficiency. He completed his expose' with 'more citizens are working, canals will be history and new towns are springing up throughout the country.' I just listened!

Preston Johnson talked about steel companies, lumber companies, and oil companies, employing thousands. While sitting beside Eugene Hamilton, who was smoking a disgusting cigar, he mentioned sporting events and the new game of football. He even tried to explain the game years ago when Rutgers and Princeton played to mark the beginning of the sport. I was really not interested, but he never let up, like he had a vested interest in the game. I just let him ramble. I sat!

When the train stopped again in Granger for another transfer, I noticed many new comers to America. People from Germany, Poland, and France milled around the depot. The group of French speaking foreigners said they were headed to Canada while the others were looking for a western adventure. Many said they were tired of all the fighting in their respective countries. 'Made me think of the 60s!'

Henry St. Clair, from Bar Harbor, Maine, was looking for work in the west but was surprised to see thousands of blacks talking the same language. He said he left Maine with his family of six looking for work in the mid-west and was overly concerned he and blacks from the south would be competing for similar work. I asked him where and what he did for work in Maine. He answered with, "On the water, I lobsta." I had no idea what he described and determined that his fishing skills might not be very helpful in the middle of the country. I wished him good luck! Before I left the train he warned me about those white hooded mean rebels. I reckon, he was referring to the KKK.

The day I arrived was sunny and warm. I reached in my pocket and secured the Amish good luck coin given to me by my brother during the war. The small town was miles from any major city. Sayersburg did have two connecting train routes, one to Cleveland and another to Louisville, Kentucky.

There were several stores on the main street. I counted three hardware stores, two clothing stores, a general store named Pete's, Randell's Bar next to Doctor Singer's office, and Will's barber shop. Another saloon next to the local town office belonging to Wendell and his brother had a sign on the front door that simply said 'Whites Only.' Immediately, I thought of Jonas! Two banks bordered the town square home to a Yankee soldier statue.

Citizens shuttled along to do their business and one grocery store with a pharmacy across from the doctor's office was busy with women buying supplies or trading their farm products while Clifton's Shoe Repair was busy with farmers waiting to collect their reconstructed footwear. Boarded sidewalks with squeaky planks provided limited safety and comfort from the mud-covered streets and freshly deposited horse manure. Two young boys exiting the Daily Journal immediately started selling the latest news as soon as they escaped five ladies standing on the sidewalk. Matter of fact as

I looked around the square, I did not see any blacks on the street or in any stores. Apparently Wendell's sign has substance!

At the end of the street Burke's Sawmill was busy. Workers covered with sawdust continually moved freshly cut timber and other supplies along as finished planks and recently milled boards in huge piles awaited shipment to some large city. I could see smoke slowly moving skyward coming from a stack. Strange odors from an industrial company filled my nostrils and wagons full of steel products slowly moved toward the train depot. The town was working. Residents were busy. The town was prospering or that's what it seemed!

There were three boarding houses and a lone hotel operated by Catherine Harris. I entered, asked for a room for the night, paid Catherine four dollars and fifty cents, and visited Randell's.

After two rounds of beer, some pork, greens, and three fresh biscuits, I asked if anyone knew where the soldier's home was located when a local resident informed me the facility was a mile up the road on Wonders Hill. Rosemary, the waitress said, "Don't hurry, pard, it's a mess!" Three young ragged looking men surrounded the young local striking adorable female covered with make-up as thick as mud as I prepared to leave! I grabbed another beer, a sausage, one biscuit, and started walking! I passed twenty to thirty residential homes before I hit the road up the hill.

The narrow dirt road was secluded from the town where oak trees, scrubby tall green bushes, and pines shaded my back as I slowly climbed the rutted passage. A recent rain made the walk more difficult than expected but I finally arrived at the Taylor Lincoln Johnson Veteran's Home. I had been warned, but what lay to my front was very, very disturbing and depressing.

I was more surprised than ever! What a horrible sight! I asked myself, this is where veterans live? Richard was wrong about the train tracks but right about the veteran's home! What a site! It was a mess!

The building was falling down! Old rotted and broken hanging boards surrounded the home's bottom. Cracked windows with shattered shutters dangled barely hanging from mangled rusty hinges. The moss covered split weather beaten wooden roofing attempted to keep water outside and appeared unsuccessful most of the time. Green moss was growing over the front porch where an American flag blew in the gentle breeze. Another flag, probably a state flag, was nailed beside the front door covering a window. Brown bushes and waist high weeds surrounded the building attempting to hide the sad structure's appearance. Dilapidated broken steps welcomed me to the front door as I looked to the side of the structure and viewed the soldier's cemetery! This place was truly a mess! Major repairs were needed and quickly! Plus, it could use a paint job too!

From inside someone hollered, "Help me please. My f__'n ass hurts and I just shit on the floor." I opened the squeaky front door and entered. What I witnessed brought immediate sadness! Disappointment set in! Surprise would be an understatement. Briefly, my mind recalled wartime hospitals! The open battlefield hospitals where confusion was the general rule of law! The huge city hospitals where doctors or nurses worked endlessly to treat dying soldiers or the prison hospitals that were identified as death traps where soldiers went to die! If first impressions are important, this place surely got my attention! Even with my experiences from war years, I was truly not ready or prepared!

Veterans wandered the halls, many with missing limbs, an eye, a foot, or fingers. Someone yelled, "Could someone find the God Damn doctor? I haven't taken a shit in three days. I need some medicine." Just about everyone carried a cane, a broken bedpost, or wood plank to support an ailing body. Broken crutches rested beside Ben Motley's door. Bare arms covered with deep scars and emaciated faces told stories too gruesome to repeat. Ragged clothes, baggy pants, and torn shirts covered some veterans as my mental anguish spread!

The scene was horrible. I was overwhelmed, sad, and confused. How could this happen? I had not read any of this kind of description in any medical journals at school. Doctors I had talked with gave me no indication of such deplorable conditions. Editorial comments were not this disturbing! Magazines such as Harpers Monthly, The Atlantic Monthly, or Scribner's hardly ever carried any article describing these conditions. I had read only one such story, but this was too tragic and depressing to believe!

I asked one of the veterans limping by if he could direct me to the supervisor or someone in charge, when he said, "Son, nobody runs this place. Who are you anyway, the new doc? We'ed broken. Nobody fix us." Another former army vet approached and said that Delores Daniels is the chief nurse. She is in room 114 next to the kitchen. I told him I could find it.

Slowly I proceeded down the hallway looking into a few rooms as I passed residents in bed reading, playing with their fingers, or staring out windows as if waiting for a miracle. One room had two veterans sitting playing cards, neither wearing a shirt or pants. A small plaque in one doorway identified the occupant as Foster Everest. Foster wanted to know when lunch was coming. I had no idea! It was mid-afternoon!

Standing in the doorway for a few seconds I wondered if she really cared. I found Delores sitting in back of a broken wooden desk and asked to talk with her.

She was wearing a white top and a skirt that was four sizes too big. Her arms were bare and I could see bruises, probably the result of some scuffle. A white scarf around her head attempted to keep her graying hair from her wrinkled forehead and blue eyes. She was writing in some sort of booklet probably reporting on her recent visit to patients when I introduced myself and said, "Hello. My name is John McMurtree." Eventually, she looked up responding with, "And what's your business, sonny? I'm busy and have to get these reports ready for the doctor and the Veteran's Commission. They'll be here shortly."

I guessed she was maybe 50 years old. I explained my purpose as she said, "Come on in. Have a seat. Don't get too comfortable." Foster walked by and hollered, "When do we eat?" "Soon," was the response! In the distance I heard, "Get that F___'n doctor!"

Delores and I talked for about thirty minutes before she asked if I would like to see some rooms and talk with some of the patients. I had explained my interest and plans. Briefly I mentioned my war experience, my schooling, my interviews with local doctors, my study of medical journals, and my concerns of wounded hometown veterans. As we started down the hall, I quickly mentioned my Veteran's group in Clinton as my focus. She turned and sarcastically said, "Good luck Johnny."

I mentioned Mr. Patterson's brother when she sadly informed me he had died the previous month. We continued to talk and walk!

We walked by Foster looking for the doctor and food when Delores described Richard's brother as a loner who talked to no one and spent his days looking out the windows. He never had any visitors or friends, ate little, and argued with everyone. He was always taking his clothes off and walking around naked. He talked and walked in his sleep every night. Some nights he spent the entire time yelling for help. One night he hollered for help as he dreamed he was pinned down with a broken leg in the middle of a battle somewhere near Chicago. Delores said he never made any sense.

"He was just crazy!" Delores said. He roamed, roamed and roamed! She constantly referred to him as 'Slick'. Jane, a kitchen worker, was always chasing him and getting him back to his room that he shared with another veteran. Bowman Bell from Wales, Illinois, couldn't stand Slick. "One night during a rain storm Slick urinated all over Bowman. Slick thought he was pissing in the rain."

"I know what you think," she finished. "Man, what a mess, we had to burn Bowman's clothes and Slick moved to another room."

Contrary to rumors, Delores mentioned doors to the veteran's home were hardly ever locked and on one occasion Slick left the home and was found in a muddy pond with leeches over his entire body. Delores finished her description by saying, "Slick was not right!" He was found hanging in the storage room and is buried in the veteran's cemetery out back. Delores said, "I think he died of a broken heart." I knew exactly what she was referencing!

Eventually, I asked her if she or anyone had notified Richard when she replied, "Hell, I have enough to do here. Most of the veterans here don't get any visitors or mail. I can't spend time trying to find a relative or report everything that happens. The Commission is always on my case. They want reports every month with doctor's reports attached. That good for nothing Stanley Sorenson is a real pain in my side. He never lets up."

Delores was rolling so I let her continue. "I have very little help. Three women volunteers from the local Catholic Church come around one in the afternoon and help with some medical needs, but they can't be counted on. When they have time doctors come by. Besides the cleaning lady, two kitchen workers, and a black driver who goes to town to gather supplies, I'm the only person most of these guys see. Ruth, the only full time cleaning lady, had a son who worked here for a while, but left when he was attacked by one of the veterans. Said he would never return. I haven't seen him since. And I could use a couple full time nurses. Nurse Virginia left before September last and no replacement has been found."

Delores said there were twelve veterans here. Two men to a room! The kitchen had room to feed everyone, but it's really tiny. We don't have good facilities here and the indoor plumbing accommodations are really not a healthy situation. The mayor and the doctor want better indoor plumbing facilities but nothing has happened in years. And the men who live here are not responsible enough to get the fresh drinking water from the nearby well, she complained. We walked! She continued! "Workers have to do it all," she complained. I asked her who owned the home. She completely ignored me saying, "What difference does it make?"

"Most of our food for the home is supplied by three farmers who are kind enough to help, but sometimes they run into problems with loss of their crops due to weather conditions or insects. Squabbles occur daily. Food fights are constant. Some of these guys throw up in the halls or in their rooms. They all think they're still in the army as swearing and profanity is everywhere. Men steal from their roommates and constantly argue over simple issues like who is bigger or better at shooting or some other item like how many times they visited the whore houses in Washington or Winchester during the war. Randy, from faraway Carson, sits on the floor in his room every night counting imaginary crickets running across his windowsill. Two nights ago he reported to Sarah, the kitchen lady, he counted over one thousand the previous night.

Some play card games while others walk or play ball. We try to conduct a quiet time at night, but that doesn't work. I live next door and usually spend my entire day in this building and many nights I have to return with my crippled husband to break up a fight or settle a dispute. Sarah lives on the second floor but is helpless when some arguments turn nasty. Wilson, the black driver, also lives upstairs and helps separate the fellows when he can, but thankfully no fight gets too dangerous and someone dies. Thank God, I haven't had to get the local sheriff! He's not much help anyway," she finished.

We rounded the corner when she complained with, "I haven't had time by myself in over two years. I don't know why I continue to work here. I really could use a vacation. Lets go upstairs and see Ruth." Someone hollered, "F__ you too. You asshole. You can't see shit." We escaped upstairs!

Ruth Anne

We climbed the steep narrow stairs, rounded the corner, and there on her knees scrubbing the floor was the greatest surprise in my life. In baggy brown pants, matted gray hair, with wrinkled lines covering her face, for the first time since 1854, I looked into the blood shot eyes of my older sister, Ruth. When she stood up, neither of us could believe what was before us! Immediate disbelief! "Where have you been, Johnny," she asked? From five feet away we just stared. I didn't answer, just looked.

Neither could believe after all these years we would ever meet again. When she left the farm in Boxford Forge with her boyfriend, I thought she was gone forever! There she stood. I was completely dumbfounded! Overwhelmed with emotion, we came closer! We continued to stare! I could not believe my eyes! She could not believe her eyes. Delores looked on in amazement, as she had no idea we were siblings. We had not seen or heard from each other in over thirty years and I never knew where she went when she left. I wondered if she knew anything about me. I knew very little of her, really I knew nothing!

We hugged seeming to never let go! Four years my senior, now she looked considerably older! "You look great," I said.

She remained silent!

The soldier's home visit took a back seat. We had to talk and soon! Delores excused herself, returned to her office, as my sister and me removed to the kitchen, coffee, and talk. "You look pretty good yourself," she said. We both had many questions.

I started with, "When did you start working here? Where have you been? Where is Garrett? How did you get to this place? I thought you were going to

Kentucky when you left us. What happen to that plan?"

Ruth interrupted my questioning with, "How did you find me and where have you been for the last thirty odd years?" We were beginning to respond when one of the residents stumbled into the kitchen asking, "When is lunch? I'm hungry." "Go ask Delores," Ruth hollered. Forest turned and left. Hot black coffee warmed our throats as we started! "I'll finish this cleaning later," she said.

We talked for the next two hours before I returned to the hotel. I located my journal filling ten pages before falling asleep that night. I was overjoyed and had to find answers to many questions.

Over the next three days and evening, Ruth and I discussed the years of separation, people who were important in our lives and expressed other concerns. It was not easy listening to disturbing events of her past and I'm not sure she comprehended the consequences of my responsibilities on the farm after pa and brother Thomas left or the horrible experiences I endured while performing my duties in the War Between the States. As we laughed, cried, let our emotions run the gauntlet, and described the previous years, I quickly realized my past was not important to her. And besides, I wanted to know more about HER past.

Ruth Anne was born in 1840 and left the farm with her boyfriend Garrett Johnson in 54. He was 16 when they departed, naïve, and determined. She also! He convinced Ruth he could take care of her! I was 10 when she escaped.

Ruth was the oldest of my sisters, a strong-headed teenager and thought she was madly in love with Garrett as they had been seeing each other over a two-year period. The Johnson farm was a mile through the woods from our farm and was easily accessed as Garrett showed himself many nights unannounced! Pa didn't like Garrett and my older brother thought he was a complete idiot. Ma never cared for him that much, but she tolerated him. Many Sundays, Garrett presented himself about church time giving Ruth an excuse for avoiding God's word. His parents were not very Christian and neither was my sister. She saw no reason to attend church or even read the Bible. The Lord's Word was a constant topic around the dinner table and Ruth knew very little about the Bible thus remaining silent as others chimed in.

Ruth hated farm work and constantly fought with pa over simple chores like collecting the eggs, working in the tobacco patch, or attending to vegetables. She hated duties inside especially helping with kitchen responsibilities. She despised housework and argued with ma constantly. She didn't even like my blue tick hound, Slappy!

Ruth was not the social butterfly, but liked escaping to the woods or the bottom with Garrett when he unexpectedly visited our farm. Brother

Thomas thought he was a waste, a general slug, and argued with Ruth to no avail! They argued over menial topics such as who would drive the wagon the next day to Clinton to get supplies and my brother never bypassed an opportunity to verbally slam Garrett. "He's a dude," Thomas repeatedly told Ruth, "He couldn't hit the barn at fifty feet," referring to shooting a rifle. Garrett wasn't the brightest scholar in Boxford Forge, but he knew enough about my brother's temper to stay away.

Pa and Garrett never got along. They hardly talked to each other and when they did, pa always listened saying little. Basically, Pa despised Garrett! "Lazy, lazy, lazy," pa would say. Eventually, Garrett made it a point to stay away. After many visits, pa politely would ask Ruth to let him know when Garrett was coming and he disappeared. Pa could always find work in the fields. Sometimes it worked, other times not! Ma was ok, but pa was constantly complaining about his presence. Occasionally, ma tried to be polite by providing chew, while pa escaped to the barn with his apple brandy.

Ruth explained she and Garrett never got married but lived in the mountains of Kentucky for a while before moving to Sayersburg around 1860. Ruth said she had lost a baby at childbirth in 55 and had two miscarriages in the late 50's. She now has two sons, Ralph, and Pierce, who work in Claiborne's Meat Packing plant over the mountain in Pennsylvania. Ralph had a job in the soldier's home before he got into a fight with one of the veterans and left. She complained, "I never see my boys. The last time I saw those rascals was at Christmas in 78."

Ruth lived next door and works at the home as a cleaning lady six days a week. She lives with Mr. and Mrs. Porter Nottoway who raise hogs and a few cows on a small farm. Two Nottoway boys entered the union army, fought, and died with Garrett during the war. Garrett's death as a Yankee soldier was a complete surprise! I never said anything to my sister! The Nottoway's have another son, Rawlins, who lives in Sayersburg and works at the iron mill. Ruth said she helps around the house as Mr. Nottoway is severely crippled from a steel mill accident and the farm work is handled by Rawlins when he has time. "I gives Mrs. Nottoway five dollars a month," she proudly said. "Mr. Nottoway is part Indian, you know," she responded.

I asked her if she remembered anyone named Patterson when she responded with a somewhat vague response. All she recalled were stories the kitchen help told and didn't pay much attention to what the veterans said. I didn't pursue the issue any more and we continued our past.

During her lunch break on my second day, Ruth offered the story of Garrett and his unfortunate death as a soldier in the Union Army. Garrett had joined the army in late 62 when Lincoln was demanding more soldiers as southern generals compounded the federals problems with battlefield victories and northern generals refused to aggressively pursue rebels in retreat. Ruth had two babies when Garrett joined Grant's Army fighting in the Tennessee region and eventually was killed at Lookout Mountain in Chattanooga. Ruth said she was told he was killed, but she never saw the body and does not know where he is buried. She complained, "I told him not to go, but he hated those rebels because of slavery. He wanted to kill them all." I said nothing. It was useless!

I was going to mention that we grew up in Boxford Forge where there were no slaves or plantations but I decided that was a complete waste of time.

To end her comments about Garrett, she complained about his sister who lives in Columbus and comes to Sayersburg every summer and brags about the money she makes working in a cotton mill. I shot back, "Don't pay any attention to her, the southern cotton farmers are not growing and selling much cotton because the prices are slowly declining." Ruth just stared. She had no idea what I meant!

On my way back to my room, I grabbed the local newspaper and read stories of Indian/soldiers fighting in the west. A battle between opposing factions described the horrible killing of 81 military soldiers at the hands of Indians some years ago and there was a recent story of a battle in Nebraska. I wondered how widespread is THAT issue. The local editor had a comment arguing Indian problems were a result of the expansion of the railroad recalling comments from Captain Steele. I blew out the candle and went to sleep. I had had enough!

Rawlins, the driver for the home, picked up Ruth one night after her twelve hours of work and brought her to the hotel where we sat on the porch and discussed what had happened to our family over the years. She had no idea what had transpired after she left.

First, I mentioned how upset I was when she left followed by my responsibilities when pa and Thomas left to work in the paper mill in Albany, New York. She didn't know where Albany was so I spent very little time explaining the situation while simply explaining pa had died in a mill accident. I mentioned Thomas had a girlfriend in Vermont (she didn't know about Vermont either) who he wished to marry, but died in a southern prison during the war. Without too many details, I briefly informed her Thomas had joined the Union Army, was a captain, and I had met him one night while I was on picket duty. And I had his prison journal in Lexington. After the war stories, I realized Ruth was not interested as she knew very little about the war. I didn't say much more!

I mentioned ma's death, the destruction of the Boxford Forge farm by

Yankee soldiers, and the move to Clinton. During the warm evening swatting flies and mosquitoes, I mentioned the sad death of sister Leighanne and the demands Samantha placed on me to read. I told her that Samantha had recently finished college and was living somewhere in Virginia, but I wasn't very specific. I told her I was going to see her shortly.

I mentioned grandpa's letters and specifically the details of his involvement in the Underground Railroad prior to the war and his untimely death. I described conditions in the south after the war with running the store in Clinton, hangings and torture at the hands of the KKK, and since Ruth knew my childhood black friend, Jonas, I described some of the unfortunate circumstances HE faced. I mentioned Jonas's pa escape from a Georgia plantation and how he found northeastern Tennessee as his home. I did not explain Jonas' pa's death at the hands of angry anti-black thugs. "Jonas moved to West Virginia and works in a coal mine. I plan to visit him when I return to Lexington," I said.

I didn't miss many words as I bragged about marrying Mary. I bragged about my three girls and son. I bragged about my education. I emphasized my wishes to help veterans of the rebel army. And by building and owning a Veteran's Home in Tennessee I could address some of those wishes. But as I talked, I wondered if she really cared. I wondered if she understood my comments. I questioned if the outside world meant anything to my older sister! And I really questioned her understanding of the mental and physical condition of those veterans she sees daily. Does she really like her work, I thought. But then, she shows up for work every day!

Ruth just looked away! I knew my story meant very little. She had other issues! Her day-to-day struggles were far more important than my past. Even with her lack of interest in my future, I still felt the need to continue.

"Mary and I are looking forward to our return to the Clinton area by the end of the year," I said. I continued to explain some wishes. I said, "My veteran's home will be a place where former rebel soldiers can meet and discuss old war stories, can get medical assistance, can get professional counseling or talk with the local preacher. They can play sports like baseball or simply relax in the comfort of peaceful surroundings. They can read, enjoy the friendship of others who share the same experiences, or simply do nothing. My veteran's home will be their HOME for as long as they want!" She interrupted!

"JT," she said, "you must be crazy. These men have no idea. They're just waiting to die and Delores and I provide the room. I come to work every day waiting for Bowman, Samuel, or Frankie to die so me and the preacher can bury them out back. They swear, fight, argue, destroy their rooms, run away one day and return the next, and generally want someone to get them more medical services. Someone is always hollering at 2am to be rescued from a battle."

"I see what you mean," I said.

"Don't get involved," she replied.

The more I talked the more I appreciated Ruth's predicament. She was struggling every day at work. Her kids were gone! She has no family!

"Ruth," I said, "I have buddies in Tennessee who are suffering from horrible battlefield experiences just like these men. They could use some help."

"JT", she angrily responded, "I see this every day. I listen to those crazy damn soldiers relive their war. I listen to their screams for help. I watch as they crawl around on my clean floors and vomit, shit, or piss in the hallways. I watch as they fight in the kitchen. I watch as doctors try to help them. They hate the doc. They hate this place, but they have no other home. Most have no family, only war buddies! I understand their needs, but me and Delores can only do so much. And then I watch as they die. Then I bury them and start all over."

"Ruth," I said, "But I have people in Clinton who will help. I'm getting people together. Matter of factor, I have already picked a name for the building. I will honor our brother. What do you think? Maybe you could come back to Clinton and work in the home? You can work for me. We can work together. Return to Tennessee." I couldn't offer the world, but I could try. She was family!

If only looks could kill, I would be dead. She said nothing. A blank look stared! She just looked across the street as four locals headed for the saloon as a mother dragged her screaming two year old into the grocery store. Her confused and simple world was headed nowhere! Nothing was said for a few minutes as we sat and swatted flies.

I was sad! She had very little money. She was just surviving. Ruth had no education! She was without reading skills. Conditions around the country meant very little to her. She could care less about Indians, railroads, oil, coalmines, riots, administrative and congressional fights in Washington over Reconstruction, sharecroppers, presidential elections, or the price of cotton. Her world was small and very local! Day to day she was surviving!

She traveled to town very little and socialized with few. At one point during our discussions, she mentioned a small gang of KKK members roaming. Frightened, she said she remained at the farm or at work! Her future was a question mark. She was just four years older than me, but looked like she has recently escaped from Camp Sumter. I felt sorry for her and tried to discuss ways in which she might return to Tennessee. "I'm staying here," she responded.

Reluctantly and hopeless, I accepted that! But, could she really work in my new soldier's home? My mind was spinning out of control! I felt sorry for her. I wanted to help! But when and how, I questioned?

As Rawlins helped her into the wagon and departed, she asked me to tell Samantha of her past. I said I would carry the information and report to everyone what I had discovered. I got the address of the Veteran's Home and told her I would write and someone could read the letter to her. That would be fine with her. As she rode away not knowing what the future had in store, I reached in my pocket and grabbed my 'Good Luck' coin! I went to my room, closed the door, looked in the mirror and said, "JT, life is full of surprises. I reckon I'm ok." Then, I located my journal making several disturbing entries.

The next morning, I ventured back to the home, talked with Delores as she gave me some paperwork, and tried to find my sister. Delores said Ruth hadn't reported to work and didn't know why. Delores had been to her residence and was told by Mr. Nottoway Ruth had mentioned she was headed to work. "She never came through the door," Delores said.

As I started thinking about her comments the previous night, I was reminded of the statements about her sons. 'Maybe she is off to find them or for whatever reason needed to escape from the home for a while. Who knows, she's complicated and has been from day one.'

I waited for two days. Ruth didn't return.

I told Delores I would write her after I returned to my family. I told her I was concerned about Ruth, but I needed to return to Lexington. I said goodbye, spent five cents on the Ohio Weekly, and wondered about Ruth Anne as I headed toward the train station. I WILL write Ruth when I get back to Mary!

I bought a ticket, transferred in Winchester and after another four hours arrived in Lexington to the welcome open arms of Mary and the children. My week away from my family was truly an eye opening experience, never to be forgotten, and hopefully not to be repeated or duplicated. I had recorded in my journal most of what Delores, Ruth, and I had discussed. I expressed to Mary my complete surprise at seeing my sister, detailed her situation, and described the last day at the home when she did not report for work. "Who knows where she might be," I commented.

I described the veteran's home and the horrible circumstances I witnessed. I had talked with townspeople, two bankers regarding loans, Dr. Poindexter about his home visits and medical supplies, two farmers about food supplies, and even spent a few minutes with the retired ticket agent at the railroad depot that repeatedly complained about being overworked. Entries regarding the home including Delores, Ruth, and veteran's personal comments covered over one hundred pages.

Mary and I talked about everything over the next few months. I wrote Ruth a letter not knowing whether she received it and was concerned if she still worked at the home. I got no response from her or Delores. Weekly, Mary and I reviewed Ruth Anne's circumstances and were fearful of her absence just before I left.

We reviewed comments made by Captain Steele and his offer for possible work in Chicago. However, Chicago was not mentioned again, Tennessee was! I had told my children of finding my older sister and what she did for work, where she lived and her two sons, and one night daughter Frances asked, "Does aunt Ruth ever celebrate Christmas?" "I hope so," I responded.

We started preparing for our return to Clinton as Mary had received a letter from Cecil saying things were ok at the farm and store. But her anxiety increased when I showed Mary the story about coal mining I had read on the trip home. Throughout the entire article, I thought about Jonas who had left Clinton way back to work in the mines in West Virginia! Plus Cecil had not mentioned Jonas or Benny in his letter. It had been years since Benny's disappearance. No one had seen or heard from him! Where did he go? However, Cecil did mention there were no Yankee soldiers in Clinton, Knoxville, or Nashville. Great Jesus, I said to myself.

Coalmining

Jonas was on my mind as I started to read. The magazine coalmining story was written by a local reporter who recently returned from Jackson County in the eastern mountains of West Virginia. The tiny community of Breakmack tucked away and isolated in the valleys was a major mining town on the slope of the Appalachian Mountains where roughly one thousand people lived and worked for the Breakmack Mountain Coal Mining Company. Its owners Stanley and Larry Wolf controlled the town. The story outlined conditions in and around the small town and specifically the coalmines.

The author described tunnels, caves, and mine shafts were unhealthy, unsafe, and extremely dangerous resulting in hazardous conditions for adults and children. Children, as young as eight to ten year olds, were employed working 10-12 hours daily for very little money. One area inside the mine he referred to a 'seam' where space for working was less than three feet from head to toe and workers had to crawl pulling the coal cars up the shafts to the outside. They couldn't even stand to work. The article described another part of the mine where a one hundred foot open area provided space for mules to work pulling the coal up the tunnels and outside where the children separated the coal from rocks.

146

The work was backbreaking, physically exhausting, and mentally draining with danger around every curve where roofs caved in, gas explosions, or asphyxiation caused mounting casualties. He argued the death by carbon monoxide poisoning was common. To make matters worse, rescue and recovery efforts were hampered because of the physical structures of the mines. Hundreds have died in the company town over the last few years and when the Wolf's supply of local workers runs dry, they simply employ foreigners from Wales, Scotland and England. When that manpower runs dry, they hire blacks for far less money and have to listen to far fewer arguments or deal with ethnic fights. However, the author explained Scots don't get along with the Welch, English despised both, and blacks can't stand anyone from a foreign country.

To one side of the small community lives a clan of Irish in twelve houses, eight to ten tightly situated in each building. Close by are about thirty Welch families, and over Settler Creek on the other side of town is a congregation of twenty-five houses where two hundred blacks reside. Close to the owner's home that is surrounded by a steel fence, is a group of white workers numbering about sixty. The train track is almost completed and according to the reporter, should be operational within the year. And located on a slight incline at the base of the mountain is the town cemetery where over two hundred victims rest.

The town sits in a valley with gray billowing smoke covering the entire area. Houses are close together and covered with soot. The local Stumpknockers Drinking Hole, Stanley's boarding houses, two meat markets, and blacksmith shop are closely situated all suffering from the constant smog covering the valley. Black lung breathing problems spreads throughout families. Everyone is a victim and deaths occur quickly. The cemetery expands!

The Wolf Company Store run by the owners gets most of the town business even though it charges high prices. Workers are paid in cash weekly with most of their wages going toward basic supplies. When THAT money runs out, owners provide "Scrip Tokens' that workers use to purchase goods and supplies. When the tokens are redeemed, it is understood in exchange for the tokens, there will be a reduction in the workers next pay. Owners control everything! The article was lengthy!

The reporter closed the article by saying, "Since there is not much competition in the small coal mining town, the Wolfs control the worker's lives. If workers don't like the conditions, they can go elsewhere!"

The topic of safety for Jonas and his family continued as Mary and I re-read the article. "Are all coalmines similar," again we asked? Was my childhood friend ok?

Sadly, I continued reporting my findings regarding my sister, Ruth, and the home, but without interrupting me too many times, Mary insisted I read the letters she had recently received, one from Jonas, one from sister Samantha!

From what I had previously read, both Jonas and Samantha appeared to be doing ok, but now Jonas seemed to indicate some conditions were not to his liking. He wasn't very specific! Many of his comments identified conditions and circumstances similar to what I had previously read on the train reducing my comfort level. He mentioned his kids were ok. His wife complained about his work. He did write befriending some blacks from Virginia. No real details! He really didn't explain or describe too much! Really, he just rambled on! He did mention he was reading a lot and I wondered if that was in reference to schooling and the small college nearby. He never said!

Following days of worrying and discussions with the children coupled with readings from the libraries regarding government regulations in coalmines in which there were few, we decided trips to both locations were needed. First, I obtained my monthly pay from the hardware store sufficient to address any financial issues and we gathered the kids and left to find Jonas. Sam would be next!

Twelve dollars for two tickets for Mary and I plus another six dollars for the girls put us in the coalmining town where Jonas lived and worked. Thomas stayed in Lexington and worked at the store plus hauling manure for Mr. Wilson.

Since Jonas and family left Tennessee, he moved his family twice and now lived in Hackett, a small town in the mountains of West Virginia. There were no connecting train tracks! The only way in to this little town was by the Cumberland and Hackett Line owned by Harold Hackett who lived in Chicago some five hundred miles away! This was the end of the line! Years ago, Harold sold out his mine to Jimmy Carroll. Harold still owned the tracks!

I told Mary someone needed to buy this line and develop some connecting routes. This mountain region is too isolated! We walked off the train and looked around.

Carroll signs were everywhere. "The town belongs to Jimmy," Nathan, one of the workers, said as we walked away. "He runs everything." That was obvious!

We walked around for a few minutes asking if anyone knew Jonas. A 'man of color' walked by saying Jonas lives over there, pointing in the direction of the hot sun. We hadn't seen each other in years and it was a welcomed sight when we said hello, even if he was covered with soot.

Jonas was surprised and I couldn't wait to hear his story. "My God," he hollered, "You look good. Mary looks even better." "Hold your horses," I responded. We began to talk.

After welcoming exchanges, some iced tea for the kids and beers for adults, we got up to date on kids and I spent a few minutes describing the circumstances in which I found Ruth. I reported conditions in Clinton were somewhat peaceful as informed by Cecil and mentioned sister Samantha while Jonas covered his movements from town to town including Hackett.

Jonas and his family lived in a tiny house at the edge of town close to the coalmines. It truly was a shack with a leaking roof, one broken window covered with boards, and a small front porch that could use some new wood. He was renting the three-room building owned by Mr. Jimmy Carroll and mentioned his rent was expected to increase shortly. "Jimmy can't keep help," complained Jonas. When Jonas asked Mr. Carroll to fix the roof, the mean looking owner simply said, "If you don't like it, move." I said that didn't make sense when Jonas agreed saying, "Nothing makes sense around here anymore."

While the kids got acquainted again and played outside breathing the stagnant smog filled air, Jonas continued saying, "Shorty Carroll owns and runs everything." Jonas referred to Mr. Carroll as 'Shorty'. He continued, "He recently hired foreigners from Ireland who speak with a funny twang. They get special treatment. Harold McClan gets extra pay for driving the wagon to Wheeling on special days." Jonas said he didn't know what Harold was buying and he didn't ask but did mention the train tracks didn't go very far. But, Jonas did mention the new train-track to Wakefield a small town about four miles away. That got my attention as I remember reading of a small community college in the town of three thousand.

Finally, I asked Jonas where Mr. Carroll came from when he shot back, "Some place called New Castle. He's been here since the end of the war. Don't cross him! That's his nice looking home over there on the hill."

Some distance away at the base of the mountains was a huge three story gray mansion with statue like pillars in the front and an upstairs porch surrounding the structure resembling an old cotton plantation home. "Nice place don't you say," he asked? "Ya, some people have it all," I responded.

After eight months of hard work and saying 'yes sir' every time he spoke with the owner, Jonas said the owner had given him and three other black families space for chicken coops in back of their homes with about five-dozen chickens. Jonas lived among twenty-five other black families that were separated from other groups such as the Irish.

Blacks live together! Foreigners live together! Whites live together. Blacks live close by one another and other groups reside within a spit. Jonas said, "Across you see the other workers, some from Canada and a large number from England." All homes in the valley looked the same, dilapidated! "Its best we stay here for just a little longer," he said. "It's a quick ride to Wake-field." But, like the boy at the train station said, "Jimmy owns everything!"

Mr. Carroll owned the mountain in back of the shacks and allowed black families to grow corn and tobacco on small parcels next to the creek. Jimmy owned the tobacco shop, the blacksmith shop and the metal shop. He owned the lone town newspaper where he wrote a weekly editorial to his liking. Mr. Carroll owned everything including the mules!

Jimmy Carroll controlled the town of nine hundred! He owned the mine, two saloons, the hardware store, two general stores, the feed store, the lone hotel, the sawmill, and controlled the bank. Interest on bank loans was an appalling twenty percent. Jonas said if anyone wanted to see Jimmy, about anything they had to visit him at the bank as his office was located in back and protected by his strong-arm kids. Plus, Jimmy was the mayor of Hackett!

All paperwork went through Jimmy. Maybe the named of this hellhole should be changed to Carrollsville or Carroll, I sarcastically said to myself. Jimmy Carroll trusted no one and had three burly sons and a mean wife to obtain any results he wanted, and on the reverse side, no one trusted him! Whites, the English, and black together despised the man! Jimmy Carroll was in charge. He controlled! Jonas mentioned Mr. Carroll even broke up fights that occurred daily. He fired a roughhouse gang a few months ago that constantly battled with his sons. The gang had previously worked in mines in Pennsylvania, had gotten fired there, than moved to Hackett. They lasted about six weeks before they were run out of town.

Jonas and I talked for some time as the kids played. Mary went for a walk with his wife when I asked Jonas about his son. Jonas said that his only boy had been killed in a mine accident a few years back and is buried under the rubble in Walker Mountain Cave where Jonas previously worked. "That was in Passage," he said. I didn't know where Passage was located. I just listened. Apparently, Passage was the first town Jonas lived in after leaving Clinton. He interrupted his explanation of his son's death to tell me another interesting finding.

That's when my childhood buddy informed me about his findings of the big city when he travelled to Louisville, Kentucky before settling in Hackett. He had spent a week there searching for work and remembered many inter-esting sites.

"JT," he said, "I got educated. I saw many things like newly founded black churches, blacks schools where black ministers and black teachers work. I saw black run businesses black owned and operated stores, restaurants, barbershops, saloons, and hotels. Black politicians spoke in city halls, in pulpits, or on street corners proclaiming freedom was not enough, as they wanted civil rights to include the right to vote. People of color informed me that many surrounding towns had black mayors."

Jonas was on a roll so I let him continue. "Black fraternal organizations assisting blacks with housing, food, and services, were not the only people helping. Other white citizens friendly to blacks like northern missionaries who formed humanitarian organizations such as the American Missionary Organization and American Freedom's Aid Commission conducted gatherings to teach the three R's. I saw a lot that week! Most people were friendly. I went into the local Frederick Douglass Elementary School and watched black kids ask questions about presidents like Lincoln and Washington and listened when black teachers talked about the 13th, 14th, and 15th amendments. I talked with blacks and whites. I didn't sleep in a black owned hotel, but rested nights in Preacher Kirby's church. That was ok, for now!

And I saw the other side also. You know JT, not all blacks in Louisville and any other big city or town looked for assistance or want to improve. I saw many blacks spending days drinking in saloons, gambling, some turned to begging on street corners while others turned to prostitution. And you know something else? There were many whites, foreigners, and others living on the streets with no place to go or incentive to improve themselves. JT, that trip is one I won't forget for a long time. It was an eye opener."

I questioned why did you not stay. He sidestepped the question when I asked, "O' Malcolm." "Ok, ok," he said.

He described the accident when a wall caved in and his twelve-year old son was covered in the debris. Malcolm had been instructed into the mine to retrieve something when the accident occurred. Wood timbers used to support the walls collapsed. Wagons full of coal were buried. Four other blacks and a white boss were also killed. That small town of Passage was about sixty miles away over the mountain and Jonas and family moved soon after the accident. Tears came to his eyes as he returned to the sight that frightful day. I told to him how badly I felt and it must have been devastating to him and his family. I couldn't imagine burying one of my children! Losing my only son would devastate me!

But the question of cities like Louisville stuck in my mine!

Jonas explained that coalmining was extremely dangerous work and many people were injured or died. Lung disease was common and everyone suffered from breathing problems. Jonas mentioned that many workers suffer from burns, bruises, or aching teeth that fall out because their teeth rot. Broken arm and leg injuries occur regularly. Bubba Callahan died when he was struggling to haul a wagon full of coal up the ramp. He just dropped dead! Mr. Carroll simply said his heart simply stopped. "Bubby was black, like me," said Jonas, "we buried him next to the other fifty-five blacks in the only cemetery in Hackett."

From what I had read and Jonas' stories, many died each year from stomach problems and mental stress associated with inside work. Workers suffer for short periods and return to the caves while others aimlessly leave or tragically die and are buried in Carroll's Cemetery. Workers are needed and Mr. Carroll is hiring new people all the time. Jonas questioned, "Want a job?" Replying I said, "No thanks." He followed with, "JT, I'll be leaving soon!"

Puzzled, I walked away thinking about his comments regarding his visit to Louisville. I had to find out what he meant about his 'leaving ' comment.

We spent two nights at the overpriced hotel and talked with Jonas and his wife when he was not working. He asked for some time off. Raymond Bassinger, his boss, quickly turned down that request! Up at five am, home at seven pm covered with soot! Work every day with Sunday off. I could not figure out why he stayed!

Jonas had spent years in West Virginia and was accustomed to the many changes, but the constant struggle with anti-black feelings still bothered him. He described nights in which he struggled thinking about being black. Rumors of beatings or fighting took place between whites and blacks every week. Blacks and whites don't work together in the mines. Blacks in one tunnel, whites in another!

They argued in the streets. They argue in stores and on porches. "Even kids fight over nothing," he said. Jonas said he feels threatened all the time. Name-calling and verbal abuse is constant! White fellow workers holler, "Go back to your plantation. Go home to Alabama. Pick more cotton. Find Uncle Tom! Go see uncle Remus, boy!" Other problems surfaced! And, Jonas had more stories.

Months ago KKK members from Clairborne and other communities walked into town and caused havoc with beatings and burnings. "It seems as though once a month someone died at the hands of the KKK and many whites in Hackett turn the other cheek," Jonas said. Jimmy always seemed to be away when the KKK shows! Over in Clax County, three blacks were found beaten to death on New Years and no one was arrested. The local white sheriff just told the family to bury the dead. Local whites care less! And the abuse was always on Jonas' mind. "If you go out at night, everyone carried a knife and pistol including me," he said! "Leave," I said.

Jonas mentioned issues that initiated fights. They erupted over who could buy certain products at the general store. He said, "Mr. Walters wouldn't sell me bullets for my rifle. Back along I wanted to go hunting and get some deer for my family." I agreed! That didn't seem right! Jonas argued blacks are treated as second-class citizens. "We earn less than whites," he complained. When he went to the bank to talk with Mr. Carroll, Mr. Carroll ignored him saying, he didn't have time. "Mr. Carroll was always too busy for us blacks," he finished.

"Why don't you just leave," I questioned? "Why have you stayed so long?" Jonas just stared looking away at the smog filled valley. "Come back to Clinton and work for me with my veteran's group," I said. There was no response but I could tell he was thinking of something! "Hell, go to Louisville," I said.

Jonas said he was making about forty-five dollars a month and money was in short supply. His wife and daughters make extra money by selling eggs, sewing dresses and jeans for white families. Jonas says he makes a few extra dollars working for some whites by fixing farm equipment and guns. That's when he again mentioned the inability to buy ammunition for his guns. However, he DID tell me he was able to acquire bullets from Frankie. Frankie is black. Frankie gets his supply from a traveling salesman who comes to town once a month selling mining supplies and other items! "He doesn't stay long," Jonas finished. Apparently, Mr. Carroll or his bodyguards don't spend much time watching Frankie or any other salesman who stroll into town unannounced. Makes no sense!

As Jonas was describing his expertise with fixing clocks, he mentioned he had heard of better job opportunities in the south in sawmills, phosphate mines, lumber mills, and foundries that were being built or opened. I hadn't read anything like that so I let him talk as he indicated his willingness to return to the south.

It took some time but eventually, I discovered Jonas had attended a local college for one year and he finally informed me of his interest in more classes specifically in Tennessee. "Why did you wait so long to tell me," I asked? "Are you moving again?" No comment!

Currently, education for his kids came from the local black school where fellow blacks taught classes and the local black church provided more classes, but Jonas wanted more for his family. "More schools are opening in the south," he claimed.

Are they open to blacks, I thought.

He continued to mention job opportunities in the deep-south. He even made reference to a section of the south called the 'black belt,' that was developing where blacks would be employed on former cotton plantations. States such as Mississippi, Louisiana, Alabama, and Georgia were developing fast and labor shortages were mounting. Was he serious, I thought, was he going there?

I didn't like the sound of that! I said, "Stay away." Jonas just looked my way and smiled! I could tell he was questioning my thoughts! Holy shit, sounded like antebellum south to me. I said to myself, Damn, Slavery all over again, only by another name. "Come back to Clinton," I repeated. And then. A few minutes went by when the topic changed drastically. I had talked with him for two days. And!

I mean with dedication and emotion! What followed was a complete surprise. Total surprise! Shock! I was dumfounded and overwhelmed. I had no idea what, when, or how my closest childhood friend had developed such insight. I listened carefully to astounding new developments.

Jonas started, "JT, I'm tired of living scared and feel as if I'm running. What I am about to tell you has taken much of my spare time. I have thought hard about what I'm about to say to you. You are my closest friend and I have confidence that you will understand and back my plans. I feel like I'm living in a cave with little to show for it. I've had enough of the coal mining business. Coalmining stinks! This lifestyle stinks! I tired of living this way. I need a change! My family needs a change! I cannot bring up my kids in such an environment or lifestyle. They will not work in caves or be treated like second class citizens." He was making me think, what was his future? Courage now had a capital 'C'.

He continued, "I don't want to fear anyone because I am black. I don't want to hide behind some curtain because of my color. I do not want to fear whites, rebels, foreigners, or someone with a title and am tired of fights. Maybe the move here was a mistake, but now is the time to move forward. We need to get out of this place. Listen to me for a minute! I just finished reading Frederick Douglas. Susan Anthony was a good read! I read Abe Lincoln. I re-read the Bible. I even read a story of the Chinese and their work on the railroad."

It truly sounded like he had some basic understanding identifying a path to follow. He continued and really impressed me with, "I feel an education for me and my family will really make a difference. I want to listen and learn what other leaders say and do while asking meaningful questions that demand sound thought and in depth expression of ideas. I want to lead rather than follow. I want to read what great leaders have accomplished and the methods they used to achieve success. I want to study the minds of the famous to understand their ideas. I want to investigate our own government to better understand what conditions were like when important decisions were handed down by legislators and courts. And someday, I want to travel to Georgia and see where my pa lived as a slave.

Just importantly, I want fairness for me and have MY family treated fairly. I will work hard to achieve those goals. I want respect for who I am and not depend on the color of my skin for favors or to have to face abuse. I will stand firm in my beliefs while asking for others, white or black, to do the same. I want to help everyone specifically blacks who feel unequal, abused, and disrespected."

That's when my ears really perked and I listened closely to, "JT that will mean every black, white, northerner, southerner, westerner, New Englander, college educated men and women, immigrant, businessman, rich man, poor man, city slicker, backwoodsman, farmer, soldier, ex-soldier, congressmen, state leaders including governors, Catholic, Protestant, or Jew will all have to work harder to establish a society where we all can live together."

He covered them ALL, I said to myself.

He took a breath. I took a deep breath with complete ignorance. I had no idea. Those readings sparked his foundation! Who else had Jonas been talking with? Apparently they had struck an emotional nerve. Preachers can answer many questions but he has done extensive research! It was obvious he had read more than the movement west or those Yankees from the northeast. I just listened as he continued. I wanted to hear more.

He continued, "JT, I feel blacks will have to work harder than others, but I think only good will come if we all make the effort. Yes, I will work as hard as I can. Who knows what will come of my plans and ideas. I don't know what or where I will finally settle or where I will work. I feel if I don't start working for my children's future by demonstrating then nothing will happen. I must lead! I have to show them we all can make a difference." Jonas took another deep breath and continued.

"You know JT, I want this for all people, not just blacks. And I realize talking with many locals and some others across the country that are not in agreement with my ideas will not be party to what I have to say. Maybe that means me and others of color will have to dig deeper, cross many bridges, and suffer more along the way, but I'm ready to put my soul and heart into it."

I interrupted him briefly to ask if his wife and kids new of the change. He smiled with complete assurance he had their support. "Those books and magazines in the back room have been read and studied," he said as he pointed in that direction. He continued.

"I may decide to become some local teacher. I might get involved in politics. I might study to work with people back in eastern Tennessee near my former home in Clinton or I might venture and settle in some big city like Louisville or New Orleans. Right now, I'm not sure but I must move forward and the time is NOW!"

We sat for another two hours and most of the following Sunday, his day off, as we discussed everything that had been disclosed. Jonas even explained his one-year of college and the satisfaction he witnessed. "Not enough," he said. Plus he never seemed to forget where he came from and our friendship, but the world had changed drastically since he left Clinton.

Throughout the entire discussions that included a long sleepless night, I continually asked questions that had no answers. Just questions, questions, and more questions! I was excited for my friend. I wanted the best for him. I wanted him to be happy. I would love to have him return to Clinton, but he sounded like other locations either in large cities or maybe a small town could answer his concerns. I did not want him in danger or abused. I was happy, but I worried!

Things were happening very fast for my friend, but Mary and I had to get moving toward Virginia.

We were getting ready to return to Lexington when Jonas brought out a church songbook and started singing. His wife and kids gathered around on the porch. He sounded pretty good as he sang four or five songs as the kids chimed in. Jonas said, "My favorites are; 'Shall We Meet Beyond the River', 'Onward Christian Soldiers', 'What a Friend We have in Jesus', and 'The Mistakes of My Life.' I jokingly asked him if he was starting a new career, when he simply replied that he sang to let his mind go and relax. He mentioned he and his buddies sang in the mines. Passes time! Sounded good to me! I never knew he could sing!

When we parted that day Jonas asked if I had heard from Benny. "Not a word," I responded.

The next morning we said our goodbyes and boarded the single tracked train to Roanoke, transferred, and than on to Lexington. Even though they enjoyed the trip and time with Jonas and his family, the kids wanted to be home. Little did they know their stay in Lexington would be short lived! Plans were in the making for another train-ride!

Fearful but extremely happy, I said so long to my childhood buddy! "Write me soon," I said. "We're leaving when I get paid," he responded, "I'll write."

Twelve

THE WAR AND FAMILY

"Man, that trip to West Virginia was more than I expected. I now have a different take on my friend," I said to Mary. "Take it easy John, He's a grown man. He will be all right," she finished. I reckon!

Samantha, had graduated from college, married Wallace Libby from Waterville, and was working in Morgantown, West Virginia. Mary and I decided we would travel north to visit with Sam before any of our future plans were started. Again, we corralled the children and headed to the Harrisburg/Knoxville Central. From the angry words of Thomas came, "Not again, I want to go hunting!" Again, everyone except Thomas boarded the northbound train. He could stay with Mr. and Mrs. Pasternak. They owned a local dairy farm and had a cute little daughter who just happened to be Thomas's age. I thought he was seriously looking at college! Well, maybe! "I can take care of myself," Thomas hollered as we departed.

Sam's letter had prepared us for the visit. She was working in a foster home where homeless kids resided. Well, some had parents, if you want to call it that! Some youngsters were placed there because of court rulings regarding guardianship responsibilities or parents unable to provide or care for their offspring. Some children had been living on the streets and were starving. Sam was employed by a couple who lost a son and daughter in a horrible drowning accident and wanted to help kids. Their twin fifteen-year old boys were away at a private boarding school in New Hampshire and the owners wanted to give something back to the community.

Prior to and during the war years the owners, Mr. and Mrs. Henry Hammer, had owned a large dairy farm in western Pennsylvania where oil had been discovered in the late 70s. Milk was their major source of income as well as corn from huge land holdings. Beside the extensive work on the farm, the couple was very instrumental in developing a local hospital just east of Pittsburg, but the discovery of oil changed everything. After lengthy discussions with John D, the Hammer's sold the two-thousand-acre property, including his prize bulls and two hundred cows to Mr. Rockefeller in 1880. Since the discovery of oil investment development was expanding throughout the north led by the Rockefeller family who were buying up any and all land, railroads, railroad cars, and any industry that affected his empire. A healthy check from John David was all Mr. Hammer needed.

In a way to escape the busy lifestyle of the past, the Hammer's decided to leave Pennsylvania and relocate in West Virginia. Mr. Hammer had received a degree in social work/finance from the University of Pittsburg and as a student had worked extensively with wandering children who were homeless as a result of the war. Hundreds roamed the streets and alleyways of Pittsburg! While building the hospital, he required a special section of the facility be reserved for such children under the age of eighteen. Plus, he wanted to expand his ideas.

By the early eighties Hamms Foster Home had been built and was presently owned and operated by the Hammers. Marie Hammer took care of daily business of schedules, staff issues, and orders while Henry handled financial matters, local and state contracts, including the constant trips to Washington to obtain updates on any new or proposed legislation that affected their home. Rules and regulations changed regularly and the Hammers insisted they stay vigilant as they understood bickering between Democrats and Republicans in DC always slowed the political process. Mr. Hammer always complained about the delaying tactics used by congressmen, but understood if he needed federal help he needed accurate detailed information. Marie argued many times, to forget those idiots, we will do it ourselves. All they do is shuffle paper from one desk to the other. "Damn politicians never agree on anything," she complained, "Plus they're never around."

An interesting comment in Sam's letter indicated that many of the residents are mulatto children from the former confederacy. They welcomed all! I liked that!

Henry didn't like surprises and on many trips he lingered longer than expected! He wanted answers from back stabbing politicians who were more concerned about maintaining their position, satisfying lobbyists, answering questions correctly or getting re-elected. On one specific visit to DC, Henry spent two days waiting for a meeting with a West Virginia senator before he was verbally 'slapped in the face' when he discovered the senator was in England talking tobacco contracts with the British. "I'll send him a nasty letter shortly," he had commented.

Samantha worked as one of the lead social workers and was right in the middle of all the decisions! As she explained in her most recent letter, she was busy all the time rescuing youngsters from disgruntled parents, hopeful foster parents, homeless vagabonds, or kids who just needed to talk. She had an endless supply of sad but true stories.

I was really glad to see her! She and her husband lived in a huge house with three bedrooms, a huge living room, a kitchen and workable indoor plumbing as opposed to what I saw in Sayersburg. She looked great! Just like the years in Boxford Forge, she smiled all the time. What a great gal! Her two children, named Wally James and Walter Lindsey were named after her husband's father and grandfather.

Her husband, Wallace, got his degree in English and is editor of one of the local newspapers. He also covers West Virginia University and it's sports programs that recently started playing the relatively new game of football. In all her previous letters, she had never mentioned her kids. I asked her why when she responded with, "I don't tell you everything about me." She was right! She's no longer my little sister, she's an adult and beautiful at that.

For two days the kids played and enjoyed one another. The younger boys enjoyed talking with older girls and my three girls enjoyed the company of the boys. Everyone got along while Mary and I thoroughly enjoyed talking with Samantha and Wallace. My little sister, who taught me the finer points of reading and always encouraged me to get better, don't settle for ok, perform at a higher level, was now very instrumental in the lives of many struggling kids. And she loved it! I could tell her rapport with kids, the Hammer family, and other social workers, was outstanding. She was extremely comfortable in her work! She had a great family. She laughed and made others laugh! I was glad to call her 'my sister.'

Wallace and I reflected on the newspaper coverage of the Civil War, as he called it. We compared battlefield reports, specifically Gettysburg and Fredericksburg. We discussed our perspectives on President's Davis and Lincoln. We even showed our intellectual knowledge of generals like Grant, Meade, Longstreet, and Lee. We had a good time enjoying each other's company. He mentioned he had a cousin killed at Little Round Top when I surprised him by mentioning Joshua Chamberlain's name. He thought I was smarter than I really am! Wallace asked, "Did you know he got elected four times as governor of Maine?" "No," I responded. I reckon I wasn't as smart as I thought!

Mary and I decided to inform them of our intentions of operating a veteran's home for disabled and injured soldiers. The next day Henry, Sam and

Wallace took us to the Marching Veterans Home located nearby. We were invited into the home, met the owners, and had a great morning. That home was significantly different from what I had encountered in Sayersburg!

I spent one night describing the deplorable conditions in Sayersburg while informing Samantha of discovering Ruth. We talked throughout the night into the wee hours of the next morning before many of our questions were answered. I supplied Sam with the location of the town as she showed considerable interest finding her long lost older sister. "Let me know when you go," I said.

While the kids attended a circus the next afternoon, we had time to discuss our plans. Henry liked our ideas! "Check Washington," Wallace suggested. "Write your congressmen and become friends with local politicians," responded Henry.

We became pretty good friends with the Hammer family and Wallace those few days in Morgantown. They liked us. We liked them. Mr. Hammer was very informative. Wallace had some good news! He was getting a promotion. He even took me to his office while describing the competition among nationally known newspapers that always vie for notoriety claiming to be 'first.'

I thought to myself, the game never stops. Everyone wants to be first, best, highest, strongest, or have the most. Competition! Competition! Competition!

Mr. and Mrs. Hammer encouraged us to work hard as our plans met with supporting eyes even mentioning his willingness to help us with finances in building the home. I told him my plans were to build the structure near Clinton, Tennessee. As we prepared to leave he surprisingly questioned, "My money IS good in the south, isn't it?" Then I thought, was he really offering his financial support?

We need to talk more! I'll ask later!

Ruth, I said to myself, 'I may need to return to Sayersburg!

I'll take Sam!'

At that point in my adventure, I couldn't be happier. I reached in my pocket and felt that Amish good luck coin I received from my brother during the war.

We thanked everyone for the visit, confirmed with each other the need to write more, and said our good byes. Everyone enjoyed the trip including my son Thomas who had spent the entire time near Lexington fishing and talking with THAT girl next door. He never mentioned her name and I didn't say anything about helping with farm chores. I did discover he had spent many long evenings at the farm. Mary wanted to know more, but I stepped in before things got carried away!

There were many topics on my mind as we returned to Lexington. Mary and the kids were preparing for the move back to Clinton. Samantha Mary-anne, my oldest daughter, had just completed reading 'Life on the Mississippi,' by Mark Twain, Roxie Marie was involved in a school science project regarding small pox, and little Frances Leighanne was constantly challenging Mary with her stubbornness. And I quickly learned Thomas had interest elsewhere. "The war," he said.

"Help me with the home," I said, referring to my future project.

Years later
Our return to Tennessee was rather smooth. Work at the store continued. We resettled at the farm as Cecil, still unmarried, relocated himself in the apartment above the store. Shortly, I would investigate and answer questions surrounding the former veteran's group. I wondered how many group members had died or moved. I soon discover many things never change, except the characters and dates.

Newspaper reports continued to cover the expansion to the west with old worn out stories of General Custer and Crazy Horse at Little Big Horn. An article from General William T. Sherman, who had been working for the government on Indian affairs, proclaimed between 1867-1884 only 565 soldiers died from fighting Indians, while he proudly described battles where thousands of Indians were displaced or killed. Mary commented, "Indians get no better treatment then blacks or southern veterans!" I agreed!

Newspapers and magazines covered everything! Rockefeller, Carnegie, and Morgan became multi-millionaires while their workers suffered in poverty. Politicians in Washington overtly supported big business. 'Money talks', they bragged. Over dinner one night, I said to Mary, "I wonder how many politicians are paid under the table?" "Too many," she responded.

In the south, thousands of blacks returned to develop land as tenant homes replaced slave quarters (In name only). Mississippi and Louisiana became huge cotton producing states while war veterans conducted huge marches to bring awareness to their plight. I had never been to Louisiana and newspaper reports at times were sketchy. Plus I didn't like the sound of it as the 'black belt' continued to expand. I need to write Jonas!

I hadn't heard from my friend in months and I wondered what he was doing, where he lived, and tried to imagine him teaching or a leader among people of color. I didn't even know where to send a letter as the previous correspondence years back had been returned. Plus, I haven't seen or heard from Benny.

The New York Times even a story about President Garfield's assassination in 81 describing the shooting and claiming that Robert Lincoln, a member of the president's staff, was near the president when he was shot. I remembered that Robert was also present in the Peterson House when his father died in 65.

And everywhere throughout the country, the railroad was expanding with Grenville Dodge's name plastered everywhere! Religion continued to influence millions as the 'Bible Belt' grew running from Texas to Virginia. Seemed like America was expanding, but I wondered if the progress was too fast and questioned whether it was for the good?

Corruption Continued

Southern states continued with many problems regarding office holders. With reconstruction came political reorganization. Political corruption was supposed to end with the end of reconstruction, but that was not the case! Corruption continued!

Elections were always a major concern as black and white candidates decided the best way to win seats was to strike deals. You scratch my back. I'll scratch yours! In local, state, and federal elections special interest groups were identified and targeted for votes. Businessmen, large landowners, and company owners were paid in cash or given favors for votes. Businessmen's taxes were reduced. Large landowners witnessed tax reduction. Prices reduced when they bought out smaller nearby vacant farms. Foundries, sawmills, and similar companies were given special accommodations regarding shipping, construction permits, or federal and state loans.

Corruption was widespread. Same stories, different decade!

Back in the mountains of southern West Virginia Jonas had commented, NOW is the time! Maybe my friend was right, NOW IS the time! My head was spinning out of control! I felt I had to act! My family, the veteran's home, and Jonas!

I asked, where has America been since he made that comment? Jonas was right then and even 'more right' now. Let's move on. Local black leader Buford Sibley the newly elected state representative from South Carolina complained in the local paper, "Can't anyone agree on anything? Why do we argue all the time?"

Mr. Sibley's comment was one of many that covered topics from politics to business and similarly focusing on social and cultural problems. He argued, how did people of color fit into the landscape of the future?

To add to the anxiety in America, women gathered expressing their concern regarding voting rights. Women were no longer willing to spend days and nights milking cows or cleaning kitchens. Working in mills or sitting at home remaining idle was not for them. Women wanted more! They wanted to he heard! "We want to vote just like men," they argued. White women complained they could not vote, but blacks could. There were other issues that surfaced surrounding the issue of white women voting.

Local newspapers in the south supported white women voting saying that that group (women) would support and defend the cause of 'white supremacy'. Editorial comments from Atlanta, Charleston, New Orleans, and Memphis agreed! "Blacks belong on plantations," hollered Ellen and James Cannon from Montgomery. I disagreed and again thought of Jonas. I argued, women in the north cannot vote! Black/white, the issue won't go away!

Thomas responded that Mr. Blake Washington, his former social studies teacher had made comments in class about a women's movement toward suffrage. That's when Thomas started asking me questions about politics, government, and the War Between the States. "Later," I answered.

With all that was taking place in America, I still had time to talk with my family. The girls wanted to discuss issues like their responsibilities around the house and becoming more independent. Mary continued her bible study with everyone and Thomas and I had time for a little hunting and fishing. Plans for the future home were reviewed nightly. I organized a search committee.

Thomas

I always thought the relationship between a father and son was special. I loved watching my son grow! Thomas was our firstborn. Over the years he and I developed a special bond. From the first time I held him and watched him struggle with his first steps, we had bonded with mutual trust that has never separated or ended. When Thomas broke his arm falling from a wagon the incident didn't stop him from chasing the chickens or the hogs. A few years later he loved riding that old mare, even when he got thrown. When we fished or hunted and came home empty handed we simply said that there would be another day. We spent numerous activities together where we spent time laughing and enjoying each other. We shared the good and bad.

I liked to think I was there for him whenever the situation arose. His schooling in Lexington was challenging and he enjoyed the town. He became acquainted with a young girl close by, but never forgot about me. Eventually, he informed me her name was Rachel. "Rachel Holly Cannon," he said one night on our walk to the barn to check on the new foal. He always wanted answers! We even talked about girls and girl friends. Hell, he has three sisters!

His interest covered many subjects and I was always honest when answering his questions. Eventually he questioned me about the war. On a few occasions, he and I had talked about veteran comments especially when I returned from a difficult meeting. He wanted to know more about the war years.

Who was such and such, he would ask. How could millionaires control so much, he inquired. Why did people venture over the Mississippi River to go west? As a youngster he would ask, why not work in a factory and make lots of money? Why go to college? The older he got, the more he began to answer his own questions. But the one question he held back came one day after he returned from a short trip to Lexington. I had always responded with, "Later." He wanted to know about the 'War Between the States' and specifically my involvement.

Later was now!

"Let's go fishing," I said. "Matter of fact, how is Rachel?"

"Just fine," responded Thomas. "We celebrated her 19th birthday last week."

My mind returned to Lexington as we grabbed our fishing poles and food.

During our five years in Lexington I had attended a few public readings where writers would read some of their books in venues such as libraries, schools and colleges, or simply halls where they had been asked to perform. Some authors were interesting while others were terribly boring. Clemens, Longfellow, and others traveled big city circuits to expose their works. I never saw either of them! Some dealt with fiction. Others focused on politics. Slavery and reconstruction were popular topics. Many reviewed the past. And some had an ax to grind! Such was the one case. Thomas just listened as I talked and we walked.

I had attended a public reading at the library about a new book recently published that described the 'Civil War.' It was still the 'War Between the States' to me! About twenty-five locals attended the proceeding. Mr. Warren, my former political science instructor in Lexington stood to the back of the room listening intently.

It was not a good night! Basically, a waste of my time!

The book was written by Mr. Langston Livingston who proclaimed the war was a direct result of a southern economic system that supported slavery and blamed the south for the carnage and mutilation of thousands of innocent people and worthy Americans.

He read a section of the book describing the battle at Gettysburg and another part of a chapter on random rebel guerrilla raids from Mosby's forces in northern Virginia. He criticized southern military tactics. He criticized southern religion and pulpit pounders. He had nothing good to say about any southerner. No one south of the Mason/Dixon line was immune! According to Canton, a classmate buddy from the area, it was obvious Livingston was from the north as he continued for over two hours to blast the Confederacy. New Yorker through and through! I had lasted about fifty minutes before I vacated my seat sneaking out the side door.

Eventually, I discovered he even argued that the south had no business asking for assistance after the war. He blasted Johnson, congress, and Grant for trying to rebuild the former confederacy. He wanted the south to provide for them-selves! "Was he all there," I said to Canton? "Sounds like he's talking out of the side of his mouth."

Howard Barnes, one of my classmates, reported the question and answer time after the reading was more brutal. He wanted to punish southern leadership, it's generals, even enlisted personnel. He hated Davis, Lee, and probably would have said something to me if I had stayed.

The title of the four-hundred page book, was 'Southern Miscalculation.' A subtitle told it all, 'Stupidity, Slavery, and Southern Suicide.' Needless to say, I did not buy the book or any other book written by the deranged northerner.

As we approached Cress Creek, Thomas said, "Pa, tell me more about that reading up in Lexington that disturbed you so much back along." I looked at him and simply said, "Thomas that northerner has a lot to learn about the war. He needs to talk to former soldiers from both the north and south. He needs to visit with wounded veterans and try to understand the trials and tribulations they encountered. Mr. Livingston's book is slanted so much it misrepresents the entire war. He has no idea the commitment young people made, the dedication they made, or the danger they endured on the battlefield or in prisons. Thomas, his book need not be read."

Thomas described his former social studies book from high school class. He thought emphasis focused on the northern perspective. He said his teacher tried to give a balanced account of the war but the book continued to take the northern view when explaining strategy, military tactics, or battles like Gettysburg, Fredericksburg, or Sherman's March to the Sea. I asked Thomas to explain what he meant when he said, "Pa, it always seemed like the north won all the battles. My textbook always showed diagrams of northern units, their strengths, and their movements in battles." Thomas went on to explain that his social studies book always took the position that northern forces and generals always were successful because they outnumbered the rebel forces, had better arms and supplies.

I decided I needed to detail some of my experience or at least give my son my view of the war. Thomas asked, "How did our southern land get so destroyed? I found an old artillery shell in the cow pasture last week. The entire south could be a minefield."

Thoughtful but with no immediate explanation, I said, "Apparently the closing days on the war were not discussed where southern information, documents, laws, and material was destroyed be retreating and evacuating forces. Information on the formation, existence, and operation of the Confederacy was burned or secured by Davis, Lee, Longstreet, Johnston, or any other important figure those finals days."

As we sat by the creek and fished for catfish and trout, I tried to explain my involvement. I started with an emotional description of leaving my ma and sisters on the farm in Boxford Forge, the enlistment, strange fellows in Clinton, and the march up the Shenandoah Valley. I neglected to mention the promise of the train ride to northern Virginia as I decided to save that comment for another time! But I did express my feelings for Mary and how her support was vital to my wellbeing while I was away defending the southern cause.

I explained in detail the eastern mountains of Tennessee where we called home, was a strong pro-union section of the south. With that being said, I tried to explain my reasons for leaving to fight for the confederacy. My strong belief in states rights, my limited understanding at age 18 of what 'dedication to the cause' really meant, and my enthusiasm to defend my homeland were all deciding factors in making my decision. Simultaneously, I explained safety concerns for the farm and family. But, ma said, "Go."

I emphasized that many citizens in and around our little community of Boxford Forge supported the union side. Locals in Clinton also provided different opinions. Not all residents in our little 'neck of the woods' supported secession. "Plus your grandpa was a true southerner," I reminded him. At that moment, I was not sure my message was understood. But!

I had to defend the cause!

While describing my disturbing camp life, dreadful long boring marches that caused bleeding blisters and continued soreness in my feet, I expressed my concern that the war itself should never be forgotten and that future generations need to know the circumstances and brutality of war. They need to know the commitment young people made. Future generations need to know the agony that accompanies warfare. They need to know soldier's mental and physical isolation associated with loneliness in foreign territory. "Soldiers marched thousands of miles with no shoes," I explained. I had to confess northern winters were nothing anyone would want to endure every year. I had never witnessed such snowstorms and blizzards!

Thomas asked, "Pa, how did you deal with being away from mom for such as long time?"

"It was not easy, " I started, "But we had great respect and love for each other. I wrote letters to your ma and tried to let her know how I was doing." I described some of the battles while watching my friends die in the Sunken

Road at Sharpsburg, Antietam in the northern history books. I described the horrible days at Gettysburg where I was wounded on day three during Pickett's Charge and almost forgot to include the days and nights at Fredericksburg that cold December in late 1862.

Thomas and I fished for about four hours. With all the attention focusing on the war, it was no wonder we didn't catch a thing. We grabbed our poles and headed back. Finally, I said, "I have something to show you. Maybe the girls would like to see it too."

Following dinner, the family gathered in the small living room. The wrinkled war torn brown booklet I call 'The Journal' was retrieved from the bedroom as I returned and sat next to Mary. I brought out my brother Thomas's prison notes. My children had never seen the journal and I decided this would be a good time to explain what had happened to my older brother after he left Boxford Forge with my pa in 1858. I was only 14 years old.

Roxie Marie questioned, "You were 14 when grandpa left?" "I certainly was," I responded, "and there is more." I spent the next hour describing how my pa and brother got to Albany, New York, their experiences in Amish territory in Pennsylvania, and their subsequent work in the paper mill. I mentioned the accident that took pa's life but refused to go into the details. I mentioned Amanda Adams who lived across the river in Vermont. Thomas had befriended her and his intentions of marrying her when the war ended.

"My brother was a captain in the Union Army," I said. The kids were surprised at the statement. They were surprised even more when I described how my brother and I met when I was on picket duty while protecting sleeping rebels. I showed them the 'good luck' coin that the Amish had given Thomas, and explained how I became owner of the masterpiece. "I carry it all the time," I said.

"Where is grandpa buried," asked Roxie? "On a hill overlooking the Hudson River outside of Albany," I answered. With tears in her eyes, Samantha responded with, "And grandma is buried in Boxford Forge, Tennessee. How sad!"

Samantha Maryanne continued asking, "Weren't you ever lonely away from Tennessee?" "Yes, I was and on many occasions I would talk with Captain Steele," I said. The captain and I talked about home life. We talked about camp life. We talked about war and killing. We talked about our future. I told the captain about Jonas and our friendship.

The captain was from northern Virginia and lost his entire family when the union forces marched through his farm." I refused go into any devastating details regarding the captain's family. The captain was my best friend before we separated and he went to command a prison in Macon, Georgia.

I did spend a little more of the evening talking about how the captain and I had met again after the war in Washington DC. "That's when I put it all together about my brother's journal," I said. "Somewhere along the line, Captain Steele figured out that Thomas was my brother."

My family had listened to me talk about my battles, my injuries, my hospital stays, and my camp life where fellow soldiers told about their respective war experiences.

Now was the time to enlighten them on the critical decision I made about my final months defending the southern cause. The weathered journal rested in my lap as I started. I had much to say!

I described how I had received the journal in the mail while resting on the train that stalled for a few days awaiting supplies near Chattanooga. I was guarding prisoners on a train headed to Camp Sumter in southern Georgia. Dejectedly I said, "I was just a prison guard." "I thought you were in the infantry," asked Thomas?

I explained I had been removed from the battlefield and placed as a guard first at Belle Island then transferred to another prison known as Libby. Both were located in Richmond, Virginia. Belle Island, located in the middle of a river, was the home of enlisted men while Libby Prison, located in an old warehouse incarcerated officers. Thomas spoke up and asked, "You mean officers were separated from enlisted men?" I responded with a simple, "Yes, including northern spies." Neither prison was a pleasant sight! Both demonstrated horrible human living conditions where inmates died every day.

Again I mentioned how northerners and southerners made reference to the same spot on a map but identified the location differently. Eventually, I said, "When southerners refer to Camp Sumter and northerners make reference to Andersonville Prison, they are both referring to the same prison." 'The hellhole of the south,' I thought.

Mary helped Frances get more wood for the stove and everyone gathered closer when I talked about prisons and my job as a guard. Roxie asked if I carried a rifle. "Of course, I responded, I was a guard." She asked, "Did you ever kill anyone?" I dodged the question by describing life inside a prison!

I talked about the lack of food for prisoners and mentioned the horrible unsanitary conditions at Belle Island, Libby, and Camp Sumter. Castle Thunder, another prison nearby witnessed similar problems, but thankfully I was never positioned inside. Prisoners suffered as I described the lack of medical supplies. Prisoners fought diseases, insects, freezing winter weather, blistering hot summers, and the lack of clothing. The clothes prisoners wore when they arrived at prison were the same clothes they escaped in, died in, or wore when they were released.

Thousands of inmates inside Camp Sumter walked around naked. I asked, "Could you live on a small piece of bread and a cup of water for your food supply for one week?" Sam responded with, "That's impossible. One piece of bread and water for a week! People can't live that way!" In respect for the younger children, I limited my description regarding indiscriminate shooting by guards when inmates crossed inside the dead zone, where prisoners were shot when approaching the prison walls.

Then I showed the children words written by my brother while he was imprisoned in Macon. Thomas had been captured during a battle in northern Virginia and sent to Georgia. As he described in the journal, the first few days of incarceration prisoners marched, many barefoot, into North Carolina before boarding a train headed further south. Thomas had written approximately every two or three days recording his physical conditions, personal reflections, and constant abuse. The entries were sad to read and hear but the children listened to every comment.

All of the topics I had covered now were open for their interpretation. The kids heard for the first time what prison life was like and it was personal. Mary took the journal and started reading. Page after page Mary read. My son, named after my brother, began to fully understand the torture. As I looked around the room, eyes expanded wide open! Tears welled! The more Mary read, the more the kids listened. Mesmerized would be an understatement. No one moved.

Roxie hollered to Frances to keep still. The girls were only thirteen months apart in age. Mary continued. Horrible words like 'no food today except black coffee' or 'blood seeping from open wound' brought immediate emotional responses. The last few pages of the journal demonstrated the slow process of dying as words like 'am dreaming', 'water, water, water', 'need rest', and 'tired, tired, tired' described my brothers last moments.

Everyone felt the anger and sadness I witnessed during my initial reading of the journal. Everyone had tears. The room was still. Lights flickered! The children sat! Mary continued turning pages. Samantha burst out, "How could this happen? Pa, why?" Frances cried saying, "Why did no one stop this? Were conditions like this in Camp Sumter or as you said a minute ago, Andersonville? Were they in every prison?" Thomas asked, "Were conditions like this in northern prisons?"

Frances tossed and turned crying and saying, "Pa, this ain't right."

I picked up little Frances and tried to comfort her when she asked if my brother was still alive. Sadly I said, "No. He died in prison and is buried in Macon Georgia." I handed Thomas the journal as he started reviewing its contents.

Samantha repeated, "Grandma, aunt Lilly, and aunt Leighanne buried in Tennessee, grandpa buried in New York, uncle Thomas buried in Georgia and my pa and aunt Samantha survived the war. Pa, do you feel lucky?"

I just looked at Sam and said to myself, I guess so! Plus we recently discovered my older sister Ruth is still alive. No one was ready for bed!

Everyone moved to the crowded kitchen when Mary said a prayer. Even Frances wanted some milk and cookies and said she couldn't sleep.

Eventually, the kids went to bed.

Even when the candles were extinguished and the gas lamps turned down, no one went to sleep. It had been an evening like no other. Everyone had a chance to ask questions and more would surface over the next few months. Days followed as I answered more questions about northern prisons without detailing specific locations or events. Thomas wanted to talk more. Sam and Roxie had many questions following their journal reviews.

Nights followed with more questions. Late one night with tired eyes I closed the journal and sat with Mary on the couch as we tried to make sense out of the events. The children's eyes had been opened. They had more questions that needed answering. They had concerns that would be part of their life for some time. We discussed the next step. Where would I begin the next time our children asked about the war?

But, my greatest concern was not talking about how many Yankees I killed or how many comrades I saved or rescued. I was not fearful of talking about battles in greater detail. I was not scared to disclose my inner feelings regarding my emotions. My greatest fear rested with how to explain to my children my untimely and surprising exit from the army. I was no General Longstreet, Joe Johnston, or Robert Edward Lee. I did not lose a leg like General Hood or my life like Stonewall Jackson, or sign any famous document. My name was not well known! I was no national hero! I had not been identified in newspaper articles or written about in magazine articles. No editor or newspaper reporter had told my story! I was a simple enlisted soldier who went to war thinking I was doing the right thing for me, defending my homeland, and my future. And I walked away from it all before the end. I had had enough! I argued with myself! I had many questions.

Was I over-reacting? Did I have a reasonable argument? Was I going to be convincing? Would they understand or agree? How important was it anyway? Would time heal my emotional wounds? In fact, did they really care?

As I discussed with myself a strategy to explain my actions, I continued to worry about Jonas, Ruth, Samantha, and Captain Steele. My mind returned to those everlasting experiences when I left Camp Sumter during the winter of 64/65 when a poorly designed administrative prisoner exchange program agreed upon by both parties collapsed. I say 'agreed upon' but that was hardly the case! THAT exchange program never worked! When the calendar changed 65, the southern landscape was covered with former Yankee and Confederate prisoners wandering helplessly!

In my mind I reviewed the final year of my enlistment at Camp Sumter, located in Andersonville, Georgia! Young innocent boys, old tired men, and former slaves throughout the confederacy, identified as prison guards, collected a few belongings and simply walked away from prisons while thousands of prisoners joined the escape. They too, became entangled in the confusion that spread across the southern landscape. And I joined the melee!

Confusion, plus lack of communication between and among the union and Confederate leaders, produced nothing but chaos. Prisoners simply walked away from stockades with no clothes or survival skills. Rebel guards lowered their rifles, turned their backs, and waited. Thousands of unguarded prisoners and lonesome confused guards plainly walked away exposed to the torn devastated south where violence, death and the unknown controlled. Danger was around every turn, over every hill, and in every town. The complete exchange program was a horrible failure! A complete disaster!

During the early winter of 65 I walked away from Fort Sumter, dodged the uncontrolled southern countryside in Georgia, and arrived in Clinton weeks later unscathed.

Weeks went by when my son said, "Pa, you mentioned that the rebel army was not ready for the war when it started. There was no Confederate Army. There was no Confederate money. There was no proven leader. When the rebels bombed Fort Sumter in Charleston Harbor, there was no efficient confederate government. Matter of fact, according to my former history teacher up in Virginia, the union had very little also. Neither side was ready for war! But, you enlisted within a year?"

Thomas and I were in the barn building a new stall when he continued with, "You said you never was given a Confederate uniform and never received a rebel issued rifle. Matter of fact you said the only new rifle you ever had was one taken from a dead Yankee or a fallen southerner at some battle. You mentioned that on many occasions you took clothes from dead soldiers, especially to keep warm during the snow covered winter months. You even took a dead soldiers boots!"

I interrupted with, "I did what I had to do to survive. Like I said the other night, I was starving one winter and had to retrieve some food from a drunken buddy who was passed out after he vomited on everything in the log shelter. I only took what I could eat." I didn't say any more.

Thomas continued, "You also mentioned the army lacked food supplies and you were hungry most days, especially during marches as food wagons had a hard time keeping up with those marching. You complained about the Confederacy as President Davis and his cabinet were never in agreement, never in control, and state governors could not be forced by Davis to supply either men or materials for the war effort. Davis was useless, you said. Governors spent more time arguing amongst themselves than trying to win the war. And you constantly complained about the lack of shoes or boots. You even mentioned generals at Gettysburg had envisioned capturing a shoe warehouse in that little town in Pennsylvania after defeating the union forces."

"There was no boot warehouse found, but I did get some oversized boots off a dead rebel at Gettysburg," I answered. I grabbed another plank and nails.

Thomas continued asking, "With all those problems, how did the south really expect to win the war? Outnumbered and overwhelmed, were rebel leaders willing to sit back and simply wait for the Yankees to retreat into the north?"

Thomas was relentless that afternoon. He had questions about the southern railroad system, blacks fighting in Rebel units, useless uneducated untrained doctors, and numerous comments regarding Abraham Lincoln. Seemed like he had spent some valuable moments trying to understand what had transpired in the 60's including what I had endured.

With all the worry I had imposed on myself, my concerns were significantly diminished when Thomas exploded with THAT barrage of comments and questions. I never answered all the questions or responded to all his comments. I never had to answer questions about some of my activities at Camp Sumter. I never had to answer detailed questions about my departure from the army. Thankfully, I discovered my children were satisfied to know I had served and survived. Samantha had commented, "Pa, you did your part."

Over the next few weeks I discovered my son had spent days with Rachel as the two high school graduates visited former battlefields and even ventured to Richmond to see the rebuilding that was taking place in the former capital. Thomas informed me Rachel had lineage to Robert E. Lee.

Thomas had brought up many issues and I decided that another lesson was in the making, so one night following Thanksgiving Dinner I gathered everyone and said, "Children I have something to say." Frances got out an old rag doll and sat beside Mary. Roxie and Sam grabbed another piece of pie and waited. Peacefully, Thomas sat close to the wood stove waiting.

I quickly made a few comments about the war itself and finished by saying that over 13,000 union soldiers were buried in the small town of Andersonville. Camp Sumter cemetery, to be exact! Something told me, they had to know THAT number! For some reason, I felt the need to say the following to my children.

"You know wars are struggles, no matter where you fight or how long the battles. Everyone has his or her own perspective about war's purpose. Everyone does not agree why we fight but no one wants to die. Citizens leave home! They leave loved ones behind! Citizens become soldiers! Fear and uncertainty welcomes them with each sunrise. Citizens invade foreign soil. Battles start!

Some battle weary soldiers turned to animals and commit atrocities. Soldiers make mistakes! Generals make mistakes. Many die! Abnormal becomes normal. Rats become food. Rags become shoes. A short march is thirty miles. One day is forty-eight hours. A night's sleep is two hours. Letters from home never arrive. Letters written by soldiers find no readers. Politicians want answers. Families are destroyed. Survival moves to first place."

I had gotten their attention, than I really got rolling.

There are lessons to learn about soldiering and I was always proud to have served. I sounded like a preacher as I moved from father to speaker. I looked around the room and realized that my four children were between 10 and 18 and I had a mission. Now was the time!

I had talked about my little speech with Mary when she responded with, "Go, do it!" Plus, Mary had her own story. I had listened to professors, politicians, preachers, and asked many questions during my years in Lexington. They made me think. I didn't have all the answers but I was intent on addressing my concerns to my family with the hope they would understand a little about my growing up years and adjustments necessary to move forward.

My next comment focused on self-identity. So I said, "Who are we really?" Frances fiddled with her doll and stared into the dark sky outside while the others looked somewhat puzzled. That was ok as I asked each of the kids what was really important in their life.

Thomas spoke first and said, "Pa, my family is the most important thing now. While I was fishing the other day, I got thinking about you and how you survived the war, as your entire family was broken apart. Even aunt Ruth up north is basically alone. I listen to my teachers as they tried to prepare me for the future. They asked tough questions every day. I understand their concerns for their students and I appreciate it. I'm not sure exactly what I want to do. Pa, I'm 18, the same age you were when you joined. You might ask me if I would fight. I have no idea. I just don't know. Things have changed. I hope for the better! It would be a hard decision. Could I do what you did? I hope I never have to answer that question about killing someone." Thomas was still thinking and finally said.

"Pa, I would love to have a big farm. I want to have a family like ours where I can have peace and respect for one another. I want to see Rachel more as we have talked about our future. I may be in love. I don't know! Pa, you always told me a good education is the most important ingredient for success. You always said to help those who cannot help themselves. I've been thinking about your ideas regarding the veteran's home."

He was about to say something else when Samantha stepped in with, "Pa, you and ma have provided for us and I want to finish school here in Clinton where I know people. I want to live in a town where there are no fights because people can't talk through their disagreements. I hate to see blacks and whites fighting over such things as what side of the street to walk on or why certain people, because of their skin color, can't get into certain stores." Sam was fifteen months younger than Thomas and seemed to know more than she occasionally demonstrated! She finished with, "Pa, what about Jonas and his family over there in the coalmining hills of West Virginia? Have you heard from him recently?"

That made me think my last correspondence with my friend was years ago and I needed to locate him. Samantha was right! Roxie excused herself, ventured into the kitchen for something to eat.

Thomas had one more comment when he asked Mary, "Ma, how did you live through the war? When Pa left in 62, you did not see him until he returned in the winter of 65, just before the war ended. What did you do and how did you feel being separated from your future husband?" Thomas continued to amaze me with interest and questions.

Everyone looked around the room. Mary prepared!

While Sam was trying to say something else, Mary spotted Roxie who was returning from the kitchen waiting for the right moment to ask, " Can I get a new dress for the barn dance this Saturday?"

Mary answered with, "We'll go shopping in Knoxville tomorrow afternoon after we clean the house." That seemed to relax Roxie somewhat as she handed out oatmeal cookies and sat. Sam said, "Later."

"I'll escort you," I said. I reckon she's really not interested. Not yet anyway! Is that all she's concerned about, a dress? I'll talk with her later.

And, this was a good time to hear from Mary!

"I was lonely all the time," she started. Mary continued with comments about our love for each other. Our commitment was strong and Mary spoke of her close ties with her family. To take her mind off me and the war Mary spoke about her work with her pa at the store, and the sad feeling she encountered when ma died. She spoke of the loss of her ma and how devastating it was.

174

Mary said, "Children, I want you to know that whatever happened to your pa during the war was felt by me as he sent letters whenever he could write. His spelling was terrible, but I could understand his comments. In many letters he described the horror of war, his friendship with Captain Steele, and his dedication to the cause. He was a proud soldier. He loved me! He demonstrated it with letters and he never forgot me. I loved him! He always inquired about Jonas."

Mary continued, "I want you to know there were many lonely days and nights. I went through periods of crying and emotional distress worrying about your pa. I had many discussions with Preacher Rackley before he moved away during the war. I prayed every night for your pa's safe keeping. Many nights I fell asleep trying to imagine what your pa was enduring. I could not really understand the degree of his mental and physical pain. I worried!

I went weeks and sometimes months without any letters and I couldn't wait to receive the next mail. But, he never forgot me! Some of those letters were horrible to read. I kept some and they are stored under my bed. When you have an interest, you can read what your pa wrote. You know, many women in Clinton never got any letters. Many ladies who live here never knew what was happening to their husbands and boyfriends. I felt I was lucky."

She had their attention and continued, "Children, I want you to know, I was not alone as other local women went through the same trauma. They worried about their brothers, fathers, and boy friends. We all feared we would never see our loved ones again. To answer some of the pain every other Wednesday night women held meetings at the local church where we found time to support one another. We shared our concerns and fear. We all had questions about the Yankee soldiers who had taken our town. Sometimes we laughed to ease the pain. Many nights we cried and left the meetings confused. I sacrificed. They sacrificed. We all sacrificed. Children sacrificed! Old men who could not fight sacrificed! President Davis even asked us for a 'food holiday' that's what I called it, where we did not eat for one day. Everyone was touched by the war."

Samantha questioned, "How did your pa feel about the war?"

Mary said, "My pa felt more obligated at home and was always around when I needed a hug. He was never called during conscription." Sam sat back as Mary continued.

"Women, like Isabelle Wakefield who lost her husband and two sons in the war, spent those years by herself raising three little children running the farm while supporting the southern cause. Could you imagine losing your husband? She spent days and nights mending clothes to send to rebel units. She even made patches for units in Clinton and raised tobacco for soldiers. Thousands of women throughout the confederacy did the same. And they were alone, and I mean, alone! Women helped in the war cause any way they could."

Frances cuddled Mary when she said, "Loneliness was my middle name, but I survived." A pause than she continued with, "Children, we all can survive. Poor civilians, rich people who lost everything, non-believers, and blacks as well as whites survived!"

The more Mary talked the more truly I appreciated my wife. An hour went by as she demonstrated what dedication and commitment really means. I think they loved her even more after she finished. I know I did!

Mary looked around saying, "You should never forget what was done there. Don't forget the people who sacrificed so you can live! Study the past! Understand the issues. Don't avoid what has taken place in our country. You may not like it, but try to appreciate what millions of citizens did including your parents, uncle Thomas, and grandparents!"

It was Roxie's turn to talk, but she was more interested in the dance and her new dress.

Thirteen

VETERANS

"Ma, it only cost eight dollars. I have two I saved from helping Mrs. Golden with her twins," Roxie argued. "Tomorrow, we'll take the train to Knoxville, Ok," asked Mary. The dress purchase was more important as talk of former years continued.

"Splintered railroad ties, mangled tracks, and blown up railroad bridges covered the landscape in the south. Soldiers worked diligently to repair the destruction completed by Yankees. Railroads were vital to the survival of the south from 61-65, but the use of the transportation system left a lot to be desired." Those were the words I used to continue my explanation/discussion of the war. Thomas had spent hours with one former teacher discussing the war. Rufus had his say. I had mine! Thomas continually looked for more information. He had spent hours reviewing journals, magazine articles, newspaper clippings that described battles, personalities, and total destruction of the south. And, I was gladly available!

When I asked the children to tell me what was important in their lives my aim was to get them to talk. Lets discuss what's important.

Well, the discussion part turned to more of a lecture and I'm not sure they had that much interest in what I had to say. But, being a stubborn southerner, I decided to continue my expose' and see what happened.

Thanksgiving had passed and plans for Christmas were getting under way when we all sat down for more of 'JT's friendly talk.' That's what I called it! I'm sure the children thought differently.

I slid into my discussion about 'Patriotic People' with a return to a few comments about the fallen south, specifically, the last few days of the war. Samantha murmured, "Not again!" Frances had practically fallen asleep.

While Mary reclaimed some hard candy and Samantha gathered her next Mark Twain book, Thomas opened his journal. Roxie said, "Pa, what did you mean when you said, Patriotic People?"

I finished my comments about politics, generals, and prisons. I had talked enough about leaving home, camp life, Captain Steele, writing letters, and my brother's journal and the children knew the close friendly relationship I had with Jonas. They had heard enough! I had spent too much time with those subjects. Now was the moment to express my concerns about being an American, even if I was from the south. I always believed I was just as much American as any northerner.

I say that only because I remember comments made during the war by editors and journalists who questioned whether a southerner could be a true American. That angered me as I always considered myself a devoted patriot. Plus, I wanted my children to understand what me and thousands of rebels did. I wanted them to appreciate the loyalty I gave to the cause.

Before I started I had thought about many rallies I had attended as motivational speakers cranked up the audience. Maybe, that's what I was doing?

That's when I said, "Children, remember who we are. I was honored to be a rebel soldier." Thomas started writing and I continued.

"Let me tell you what my grandfather told me before I went off the fight. The first thing he said was 'hold your head up high and be proud'. For the years I was away from my family, I always thought of my responsibilities as a soldier. I know what you may think after what I had just explained about departing before the war ended, but I was still honored to have served. Yes, I walked away from Sumter! Yes, I wondered what other guards thought. Yes, I feared for the prisoners and I thought about that civilian sketch artist from Chicago who was captured and spent long days and nights in captivity. He wasn't even a solider. Just in the wrong place at the wrong time!"

I continued, "I never forgot the struggle at hand. I never forgot that thousands of young and old had fathers, brothers, sisters, and friends who fought. I never asked for a medal, plague, or special favors. They did not! We just woke up every morning to do our job whether it was marching 30 miles, digging a latrine, pitching horse manure, or killing the enemy. Many hollered the rebel yell as they ventured into enemy bullets. Some survived, many did not. Some would say they were stupid, others would say they were loyal to the constitution and defenders. But, no matter what you think or what you believe, they were fellow soldiers who helped others when times were tough. We watched out for each other!

Yes, there were deserters who left battles and ran to the safety of the woods never to be seen again. Yes, there were soldiers who stole from their friends and yes there were soldiers who went crazy, but on the average the common soldier in the southern army did not turn his back, he stood his ground and fought."

Thomas asked, "Pa, you said to never give up. What does that really mean?"

"Son," I said, "we all get setbacks in our lives at times. Normal citizens watch as their homes and families are destroyed, but they rebound. They rebuild. They dig deep in their hearts to find ways to move forward. They don't let one or two disastrous days, months, or years control their future. They look beyond and think positively. I will stand by my thinking that all of us have the strength and knowhow. For some, it simply means, 'doing it'. Others will have to be convinced and prodded. Some people find preachers or consultants, while others find encouragement from within. God helps! And I will never try to convince you that moving forward is easy. Life is not easy. Decision-making takes courage."

Mary handed me some iced tea and I grabbed a piece of chocolate cake. Frances rolled over on the couch and I got ready to close my little talk for the evening. Sam and Roxie wanted to know more about my intentions for the soldier's home as Thomas made more entries in his journal. And, I knew Roxie wanted that new eight-dollar dress! The barn dance was a few days away!

Mary said, "JT, tell them what your grandpa told you about supporting your fellow soldier." I had read some of my journal the night before to Mary and specifically the letter grandpa Phennessy had written as he described his involvement in the Underground Railroad. I had received the letter while fighting in northern Virginia and it was a total surprise, as I had no idea the dedication grandpa had made to free slaves during the 50s. Even though, grandpa was born in Europe and came to America when he was very young, he despised and truly hated slavery. It was during the 30s and 40s when he became interested and developed schemes and ideas to help slaves escape. He helped organize the local community and got others to join.

The letter described in great detail the fundraising, the secrecy, and the movement of slaves from plantations to houses along the way to northern safety. Grandpa even explained the dangers he and his group faced. He described dangers run-a-way slaves faced.

I grabbed my old soldier's journal and read a brief section of Grandpa's letter. Everyone looked at the journal when I set it down and asked, "What have YOU done for somebody else today?" No one said a word! "Grandpa was constantly thinking of others," I said.

I continued, "Every day that I wallowed in a mud march, dragged a wounded soldier from the battlefield, or force fed a prisoner, I thought of grandpa's comment about helping others. Many letters I wrote included comments about other responsibilities I had that required some involvement with other soldiers. Many buddies were younger than me! Many had no idea what soldiering meant! Many worried about the next battle and killing someone! Many had no idea how to cook a meal, clean a rifle, or simply write a letter. Most could not read! Some had no families." Thomas spoke up and said, "Pa, I read one of ma's letters you wrote. You never mentioned helping others.' Many didn't mean always," I responded.

I continued, "Thomas, I never wanted any pats on the back. I understood we all had a job to do, but I realized many soldiers had very little knowledge and if I could help them survive then I would have done my job. But, I was not the only one who performed that way! Thousands of rebels helped one another. We watched out for fellow soldiers, not as killers of the enemy, but as human beings. Even with all the killing that was taking place, we found in ourselves the devotion to help our fellow man."

I rested for a few minutes before I said, "Take the Battle of Sharpsburg. After the bloodiest single day battle of the war, soldiers rested that night, but the next day under a white flag of truce, both armies sent soldiers to the battlefield to gather fellow wounded and dead. Yankees and rebels walked the battlefield, talked with each other, shared whiskey or tobacco, swapped belt buckles, trinkets, or other souvenirs. Eventually, after securing their respective fallen comrades they gathered themselves, said good-bye, shook hands, and returned to their units to fight another day. Was that crazy? Maybe! It was a strange war! Were they saying 'respect each other. Maybe! Maybe they were!' Even with all the blood that covered the small town in Maryland that September day, both armies took the time to honor those fallen buddies. I spent time that day looking for a buddy of mine. I found him. He was dead on top of two fellow soldiers laying in a ditch that became known as the Sunken Road or more commonly referred to as 'Bloody Lane'." I finished by saying that everyone had a story. That was one of many!

Samantha sat her book aside and spoke up saying, "I never heard you speak of that day when soldiers reclaimed their friends. I had read a little of Antietam (Sharpsburg) but never knew what you just described."

"Strange war was it not," I asked? "But, more often than not, soldiers took responsibility for their buddies." "I reckon you're right," commented Mary.

I spent another hour or so and reminded the children the responsibility of looking after one another. I talked about honor, respect, and the enjoyment people receive from helping others. I was getting winded, the younger children were almost asleep, and Mary had wrapped a blanket around Frances when we all decided there would be another time for more discussions about similar topics. I was tired. They were tired. I had said enough!

Snow started to fall when I closed with, "Every day, do something for you and do something for someone else! Good night." I heard 'ya' as they descended down the hall.

We woke the next morning to about a foot of snow. After some biscuits, sausage, and eggs, the kids and I ventured outside for some fun. Thomas and I shoveled off the front porch and helped Mr. Stephens next door clean his front entrance before noon. I spent the afternoon at the local library researching government loan programs and tried to write a letter to Captain Steele. Neither was very rewarding as I returned home and discussed with Mary my disturbing news.

I had received a letter from Jonas who was living in Memphis, Tennessee. Now I knew where he called home! Mary insisted that I read it before dinner. It appears his life was getting more complex and he was in extreme danger. There had been a number of accidents with numerous blacks killed and Jonas feared whites were planning the destruction. Jonas mentioned a big burly white 'thug' who had recently ventured into Memphis was singling out blacks to punish for stupid mistakes. Stupid, what did he mean? William Logan, one of Jonas's friends, had been found under a pile of rubble and eventually bled to death. Jonas wrote it was no accident. It was a set up! He was killed!

In his first letter in years I discovered some amazing information about my childhood friend. He had left West Virginia and moved to western Tennessee! Jonas had finished college and was working as an assistant in a small law firm in Memphis while working on a law degree. I had not heard from him in years and now realized his desire to become a lawyer. All my worrying changed for a moment!

That black/white issue again?

Even with a new decade approaching, life for many blacks had not changed! The letter contained stories of local restrictions and more abuse to blacks. His job at the firm focused on proposed new or recently passed local, state, and federal laws.

I thought about how widespread was the anger? I wondered about the other groups such as families from England, Germany, or Scotland, and those French-speaking strangers from Canada. Were they getting any of these threats or abuse?

I had just completed talking to my family about helping others, and now this!

Jonas finished by writing he and his family may be headed south in a short time. I wondered if he was really serious about going to Louisiana or Mississippi, as he had mentioned back along. I hope not. Eventually, I wrote

Jonas a letter inquiring about everything!

Days followed when I received a letter from sister, Samantha, and decided to write her. I tried to be as polite as possible without asking for financial support from Mr. Hammer, my sister's boss. But I had to entertain the idea that money for my future soldier's home was not forth coming and I might need assistance. I continued explaining my research, identified contacts in Clinton who were interested but lacked funds, and described my unsuccessful attempts at convincing businessmen of my plans. I even mentioned I had written to Captain Steele inquiring about ideas for funding. With his background in finance, I thought he might have some suggestions as he was now working for the Pullman Car Company as an accountant. The captain had suggested that I contact a local state representative and see if there were any state funds available.

I had to admit that that angle may not be very productive, and in a follow-up letter to the captain, I didn't ask any more. State governments in the south were still without sufficient funds. I would have to look elsewhere!

Years Later

I was sitting in Mathew's Bar with five other veterans. Gray hair, wrinkled faces, and long gray beards surrounded the small area where beer, whiskey, and sausage covered the table that helped relax the group. James spoke up reminding everyone that we were celebrating the anniversary of the death of General Grant. I didn't think that's what we had gathered for. I just listened!

The bar, located in Hampton Crossing some ten miles north of the Tennessee state line in Kentucky, was the sight of our monthly meeting. We actually alternated monthly between Clinton and Hampton Crossing! The veterans group had dwindled. Veterans were dying faster now that age had become a significant factor.

Many veterans had difficulty remembering names, units, or locations from war years. Certain leaders stood out, but simple names of battlefields had disappeared. Chronic physical and mental problems persisted. I had suffered through two recent winters with reoccurring pneumonia, but survived. Even though certain aspects of the past had disappeared from some members, a few individuals still had disturbing memories to share and could not distance themselves from THAT decade. Plus, my plans for the soldiers home was still taking shape and from my perspective, too slow!

James' comments about General Grant were somewhat accurate. He had died in 85 and Mark Twain had indeed helped write his biography and there were other events taking place in America as my mind wandered thinking of my most recent readings. Clara Barton started the Red Cross. Indians out west were still being herded onto reservations by former war generals and buffalo populations were being reduced to nothing. Billionaires continued to controlled monopolies, congress in DC and state governments in the former confederacy still suffered with political battles. Big city life was brought to a standstill with riots and poverty spread like a wildfire causing food fights and labor disputes.

This was the late 80's! The KKK was still creating fear everywhere. Three more blacks had been brutalized in Baldwin. Was anything positive, happening in this country? O' parades were being planned for the twenty-fifth anniversary to celebrate the end of the war and everyone was invited.

I tried to look on the bright side of life when William Mitchell from Bakersfield, Kentucky spoke up and wanted to know if there were any good tobacco farms that had an extra supply. No one answered. The smiling young lady reloaded the beer pitcher, brother Augustus brought out his flask with fresh brew, and the sausage plate was refilled. We talked for hours before we returned to our homes with the promise of returning in another month to continue our friendships!

My life is still focused on working at the hardware store with CA, that's how Mary refers to her brother, while attempting to obtain initial funding from Mr. Hammer. I began to feel he's really not convinced of lending me any money as he had been back along, but I continued to write. Maybe I needed to venture up north to talk more! When thinking of the veteran's home, Ruth comes to mine.

On a more pleasant note, Mary and Roxie had a bake sale to raise money for the home and Sam sold the mare and gave the funds to Mary. "For pa's home," she said.

Mary was working in a dress shop. Thomas was off to college in Roanoke, Virginia. I don't now what he is studying, maybe Rachel! He never writes home. Sam finished high school and is trying to find herself, whatever that means, and Frances still tries to get her way while working at the local hat shop. Roxie, who dresses as if she is going to a 'ball', is in her final year of schooling with dreams of visiting Europe specifically, Paris.

I still write Captain Steele who is now a 'big wig' in the Pullman Car Company. My two sisters, Ruth in Sayersburg and Samantha in northern West Virginia, are ok. I may be assuming a lot! I still think about Ruth and hope for the best. I sent her a letter last month in the hopes that Delores found time to read it to her and have received nothing in reply. I often wonder if Delores is still there! Maybe I can do something for Ruth after I get my veteran's home up and running! At last month's veterans meeting, I mentioned

I had received a letter from my childhood buddy Jonas. "That Blackie," hollered Teddy. "Ya," I answered.

Veterans

Months passed rather quickly as the veterans returned regularly for more beer, sausage, and talk. The dynamics of the group had changed as I shared with everyone my childhood in Boxford Forge and centered on my relationship with Jonas. Teddy asked, "You the same age?" "Close," I answered. I mentioned some of the abuse Jonas had faced in and around our little town and in Clinton before he moved to work in the coalmines. "Good for him, hollered Teddy, he should stay there." I mentioned I had traveled to see my friend and had talks with him about the new south. Teddy questioned, "Where is he now?" "Memphis, Tennessee, studying to be a lawyer," I responded. I had no reason to say more. Really, I thought no one was interested!

According to my last letter at Christmas, Jonas had indeed moved to New Orleans, Louisiana working in the law office of Caldwell and Baker. That's all the letter said, "He worked under the watchful eye of Randall Caldwell, a well known black leader of New Orleans and current state legislator."

I had made the mistake of mentioning Randall when I heard. "How's the fancy new lawyer doing," asked Teddy sarcastically? I responded with, "Just fine." I didn't say anything about the abusive conditions still prevalent in big cities and small towns in the south. Recently I read in the local scandal sheet that restrictive measures against blacks were still common.

I remembered warning Jonas, but he said he could take care of himself and family! Newspaper reports from Memphis and New Orleans had displayed pictures of blacks marching down main-street. On numerous pages were pictures showing blacks beaten and lying in the street. "Serves um right," hollered Teddy. I should never have said anything!

It was obvious Teddy did not like blacks. He was relentless! Every time I mentioned something about blacks and specifically, Jonas, Teddy always had some negative comment or jester. "Those dumb F___ers belong in Africa or back on my grandpa's plantation," he responded.

Maybe, I should reserve my comments about blacks for another time and place? But that's not right. Blacks are humans! We all breathe the same air! They can vote. According to the constitution, they are citizens. They have rights! Well, they should have rights like whites!

Teddy needs an education! I know he was injured in the war just like many of us but why does he think he is better than blacks? I know Teddy is missing an arm. His mind is warped! I'll ask him if he owned slaves growing up. He's been reading too much garbage or maybe he doesn't read!

Slavery was the past. This is now! Let's move forward!

Eventually, the veterans had had enough beer and sausage for one afternoon and decided to meet again. I would try to get more information on the veteran's home and bring it to the meeting while asking them to spread the word to get others who survived the war to attend. My plans for discussing the home had taken a back seat to the discussion that day, but there will be another day. Maybe, I should write another letter to Jonas. And I definitely had had enough of Teddy!

Fourteen

McMURTREE'S HOME

A letter from Captain Steele arrived. Not a pleasant letter, but a letter! He quickly described his new promotion and mentioned he was looking for workers as he had been promoted to sales director and chief accountant in the Chicago office. The company was expanding. The owner and Steele's new superior Robert Lincoln were providing bigger and better accommodations on trains and more people were needed. But, the captain had deeply disturbing news.

His twenty-three year-old son John Edwin had recently been killed in a brawl between blacks and whites. When the captain left Virginia after the war he and his young son went west as his wife had died and he wanted no more sadness that had spread through his life.

The fight that killed Edwin started over some girl in a saloon near the steel plant where John worked. According to the newspaper accounts, blacks had ventured into the bar where a sign had been posted that simply said, 'whites only.' A group of fifteen blacks came through the front door asking for beer and Sally. One angry black hollered, "Where's Sally?"

"Who wants to know," responded one white? "She's not here!"

Whites led by Horace Plunkitt approached the blacks hollering, "Can't you read, stupid? You're not wanted in here. Get out, Blackie. Get out, now or else! The doors behind you! This is a white man's bar." In unison, three other whites hollered, "Get out Nigger, Sally's not here! Go on home. Blacks ain't welcomed!"

The group of 20 whites surrounded the blacks. Insults continued! No one moved. More words were exchanged. Eventually, pushing and shoving led to punches being exchanged before long handled knives were brought out as everyone had something resembling a weapon. People started swinging! More shoving with more insults were passed among opponents. Swinging continued. Pistols were drawn. More shoving! Tables and chairs were kicked over. Shots rang out. Beer drinkers dived for the floor! Bullets split the mirror behind the bar. People screamed! Innocent citizens ran for the nearest exit screaming for police help as they scrambled across the sidewalk! Beer mugs turned to weapons crushing hard against black and white faces. Horace took a beer mug to the arm and another to his face. Blood splattered across the wet red floor.

More patrons escaped out the back while others pushed aside one another before exiting the front door. The fighting continued for twenty minutes before help arrived. The mêlée slowed as seven slow moving white Chicago policemen with guns drawn entered the front door. But, before the fighting had stopped, four blacks and three whites were dead, one being John Edwin Steele. He had been shot three times in the chest. Horace, the self appointed white spokesperson, was carried from the premises bleeding with extensive facial wounds only to die before he reached the sidewalk.

The newspaper article accompanying the letter never clarified who Sally was or why the blacks wanted her. Captain Steele did mention in the letter that Sally had been a worker in a cotton mill but didn't mention what she did or what angered the blacks. Hundreds of blacks worked in the nearby cotton mills and other places in Chicago as over thirty thousand blacks lived in the south side of the city.

The article was reread and reread! The captain repeated three times, 'John is dead!' Six blacks and two whites, including the white bar owner were arrested! Captain Steele's last line said Sally was black! She was found 24 hours later in the back alley, beaten to death!

What was she doing in that bar anyway, I asked myself as I grabbed my journal recording as much material as I deemed necessary or noteworthy! How much more tragedy can the Captain endure?

My mind continued to wonder if blacks would ever be considered equal. Man, the hatred is so widespread beyond belief! The southern Black Belt is one thing, but in the north? I feared for the south, now the north. Are other big northern cities like Cleveland, Pittsburg, or Providence seeing the same discrimination? Are there 'whites only' signs spread across all northern big cities and small towns? Are workers and owners in oil businesses and steel companies seeing the same behavior? And what is happening in Nashville, Jacksonville, New Orleans, and Louisville? Where was Benny? What happened to him? How safe is Jonas? Should my soldier's home be open to all veterans, white and black? Definitely, yes!

In my next letter describing my sadness, I asked the captain what he would do. I thought of his mental status and his loneliness. I thought about all the horror he had encountered in his life. Much too much for any one person! The death of his son was overwhelming. I limited my questions while changing the subject expressing my concern for Jonas and his family.

Over the war years, I had spoken with the captain about Jonas many times, so my comments were not new. But, even now with his college degree and continued education towards the law profession, I still worried about my childhood buddy.

What did those recently passed amendments really accomplish for the blacks? Anything? Whites Only signs! I had seen only one such sign in Clinton about fifteen years back, but nothing since. Was America stalled in Antebellum?

I got thinking about blacks riding on trains, working beside whites in mills or factories, or residing in neighborhoods near or close to whites. I read articles about foreigners from Europe, Japan, and China migrating to America. People with different ideas, values, beliefs, and lifestyles living and working together! I was concerned about Canadians coming to our country and wondering if everyone could get along with one another.

Where was America? Were we moving forward? And what about those southern veterans from the war? Maybe, I needed a trip to the warm mountain springs on the outskirts of Lexington! I'll ask Mary if she would like to take a trip!

Samantha stayed home with Roxie and Frances as Mary and I headed to the Lexington area for some relaxation. While Mary and I sat in the Virginia springs letting the warm water bring some comfort to our tired bodies, we discussed Captain Steele's letter and tried to understand what was taking place in America. We weren't well versed in politics or business, but attempted anyway. We discussed plans for my future veteran's home. I had written some letters to our US Representative Baker Fitzpatrick, in Washington but have not had any response. Correspondence from Washington was always slow! I'll just wait! Monthly meetings continued.

Mary asked about Jonas. "Haven't heard from him lately," I responded.

While in the Lexington area, Mary and I revisited Washington and Lee University and specifically recalled the famous church that houses the famous General Lee. I went to visit two of my professors and we talked at length about the country. "Treading water," said Ansel. Mr. Ferguson still teaches political science and Mr. Yardley retired to the boring life of studying plants and insects. He said he wanted to visit Africa in the near future. "Good luck," I said. After three days and nights away from our girls, we headed south stopping in Roanoke to see Thomas before arriving back in Clinton.

Three weeks later I wrote another letter to Mr. Hammer in West Virginia regarding financial assistance for the construction of the veteran's home. It took about a month before I got any response and when I opened the envelope, all I got was an application for lending or as I said, "Boring." The huge envelope had a six-page application, two pages titled 'Plans', and pages listing the names of my committee members. Whew! What committee, I said to myself? Holy Moses, I wasn't looking for the world, just a few thousand dollars to start my home!

The application wanted to know who would own the establishment, who would manage it, and who was responsible for the staff. Would the home have nurses? How big was my projected staff? Would it have a complete full time staff or part-time people? Would we have volunteers? Who would hire and fire? It wanted to know how it would be funded. Where was the operational money coming from? There were questions relating to my contacts in DC and Nashville. There were questions about local veterans and how and who would qualify. Would the home accept any veteran, north or south or was the home strictly for former rebel soldiers? Were veteran blacks accepted? Were there qualifications regarding length of service, reserve status, or units that never left their respective states. Were they talking confederacy or state militia? Hell, I didn't know! The questions were endless!

The application wanted to know more about my background and experience, my military service, and specifically where the home would be located. It wanted to know how many veterans it would hold. The application wanted to know where I would live, either in the home itself or in my private home.

After re-reading the application three times, I looked at Mary and said, "I need to talk with someone. Maybe, a lot of people." I had seen applications in journals and magazine articles, but this application was overwhelming! Did Mr. Hammer design this application or was it a general application applied specifically to the business? Too many questions as I placed it on my night stand and fell sleep!

For the next month I made a list of people I would contact. I would get names and addresses. I would write letters and personally visit hospitals and maybe even take a trip to Nashville and eventually, Washington DC. I would obtain documents outlining qualifications for administrators, nurses, and contact someone with knowledge regarding federal and state laws. I even decided to visit the local lawyer, Mr. Marvin Meredith. Quickly I discovered local was relevant!

Mr. Meredith was an interesting fellow to say the least. After some small talk about Clinton, the new black church, a new black elementary school run by a small groups of blacks, and the new post office that now had a building all it's own, I asked the lawyer about some local laws and rules regarding my veteran's home. My focus was the home while his turned to local ordinances and regulations. He was basically vague without specifying any particular rules as his office was in Knoxville some twenty-five miles away. He did say he would look into it and said his fee for my one time office visit was fifty-five dollars. He didn't tell me anything I had not heard before and he charged me for sitting in his office. This thing may be costly, I thought as I grabbed my bags, handed him his due, and left.

Committee Members
One year later

Gathering my list of perspective advisors for my project, I decided to contact as many as possible. I set a day for our first gathering and asked Mary if she would be the note taker. I also wrote a letter to Mr. Hammer in West Virginia and explained my plan. I even invited him! I got nothing back and assumed he wasn't interested or was waiting for my next correspondence, completion of the application he had sent me. Maybe he thought I was still preparing the ridiculously long and complicated paperwork. Anyway, I had more immediate local concerns to consider.

I had to spend some time at my new job at the feed store. CA and I now own the hardware store and the new feed store. We had bought the feed store back along and business was picking up. Before I left for home one night I picked up the family mail and received a letter from Jonas. I had not heard from him in over a year and wondered if he was okay as I reflected on comments I had made regarding his safety.

My friend was doing fine with his new employer, the law firm of Caldwell and Smiley. His responsibilities consisted of being a watchdog of developments regarding enforcement and abuse of the local 'Jim Crow' laws. He and his family were completely settled in New Orleans and Jonas was spending considerable free time working with poor blacks who were looking for work. Jonas continued informing me he was watching social and employment issues facing blacks in southern cities while scrutinizing major decisions coming from the U.S. Supreme Court. Sounded like a full plate for new member of the firm, I thought!

His letter described horrible living conditions in big cities as low pay for blacks, and continued dissatisfaction with safety issues were major concerns among thousands working cotton tenant farms in Louisiana and Mississippi. Cotton was still 'King' in that part of the south! He had traveled to Natchez, back to Memphis, and Vicksburg a number of times to look at other work opportunities, but blacks were not being hired. His neighborhood friends, George, Hiram, and Samson asked why?

On page three Jonas mentioned protests conducted by blacks regarding the Jim Crow Laws, were taking place in New Orleans and elsewhere. On many occasions riots followed with injuries and deaths. Blacks were simply asking for better treatment in their neighborhoods. Refusal to sit anywhere on a train was a great concern as well as fair treatment in the work areas. *Some blacks fortunate to find employment work 16 hour days with only a short 15 minute break,* he wrote. And many refuse to work fearing intimidation or physical abuse. Thousands just sat!

I remember warning him of such conditions in other parts of the south, specifically in Mississippi, and Alabama. Blacks were no better off than before the war! That's when the letter offered more disturbing conditions!

Jonas and his wife were living near tenant houses where families worked cotton farms owned by Herman Blackwell, a banker who lived in Vicksburg. Each tenant farmer has a small house and there are nine families around the farm who shared five common wells. There were nine outhouses, as no indoor plumbing has been installed. "My house has indoor plumbing and we are fine," he clarified. Each tenant family had their own small garden while Hiram and George also work a bigger vegetable garden to make a little extra money selling their goods to the locals in the town square. Jonas wrote, George takes care of the twenty mules on the farm.

As he continued his social responsibilities, Jonas was working on a big project at the law firm. Talking with local black businessmen, factory owners, and church leaders to develop ways of improving unhealthy relationships between disgruntled white factory owners and black workers were his goals. Verbal and physical abuse in the workplace surfaced as a major problem. Some blacks are asking for work in white factories. White factory owners want workers to do as they are told. Even the mayor was invited to sit in on a meeting prior to Christmas and as Jonas wrote, "That was a waste of time." The grueling meetings last forever with little accomplished, but I will not relinquish, Jonas wrote. Jonas continued writing, "I have to get people talking to each other."

The letter was informative but disturbing as he closed by saying he and his wife were now living by themselves, as the kids had all grown and left home. "Sunday was a day off from work and many blacks gather to play baseball in the fields. I pitch," he finished. Jonas never did mention where the kids had gone or what they did. 'They just left," he wrote.

I decided to start reading the Nashville newspaper more often and maybe gather some widespread New Orleans papers to get a better understanding of what was taking place. I said to Mary, "Maybe after we get our project underway we can take a trip to see Jonas and his wife."

She responded, "When is the first meeting?" "Shortly," I responded.

I had completed my hours of work at the feed store and went upstairs to the wide-open room above. The twenty by forty room was plenty big enough. I had invited twelve individuals to become members of the advisory committee, but not all showed for the first meeting. It was Saturday, July 20, 1892. I was excited!

Eight individuals gathered. Mary and I made ten! I was nervous. Mary was nervous! We had discussed who would run the meeting and Mary said, "You, of course!" Roxie appeared with three pitchers of iced tea, two large watermelons, and a coffee cake. It was hot! Mary handed out fans!

After introductions and friendly conversation, Marvin Meredith the lawyer from Knoxville said, "Lets hear from Mr. McMurtree. I have business in Knoxville. It's a long ride back."

Seated around the table were:
52 year-old Marvin Meredith, lawyer
51 year-old Gary Norton, Clinton banker
39 year-old James Corrigan, local state representative
54 year-old Howard Spencer, Tennessee US Senator
44 year-old Kenneth Spaulding, local war veteran
44 year-old Rufus Appleby, local war veteran
42 year-old Nicolas Shelley, local war veteran
35 year-old Kathleen Ashford, social worker

Mary sat beside me! I needed all the support I could muster! The Knoxville hospital administrator and the lead doctor had been invited but refused my offer.

I opened the meeting by describing my plans for the Veteran's Home. I went on to detail the proposed sight on a hill outside of town and even suggested a name for the facility. I addressed practically every topic covered in Mr. Hammer's application! Everyone had a chance to comment, make suggestions, and many questions were asked and answered before the committee broke up just before 9pm. Just about everyone was polite and courteous, except Mr. Norton, from the bank. 'A little grumpy', I thought. I'll talk with him later! Everyone was asked to investigate information pertinent to their respective titles and I asked if we could meet again in a month when Marvin spoke and offered his office in Knoxville. We all acquiesced.

I had asked everyone to fill out a questionnaire I had prepared and after Roxie completed serving her delicious late night snack and put away the dishes Mary and I sat down to review what they had written. A pretty diverse group!

Marvin Meredith is a local lawyer from Knoxville. He was born in Lexington, Kentucky and moved to Carthage Tennessee when he was 6. He is married with four kids, his third child at Vanderbilt, and his youngest is one year old. He's 52 now! He was 22 when he enlisted fighting for the confederacy and was immediately elected Captain by his company before they left to fight. He was a veteran of battles at Seven Pines and Winchester was wounded four times and is missing his fourth finger on his right hand and he still wears his CSA belt buckle!

He was a graduate of Vanderbilt where he majored in Real Estate and Business Law. He worked in Nashville before moving to Knoxville and was instrumental in building the 'Better Business Bureau of Knoxville'. He presented himself as being very intelligent. Well, that's what I thought! He wore a dark pin stripe blue suit with a brilliant bright red tie. He was extremely concerned with local rules and wanted everything in writing with signed contracts. I liked his attention to detail! Other issues concerned him were the location of the home, resident access to services, thus providing the best care possible. He even mentioned his concern for nurses. He wanted experienced nursing care. He went into detail questioning medical, physical, and dietary guarantees. Guarantees, I questioned? There are no guarantees in this world, I thought!

The only concern I had about him was that foul smell of alcohol and when he left he grabbed another whiskey bottle from his belongings. Those horrendous smelling 'bad cigars' that he smoked during the meeting spreading ashes everywhere were downright awful, but I liked him. He seemed honest with a great background! I can deal with that! My initial meeting with him was ok. This one much better!

Gary Norton was another story! I will have to keep my eye on Gary! Gary is the local banker who came to Clinton during Reconstruction and never left. He is from New York City and could easily be described as a 'Carpetbagger.' He is 51 years old, not married as he divorced in 75, but has ten kids roaming America.

He never smiles, always has a frown on his face! He appears arrogant, abrasive, egotistical, regular know it all, always right. Plus, he loved to brag about the domineering north. He loved Lincoln and Grant, hated John W. Booth, as he argued Booth was part of a massive federal government conspiracy. At one point during a break in the meeting he said, "I told you so," referring to me! He despised Lee. To make matters more interesting, I discovered he disliked blacks, thought they were all stupid, but despised former plantation owners even more especially those who lived in Carolinas. That's interesting, I said to myself!

Gary had moved to Baltimore before the war and was in the city as all hell broke lose when Yankee soldiers from Boston came marching through on their way to DC in 1861. He said he quickly moved to Philadelphia for the rest of the war! He bragged about his ability to make money during the war as he described his scheme regarding contraband. His moneymaking ideas centered more or less on gathering army supplies that were going nowhere. He would purchase the army materiel at ridiculously low prices and resell it to anyone, even unsuspecting rebels. "Just a little extra money", he said. "Quadrupled my money," he bragged.

As I reread his information sheets, I had my doubts about his contributions or even if I should want his services! Maybe, I need to check out other banks in Knoxville!

Gary dressed in a spiffy suit considerably too small for his overweight frame and bulging stomach. He smoked constantly while sucking on hard candy and according to the locals was considered tight with lending money. He was the committee pessimist and antagonist with endless questions, why, how, who? Mary questioned me saying, "Maybe we DO need someone on the committee to ask the dumb questions." "You might be right," I responded.

Now here was a person I really like! Thirty-nine year-old James Corrigan was the local state representative from Clinton. He lives in town with six kids. His wife died of scarlet fever in 1888. His information sheet said he grew up in South Carolina moving first to Knoxville before moving to the area after the war. He never attended college. I had met him on a train ride four months earlier and I liked him. Seemed like a real true guy! He had mentioned he was not really fond of people above the Mason/Dixon Line. I understand! I just let it go.

James is a friendly fellow who raises hogs and tobacco, loves to race quarter horses, and trained Tennessee Walking Horses on his three hundred acre farm. His closest neighbor is the Brown family. They are black and their 19 year-old daughter Suzie, helps James with the younger kids. James is very interested in veteran's home idea and willing to help find money to fund the project. "I'm looking for any state money," I said.

We had talked a little politics when he said he hated the train trips to Nashville every spring and fall. Politics in Nashville are really slow. Cotton owner representatives from Memphis always try to slow down the process and get what they want. Tobacco growers in eastern Tennessee always have their issues. He spends lots of time in Nashville in the back rooms and hallways trying to get bills introduced or passed and many days are long and boring.

Nights come with no progress. State senators and representatives argue over simple procedural issues such as who speaks next or how long Mr. Smith can speak. He said, "I'm glad I only have to go to Nashville twice a year."

Anyway, he dresses nice, carries himself like a gentleman, and I like him. He chews and spits a little. That's okay. He'll still be a good asset to the group.

It was getting late but I was on a roll so I continued to read more information packets.

Fifty-four year-old Howard Spencer, is our US Senator in DC. He was first elected to congress in 68 and had been there since. He's from Baillie, married with eight kids, and proudly explains he was 23 when he went to fight in 1861. He was elected Captain by the 8th Infantry Volunteers, was wounded at Pittsburg Landing (Shiloh) where he spent two months in a rebel hospital. And with all that had taken place during those violent war years, Howard did not like to talk about the war.

He was a graduate of The College of Charleston in South Carolina and said he would help with the project but was extremely busy in Washington. On the comments section of the questionnaire he explained his extensive time in DC has been beneficial, as he has argued every session for more money for southerners starting with the Reconstruction years. He has argued for businesses, farmers, factories, and specifically has devoted considerable time financially rebuilding cities and towns. Currently, he leads an initiative to rebuild many of the railroads and depots throughout the south and he is chairman of a committee rewriting the discrimination laws. I thought of Jonas and wondered if any Louisiana Congressman might be on his committee!

I looked forward to his input, even if it is spotty. Howard described a situation where Maine congressmen representing fishermen, Louisiana ship builder representatives, and cotton grower representatives from western Tennessee had stopped fighting and more bills were passed and progress was made. You slap my back. I'll slap yours,' I thought.

I liked him. He's dedicated to helping the south move forward. I specifically asked Mr. Spencer to look for any current government sponsored loan programs that I might apply to the project. I also asked him to explain the new anti-discrimination legislation known as the Curran/Rumford proposal. He said it was still in the design stages but he would get back to me. Everybody on THAT committee wants a voice.

In my next letter to Jonas, I'll mention Mr. Spencer and ask Jonas to keep an eye out for any new bills coming from DC. I'll keep my eyes open too!

Kenneth Spaulding, a forty-four year-old ex-soldier, has a record that really appeals to me! He lives locally. He has been to every monthly veterans meeting since my return from Lexington in the 80's. He always has a joke or two, loves Jack Daniels, and flirting with any beautiful women, Mary included. He enjoys life. He laughs all the time! I told Mary he would be a good adversary for the veteran's home. But his service record could destroy most men!

He is married with five kids and his wife Kelly works at the local bank. (She didn't care for Mr. Norton, thought he was too bossy) Ken works in the local iron works mine and has a breathing problem that Doctor Glasgow told him had developed from working inside the caves. He constantly has coughing spells and has to travel to Knoxville regularly to get more medication.

Kenneth proudly said that he joined the Confederate Army when he ran away from home at the age of 14. That was in 1862, he wrote! He saw the elephant in battles at Malvern Hill where he was wounded twice, Gaines Mills got just a leg wound, Winchester where he escaped unscathed, and Petersburg where he was wounded three times. As a result of all those wounds, which he does not talk about at any great length, he is missing two fingers on his left hand, has trouble seeing out of both eyes, and concludes his section on injuries by noting that he also has trouble hearing. Too many bombs, he added. Plus, that tunnel explosion at Petersburg almost killed me just before the war ended. And he had other problems.

The four-year veteran briefly described he wakes up nights with nightmares and has been accused of beating his two boys. Not true, he insisted. Dr. Abramson, the highly regarded psychiatrist from Knoxville, sees Kenneth once a month, but Ken says that will stop soon. I'm okay!

In the comments section on the final page, Kenneth made mention that after Petersburg, he and his buddies traveled west with General Lee as thousands of barefooted and hungry soldiers shuffled toward Appomattox. There were too many Union soldiers. We were surrounded. We were all starving when the general signed the treaty and Kenneth was resting on a log crying when Lee rode by to announce the war was over. He wrote, Twenty-four hours later I sat beside Private Lenny Knapp, from Montpelier, Vermont as we exchanged souvenirs. He gave me a Yankee belt buckle and I gave him a counterfeit confederate note.

Even with all that had taken place in Ken's life he still carried himself as a 'proud southerner.' I like that!

Then there is Rufus!
Rufus Appleby, a veteran from Rocky Top, Tennessee, wanted to be involved in the group when he said his experience in the war would provide background for what he described as 'decision making'. I'm not sure that Rufus actually understood what that meant, but I invited him to the

first meeting anyway. Plus, he was a regular at the veteran's meeting every month where he chewed constantly and his shirts were always covered with tobacco juice, especially when the wind was blowing in the wrong direction! He was a mess! His old confederate shirt he had taken from a fallen South Carolinian in 65 always changed color before our meetings ended! THAT shirt was over 25 years old!

Rufus was 15 when he went to fight just before Gettysburg in the summer of 63. Rufus was his own man! He ran away from home after his fathers farm in Greenville had been destroyed by Yankees. He rode with the cavalry of Jeb Stuart until the general died from wounds in 64. Rufus loved to tell stories and shared a few with the group when breaks were taken. He loved riding horses, loved the cavalry experience, and was extremely proud of his success with the pistol when confronting Yankees. Cavalry rifles were not accurate enough. Fighting on horseback was easy, "Was always moving," he explained. He even described methods used to sneak up on union pickets and killing some while stealing from others. Blowing up trains and bridges were fun.

Rufus never married. He adored army life and bragged about sneaking into cities to see the women of the night. "Gorgeous," he had said, "the houses too!" It sounded like he was a real prankster sneaking into camp where he described how he and his buddies filled coffee pots with sand or stole infantry company rifles. "You could get hanged for that," I said. He just laughed.

I soon learned Rufus had some emotional problems when he complained about army doctors. He had been wounded a number of times and in one incident while lying on the ground, a doctor rushed to his side and wrapped his wounds with the leaves from corn stocks. He complained the doctor didn't even have any dressings in his wagon. Leaves were useless but they were available. We were fighting in a cornfield.' "That was late 64," he said. Rufus survived!

Mary and I decided we would allow Rufus to continue with the group and agreed we would have to keep an eye on him. He might get sidetracked during the meetings! I really don't think he would make trouble. I'll see what happens. He said he was a proud soldier and would have stayed in the army if Lee hadn't surrendered.

Rufus lives by himself on a small ten-acre farm where he raises tobacco and races horses on the weekends. He attends the monthly veteran's meeting and sees Dr. Jenkins, a psychologist from Greenville once a month.

Nicholas Shelley, another veteran originally from southern Georgia, is 42 years old, and married with five kids. He owns a six hundred fifty acre hog farm and is business manager for the local Baptist Church. He also spends many hours organizing fund raising projects for Baptist Hospital. Nick is on the Board of Directors for an organization known as "For Southern Veterans Only." He even finds time to be a substitute preacher on many Sundays. 'Busy' is his middle name!

Nick writes he entered the rebel army when he was just 14. He simply ran away in the winter of 63/64. I discovered his father was a former mayor and very important in many community organizations in White Junction, Georgia, during the fifties and sixties. His dad died when Yankees stormed the small town during Sherman's March to the Sea. Nick had recently joined the veterans group meeting within the last month and is well liked by everyone. After the war, Nickolas attended Auburn University in Alabama and earned a degree in Business Management and an advanced degree in Theology.

Nick's paperwork described his wounds from battles at Chattanooga and Nashville. "We didn't have a chance in Franklin," he wrote. He lost his lower left leg on the approach to Nashville and gets around with the help of a wooden leg manufacture by the Brass/Wood Company from Pittsburg, North Carolina.

Of all the members of the group, I will depend on Nicholas for timely help and comments. He's always very positive. Good financial background! He even invited Mary and me to join him at church the following Sunday.

Kathleen Ashford is a Social Worker from Boston who moved to the area in 1879 following reconstruction. Her father, James Eugene St. Clair originally from Canada, was a priest in the local Catholic Church in Albert, Massachusetts. He had been a priest in the union army and was at Second Manassas, Chancellorsville, and Gettysburg before he was killed in a train accident near Washington DC during the winter of 63/64. Kathleen said the train had been attacked by a band of rebel guerillas. "Mosby," she insisted.

Kathleen is 35 years-old married with three kids. She and her family live on a farm with cows and work horses that are raised to sell. Kathleen is a graduate of Boston College with a degree in Social Work and an advanced degree in Business. Her husband, also a BC graduate owns the local Pharmacy and Chairman of the local Chamber of Commerce. Both are very smart people and loved by everyone. Well everyone, except the local banker. Apparently, there was some disagreement when Mr. Ashford applied for a loan to build the pharmacy. Eventually, he and Mr. Norton worked out their problems, but the Ashford team doesn't spend a lot of time at the bank!

Presently, Kathleen works about fifty hours a week at the local hospital and finds time to work at the newly constructed Catholic Church, the first one in the area. She and her family are very religious attending church every Sunday. Kathleen teaches a class to adolescent youngsters after dinner on

Wednesday nights and finds time to take care of the church money. Recently, she took over responsibilities as the principle fundraiser for the Catholics and now has agreed to become a vital member of our group. A stabilizing influence! Man, what responsibilities!

I couldn't be happier! Eventually, I sat the papers aside and went to bed.

Over the next month I wrote letters to committee members thanking them for their time and effort while expressing my concerns. I got together some drawings that I determined could be used for construction, and I mentioned the name 'Junior Thomas McMurtree Soldier's Home' in honor or my brother. 'Thomas Junior McMurtree Soldier's Home' would be better, I reckon!

I mentioned procuring the land for the project and asked Mr. Spencer about any bills or funding that might come from Washington. He replied back with a real short letter, "Nothing yet!" I'll keep track of any new bills from the state capital in Nashville and will talk with Mr. Corrigan about available local monies.

I spend time attempting to complete the application for Mr. Hammer, but I could not find the enthusiasm as my interest and focus had switched. "Let's keep it local," I said to Mary. She agreed and veterans continued meetings!

Mary and I got a letter from my sister Samantha who was still working for Mr. Hammer. She mentioned nothing of the application that I was struggling with! I found an old letter from Captain Steele lying on the corner table and re-read the loss of his son. Walking down the streets of Clinton I would occasionally hear someone say nigger or something else that was earmarked to slam or degrade blacks. Can't the races get along?

I thought about sister Ruth up there in Sayersburg working in the rundown soldier's home and living on very little, and I spent my leisurely hours fishing, hunting and reading the newspapers. For Christmas that year, I got a book from my daughter Samantha titled, 'Frederick Douglass, The Activist'.

Plans change!

Fifteen

SAMANTHA WRITES

Clinton still had one bank in town, as the new-year got under way. A blizzard stalled business for about a week following Christmas and I had time to read my new book about Mr. Douglass, a former slave born early in the 1800's. The author of the book claims Douglass's father was white. Not uncommon, I said to myself. And when his first wife died, I discovered he married a white woman twenty years younger than he. Interesting! After his escape from slavery, he became an avid supporter of human rights, women's rights, and traveled extensively throughout the country where he delivered resounding motivational and sometimes controversial speeches. He endorsed the thinking of William L. Garrison, an anti-slave activist from New England, and developed a principle that he carried with him on the lecture circuit. "Truth is of no Color," he wrote. I liked the book!

I gave it to my daughter Roxie to read. I said, "Give it to Frances when you finish."

The newly remodeled bank looked considerably bigger when I walked in for my meeting with Mr. Norton. Even the outside bright red bricks, flashy new windows bordered with local rocks from the nearby creek, and the heavy shinny oak door that weighed over two hundred pounds looked impressive. The cobblestone walkway looked suburb as I walked in! Actually, I was deeply impressed!

Unusual ornate decorations surrounded the inside of the refurbished bank. The tellers welcomed customers as they rested their arms on Italian granite and Greek designed doorways led to the back where the bank's vault secured vast holdings. 'Well, that's what I thought!' The sparkling new floor shined brightly as I shuffled across the surface looking for the manager. Mr. Norton was sitting in a leather-covered chair in his office behind his new oak desk and looking out as local citizens strolled by. His desk was covered with paperwork, giving the impression he was extremely busy. That's what I learned from my political science instructor in college. Cluttered desk shows one extremely busy!

Mr. Norton, the self proclaimed expert on money, was smoking a foul smelling Havana cigar and it's a wonder he didn't burn himself as his new grey beard was now covering his entire face. His shady eyes were surrounded with wrinkles and he looked considerably older than he did the last time I saw him before Thanksgiving. His new blue suit, white shirt, and red tie were wrinkled so badly it gave me the impression he had slept in the complete wardrobe. I said to myself, looks like he's been in a fight with a bear!

Mr. Norton welcomed me into his new office as I fought through the thick cloud of grey smoke, coughing, as he explained he had just returned from New York where he had spent time visiting his ailing ninety-five year old mother. "She still smokes too much," he said. I questioned, "Has she smoked all her life?" "Since she was ten," he replied. "Let her continue," I said.

To ease into our deeper topics, I asked him where he was when the blizzard hit. "Stuck in the train depot in Washington, DC for two days and another complete day in Richmond," he responded, "So what's on your mind, John?" The banker leaned back in his chair, grabbed a flask of whiskey, and poured himself a shot.

I spent the next thirty minutes detailing my project updates and the correspondence I had had with Mr. Meredith the lawyer, Mr. Corrigan, and Mr. Spencer. I also mentioned my letters to Mr. Hammer, but was really interested in getting a loan from the local bank. During my explanation, I never felt comfortable or very positive about my chances as he frowned and asked questions. At one point, he wanted to know more about my work at the hardware and feed stores and what Mary was doing with her sewing. I told him CA and I had bought the feed store years ago. "I run the feed store. Cecil runs the hardware store," I informed him.

He wanted to know how my son was doing and WHAT he was doing. The only thing I said was Thomas had graduated from college and worked in Roanoke. He wanted to know about my daughter Samantha who had been sick the previous summer and how old Roxie was. "Fine," I responded. 'He never asked about Frances.'

I never saw any connection! I was simply asking for a starter loan of four thousand dollars! I wasn't asking for the world! He poured himself another shot! "Want some," he asked? "I'll wait," I responded.

After I had answered all his personal questions and was about to ask him about his new surroundings, Mr. Norton asked me questions about financing or as he put it, mortgaging. "Backing the loan," he said. He wanted to know more about Mr. Hammer north in West Virginia. He mentioned a loan of three years as I had made reference to a ten-year agreement. He said his interest rate was a little over twenty percent, twenty-two to be exact. The more he talked the angrier and more discouraged I got.

I finally left the bank, got on my mule, and rode to the top of the hill, overlooking the sight of my project. We had not settled anything. I had not signed any agreement, loan, or anything that resembled a contract. Mr. Hammer had educated me regarding contracts and signatures and said not to sign anything unless I understood all that was written. Even though Mr. Norton was on the committee, I still had reservations about his interest in my soldier's home. I was going nowhere, fast!

Mary and I talked about our next attempt as we decided a trip to Sanford Bank in Knoxville could provide more insight into our future. Roxie was still reading about Mr. Douglass and continued to ask questions regarding slavery, reconstruction, and the current anti-black sentiment covering the country. I picked up the Knoxville Times with the headline on the front page, 'James Blackwell Hung in Charleston, West Virginia.' Mr. Blackwell, owner of the local ironworks, was black! But, I had more pressing issues controlling my family!

Sam

Samantha, my oldest daughter was recovering from the whooping cough and sweating profusely. She had been extremely sick the previous summer spending the entire hot months in bed and vomiting blood. She complained about headaches and was exhausted with aching muscles. She lost fifteen pounds last year and has not regained any weight. Trips to Dr. Rowland proved at best, limited.

For three months Sam drank enough water to drain the well. Sweating continued. She needed some help and another trip was in the making.

My oldest daughter had always been the leader of the girls, always supporting them while insisting they complete their homework. Frances always whined. Sam was persistent. Sam always helped Mary with housework, and she even spent time learning enough at the hardware to be an asset. She reminded me of my sister, kind, considerate, willing to help. Even when her big brother left, they remained close by writing on a regular basis. Thomas was not good at writing me or Mary and Samantha became the connection.

While she was resting last summer she received a special letter that mentioned Rachel was spending considerable time in Roanoke and the two were talking marriage. Maybe, she didn't know they had married.

Samantha never let me forget my lost friends, Jonas and Captain Steele. Never a month went by without her encouraging me to write or visit them. She never let me lose track of friendships instrumental in my life and the more she asked about Jonas and the captain, the more I considered a trip to see both of them.

On one special night last summer, we had an extensive talk about grandpa Phennessy and his creative way of making a point. She really made me think!

But, she was not well. She was suffering every minute, everyday!

Everyone was upset and concerned. Mary cried nightly! Roxie and Frances wanted to help but were confused. Cecil stopped by to help in any way possible and Thomas wrote to explain his concerns. Local doctors had no answer!

Eventually, after many sleepless nights coupled with excruciating pain Mary took Samantha to see Dr. Richey Rowland, a local boy and recent graduate of Vanderbilt. After a complete exam, Dr. Rowland said he was really concerned about our daughter and asked us to watch her closely. "If things get worse, I recommend you take her to Nashville," he said. "Its only a five hour train ride," he finished.

He had given Mary medication that resembled horse pills as we put Sam to bed for days. The fever persisted. Coughing continued! Vomiting started again! Her face was on fire as she developed a red rash with swelling around her eyes. Her arms swelled and were inflamed. Her arms started bleeding from excessive scratching. Her arms peeled! Sam complained about a sore throat and refused to eat. More sweating as daydreaming followed. She got worse. Back to see the doctor!

Dr. Rowland gave Mary more medication and some white cream to put over her arms and anywhere Sam had the rash. The doctor continued advising us to watch her carefully and return if her condition went 'south'. I guess that meant to return if she got worse! "I know a good doctor at Vanderbilt," he said.

Well, her condition did get worse and Sam remained in bed for over a month. Nothing improved. Sam lost more weight. She hallucinated. She became confrontational! She screamed with pain! Thomas returned from Roanoke for a week to be with his sister. I wrote a letter to Sam's aunt, Samantha, and she came to Clinton for a few days. Even Doctor Rowland came to the house on six different occasions. Roxie asked what was happening to her older sister while young Frances looked to us for support and wondering why. No one in the house was comfortable!

Everything regarding the veteran's home was put on hold, but the monthly meetings with the ex-soldiers continued. The former confederate believers told stories and asked if any progress was being made with Sam. I had to answer in the negative, but reassured them I would continue work on my project.

Eventually, Samantha, Mary, and I boarded the Nashville bound train and headed west. Sam's condition was progressively getting worse as we all hoped someone had an answer. Even with assistance from three doctors, two weeks at the medical center where evaluations and recommendations were endless and under watchful eyes of expert nursing care, results were not positive. Sam's lungs were weak. Her heart was failing. Her joints swelled! Coughing blood after every meal reduced her strength! Weight loss continued. She did not improve as we returned from Vanderbilt.

During those months of attending to Sam, I returned periodically to see Mr. Norton at the bank with little movement on his part and continued frustration on mine. The only positive sign was the hardware and feed stores were doing quite well and I started to sell other farming supplies, specifically newer chemicals for tobacco. I even got a visit from a flashy looking salesman that wanted to sell me some bow-weevil pesticide when I informed him the area was not a cotton producing empire. He must have been from New York!

In order to isolate her, Mary and I had placed Sam in a small room off the kitchen praying she would get better. Dr. Rowland contacted another doctor in Knoxville and the two agreed Sam had developed 'scarlet fever'. Her condition worsened. She went into a coma! The end was near!

During another nighttime snowstorm in mid- February, Samantha Mary-anne McMurtree passed away! Everyone was devastated.

I decided it was time to follow my conscience, so I contacted Simpson Sharpe the black preacher from the Baptist Church where Mary and I had become members, and made arrangements for my oldest daughter. His funeral home was right next to the church! I wrote my sister, Samantha and Thomas. They returned to Clinton with their spouses! I wrote letters to Jonas and Captain Steele. Neither came to the funeral but sent thoughtful comments I arranged in my journal.

When the snow melted and the ground had thawed, we buried Samantha in the St. Cloud Cemetery. Blacks and whites carried the casket! Blacks and whites surrounded the grave sight. Blacks and whites dug the grave! Blacks and whites read the Bible! Blacks and whites said the prayers! Blacks and whites celebrated Samantha's life! When Preacher Sharpe read the 23rd Psalm, it never sounded so good!

A Week Later

The cemetery, located at the bottom of the hill where I hope to build my home for Confederate Veterans, is visited daily by Mary, the girls, and me!

One night as Mary and I were cleaning the room where Samantha had spent her final days, I located a sealed envelope addressed to me. It was a letter from my oldest daughter. I went to my bedroom, closed the door and read a letter that Samantha had written just weeks before her life on earth ended.

Dear pa,

I really don't know where to start as I have so much to say to you and so little time left. I know I have but a few days left on earth and I know you and ma have done everything possible. Dr. Rowland is a nice man like the doctors at Vanderbilt, but I feel bad all the time, even with all the pills and that foul smelling cream all over my body. I'm sorry about all the mess with throwing up and feel bad that I have not been able to help you in the hardware or feed store or help ma around the house. Pa, I'm extremely proud of you and appreciate you more each day. You have often said to me that the wartime experience brought a lot of thinking and changes in your life, one being 'to do the right thing.' Now, I know what you mean!

As I lay here in my bed with open sores on my bottom, swelling around my eyes, and cry from the excruciating pain over my entire body, I have reflected on many things in my life. I have always thought one of the most influential moments in your young life was when you received your brother's prison journal. I can't imagine trying to survive like my uncle did! The journal! How could anything be more important? Maybe, that's the reason for some of your untimely nightmares! He wasn't even twenty-five years old!

I now realize all you have done for me and our family and I hope the veteran's home gets built soon to help all those injured and wounded soldiers.

I must say thank you and don't know where to start. I appreciate you more than you will ever know. A few months before I got really sick you took me to the veterans meeting and it was awful seeing those men who were missing fingers, toes, arms, or legs. Seeing Rufus Appleby struggling with his mind. He was angry and swore all the time. I thought he might shoot himself that night as his pistol on his hip was loaded and ready. Almost all of those men looked like they had not shaved in a year or had a good meal in a long time! I'm glad I took the apples and pumpkin pies! But, the best part of the evening was when

*you tried to reassure the men that the monthly meetings were helpful
and the future home would make life easier. Those are positive things
taking place in their life. Pa, you are an inspiration to those men!
Don't you let anyone tell you different! Get that banker to help you!*

*Pa, I know you have always wanted me and Thomas and the others
to get a good education. I'm sorry if I disappointed you by not pursu-
ing an education like my namesake. I'm sorry if I did not live up to
your expectations. I'm sorry if my lack of attendance at church has
disappointed you. I do remember some of those Bible stories you use to
read to me. I even remember Cain and Able! Wasn't that their names?
And I'm sorry about all the trouble I have caused you and ma. A good
slap on the bottom never really hurt! Those individual discussions,
as you called them, never hurt too bad! You always made your point!
Thankfully, Frances got more than me! Besides, I still love you with
all my heart.*

*The girls I met in school while we lived in Lexington thought you
were the best. We were good friends! We shared the same teachers. Rebecca Alexandra, Ava Newly, and me used to sit around and discuss
our lives, home, and siblings. Rebecca and Ava thought you were 'just
the cat's meow.' We used to go horseback riding and discuss boys telling each other about boys we wanted to marry. Ava said she wanted
someone like you. What a compliment! I agree. Rebecca said she hated
history and our teacher Mr. Brookes, but she liked listening to you tell
stories about Captain Steele and how much you respected him. Pa,
you're the greatest!*

*Unfortunately, I will never get the chance to marry! I know I am
getting worse every day and have but a few days left. Last month I got
a letter from Ava asking about me and wanted to know about you and
your veteran's home project. She is married and lives in Fredericksburg. She is expecting her first baby in two months. I would love to see
her, but I have my doubts!*

*You have been a wonderful dad. You have given me values that I
cherish. Truth, honesty, and dedication stand out! I hope some of my
love for you has shown. I hope I have represented our family even with
all my shortcomings. Do you remember the night you asked about my
future? Well, if I remember, I wasn't very clear or specific. Maybe, it
was my age! Who knows? But, I remember your concern. You asked all
of us to think ahead. Plan! Be positive! See the cup half full! You said,
don't ever think you can't do whatever it is! Pa, you did a great job.
You are a great person and I hope others recognize that! I don't know*

where I went wrong! I love you dearly!

I know my handwriting is not very good but I'm going to continue.

Over my young years I have watched you work around the house, the determination you demonstrated while getting a college education, and the way you always had time for your family. Even those years in Lexington! You even found your lost sister, Ruth. I wonder if she would like to return to Clinton. Maybe, you can ask her! Has she seen her sons lately?

Thomas and I have talked about it often. The way you and ma always seem to iron things out! I don't know how many times you and ma have disagreed on something but I don't remember any arguments or fights. You always seem to have a level head. Were you just hiding something? I think not! I love you for putting us first, you know, your family. Heaven has a place for people like you. I know I'll see you there someday.

I don't remember saying anything to you about discussions you and ma had when all us kids went to bed. But, we all could hear you discuss many concerns such as your frustration with all the violence taking place at the hands of dangerous members of the Klan. I remember your comments about fearing for Jonas and his family. I remember you saying you could not save the world, but somehow you felt the urge to help your boyhood friend.

Before I got extremely sick right after Christmas, I was thinking about a trip to see your childhood buddy, Jonas. I know you miss him and want the best for him. I know you worry about his condition, living down there in Louisiana near that cotton farm watching black workers slave with other white tenant farmers. I have seen you reading the paper and know it bothers you when you read stories of abuse to blacks. I remember hearing you and ma talk about Captain Steele's son and how he died in a brawl between blacks and whites in Chicago. Maybe with the summer approaching, you and ma can find time to visit Jonas and the captain. Frances and Roxie may want to go! Jonas and the captain would love to see you. Your veteran friends will understand.

One night the topic turned to funding and starting the home. You discussed your dreams and how they would help the locals, but you were frustrated with the initial starting cost. And my aunt of the same name had a boss who could help, but you were reluctant to ask too much from him. Keep trying!

As I close this letter, I want you to know that my love for you is and always has been very deep. I could not have had a better pa. You have made me feel proud. And don't worry about me. I have had a great life. Even at my young age, I knew I was blessed with great parents and you were the leader. If there is one last comment, it is that I will love you always. You lead by example. What more could a daughter want?

Take care! I will see you later, much later, as you have a lot to do here in Clinton.

I love you always,
Samantha

Epilogue

Over the years JT never forgot that letter from his daughter he described as extremely moving and heartwarming. 'Follow those dreams,' she had reminded him. Years followed with visits to the sight of the future home that always included a side step to visit Samantha's grave. He constantly said to himself, I will live up to her comments!

A month following the burial JT received a letter from his sister, Ruth Anne, inquiring about a return to Clinton and work in the soldier's home. Immediately he wrote back that plans were still being formalized and he would love to have her return even without the home. Two months later he ventured to Sayersburg and returned to Clinton with his long lost older sister. She became part of the family, again!

John constantly recorded significant events in his life and the following is dated, August 23, 1895. The journal reads:

> As contacts with the veteran's group continue and letters to committee members fizzle I am overly concerned about the prospects for the home. Visits with Mr. Norton, who had recently been informed that his mother left him two million dollars in her will, proved to be a waste of MY time. She had owned a dress manufacturing mill on Long Island, New York and left it all to him. Even with all his money and his position, I got nowhere with him and wrote letters to Mr. Spencer in Washington and Mr. Corrigan down in Nashville, and again got no positive results. While Ruth keeps the house clean and does most of the cooking, Mary, Roxie, and Frances continue to hold bazaars and cookie sales each weekend at church and I work extra building wagon wheels. We continue to put money aside for the home but the balance is not increasing extremely fast.
>
> I said to Mary one night as we shared some chocolate cake that

something was missing in my life. Yes, I am still conducting the month-
ly veteran meetings coming home with confusion on my face. Meetings
turn ugly as rowdy veterans continually express extreme anger with
no progress. While members continue to recount their torturous war
days they argue they had nothing to show for their service except scars
and mental disease. That's what they call it 'mental disease.' Alton,
a new member of the group, spoke up with, "This damn Confederate
Government never gave us assistance when we left that f___'n army
and now rumors are circulating those stupid former southern officers,
especially generals, are planning a reunion." Rufus chimed in with,
"That's stupid. Give us some God Damn help. I'm tired of living in a
shed. Those bastards live like kings. Let me put some gunpowder in
their f___'n black coffee like I did in 64."

Rufus Appleby didn't attend the next two meetings so one night af-
ter everyone had disbursed I walked over to his living quarters and
found him hanging from a tree. He had been there for some time as the
odor was atrocious. The note inside his home simply said, "Enough
is enough." I buried him near the sight of my future soldier's home. I
WILL build one!

I talked with Kathleen Ashford, the social worker, regarding Rufus
and her perception. Kathleen had been to see Rufus a number of times,
but when he became confrontational, she curtailed her visits. She men-
tioned she liked the man but had to stop.

Kathleen informed Mary and me she would help raise money,
but except for helping Mary and the girls on Sunday she had very
little time as her daily work demanded nine and ten hour days. Plus,
she may be moving to Cookeville where her husband called home. I
grabbed my mail.

My immediate future was uncertain and the letter from Jonas ad-
dressed my anxiety very quickly! I didn't like what I read and needed
to make some changes. The soldier's home was becoming a nightmare
and I worried about my buddy.
    JT

His buddy had much to say!

By the 90s, Jonas and his wife were by themselves. Jonas worked long hours for the law firm investigating cases for court proceedings. He did most of the legwork while leading attorneys argued the cases and had moved to another section of New Orleans. Closer to work, he wrote. His free time became more focused with 'Jim Crow Laws', abuse in cotton fields, and labor unions.

JT kept reading to discover that Jonas' group meetings had turned disruptive and at times useless. White factory owners and railroad car owners were his monthly antagonists.

Continuing, the letter described the Ku Klux Klan had resurfaced spreading anger among the white southern anti-black population and fear within the black community. Segregation surfaced as a primary topic. Separating blacks from whites was the overwhelming concern of whites as they controlled many governmental big city offices, major businesses near the waterfront, huge iron factories and other establishments like bars, hotels, and railroad cars. When the Klan didn't control the scenes, hoodless angry whites, many former confederate soldiers with sticks, pipes, and weapons took over.

On a similar topic, in Boston, Frederick Douglas continually gave speeches encouraging blacks to get educated, vote in numbers, and stand up for human rights. He journeyed south spreading his campaign. An editorial in a local Atlanta paper blasted Douglas and told him to go back north. He stayed!

Everything mentioned in that letter was recorded in his journal and JT had commented to Mary, "How far has America come since the war?" "Nor far," was her response.

By the turn of the century John's life had taken on new meaning as he became increasingly concerned with the plight of 'people of color' specifically his friend in New Orleans. John was still a member of the small black church that he and Mary had joined prior to Samantha's death. Verbal and physical abuse had almost disappeared from his life, but he worried constantly. Mary had become socially comfortable having become involved in many local groups, but was suffering from some heart issues that were never explained by doctors in Clinton or Knoxville. Just before Mary died of a heart attack, she and John ventured to New Orleans to see Jonas. Upon their return home the comment in his journal confirmed his anxiety but he finished with, Jonas can handle whatever crisis he encounters.

PLESSY VS FERGUSON

But a very significant event took place in the early 90's. In 1890 the state of Louisiana passed laws simply stating: "Equal but separate accommodations for white and colored races" on railroads would be enforced. John made comments in his journal describing early developments within railroads.

During the 60's, 70's and 80's when riding the trains blacks were seated in the front cars of the trains directly in back of the engines as smoke from the burning fuels, wood in the cases of the southern trains, was stifling with passengers getting extremely sick. Whites rode in the back cars. However, as trains perfected the exhaust problems, blacks were removed to the back cars on trains. Whites moved forward. According to Louisiana law, blacks were regulated to the back cars and prohibited from sitting anywhere else.

Louisiana resident, Homer Plessy, refused to sit in the back train car section and was arrested for breaking the law. The case went to state court in New Orleans with Jonas and his firm defending Mr. Plessy. State Court upheld the recently passed law! The state court led by Justice John Ferguson ruled, "The purpose of the 14th amendment was to enforce the absolute equality of the two races before the law and laws requiring their separation do not necessarily imply inferiority of either race."

The case was appealed to the U.S. Supreme Court in Washington where Jonas and his firm were present when the court handed down the 7-1 decision stating, "Separate but Equal was Constitutional." Former Kentucky slave owner and Union soldier, John Marshal Harlan was the lone dissenter saying: "The white race deems itself dominant, but the Constitution recognizes no superior dominant ruling class of citizens. Our Constitution is color blind!"

Even though Homer Plessy was 7/8's white and 1/8 black, by Louisiana Law he was considered black. 58 years later in 1954 Jonas's great grandson attorney Jonathan Trent Manford, helped overturn the findings of the 1896 decision in the Brown vs Board of Education case stating "Separate but Equal was Unconstitutional." Jonas would have been extremely proud!

John and Jonas

Following newspaper reports and letters from Jonas regarding the Plessy cases and the unfortunate untimely death of Mary, John and Jonas spent many summers and vacation time together visiting one another. And on a special trip after the turn of the century, they ventured to Chicago to meet Captain Steele who was happily married and the father of a new baby girl. "The Windy City," according to the captain. Captain Steele had shown his history knowledge mentioning that his boss, Robert Lincoln had been in the vicinity of all three of the assassinated presidents as President McKinley had recently been killed by a deranged angry madman. Before leaving Chicago the two ex-confederate soldiers agreed to meet in Gettysburg at the 50 Anniversary of the famous battle.

After many very successful years in New Orleans and before the death of his wife, Jonas had relocated in southern Georgia where he discovered the plantation where his father had been a slave and escaped. Sadly, Jonas never found his friend Benny, who had left Clinton to protect his family in the 70s.

John Trenton McMurtree

Years passed as John, the captain, and Jonas corresponded regularly. But

John could never forget the War Between the States. Living by himself in Clinton and working with Cecil at the hardware and feed stores and with the hopes of the Soldier's Home, he continually redressed the war years. Nightmares many nights! Pneumonia every winter! Sitting alone at night or daydreaming while working, he constantly revisited the stonewall at Fredericksburg, the Sunken Road at Antietam, the charge across that half mile field at Gettysburg, Libby Prison, and Camp Sumter in Georgia.

He constantly reread his journal where he recorded the war and more. One entry simply said, "Moral Majority, God's Will Will Prevail." He reread his brother's prison journal and recalled meeting him in the woods of northern Virginia while on picket duty. John reached into closets to retrieve dust-covered letters from Mary, Samantha, and grandpa. And he never forgot that day in 58 when his pa and Thomas left the farm. All he had were memories of his pa buried outside of Albany.

But he continued his wish of building the veteran's home with visits to banks followed by committee meetings, letters to local and state government leaders, and extensive study. He always felt he had an obligation to fellow comrades. Visits to Mary and Samantha's graves never satisfied his emotional needs. Visits to the local preacher coupled with trips to Knoxville never solved much.

Finally, a letter arrived from Mr. Hammer! Enclosed with an explanation was a check that provided the initial funding for the soldier's home. Check date 1-19-1904. JT's birth-date! He was 60 years old!

Coupled with funding from Washington, small loans from two local banks, and agreed upon sales of the hardware and feed stores, John's dream came true. With the help from Cecil, the local Amish people, a few able veterans, and his son Thomas who had returned to live in Clinton, the soldier's home honoring his brother was completed the year Howard Taft entered the White House.

In 1913 while thousands of former Yankees and Confederates were dying annually, many survivors with missing limbs or an eye and some walking with new oak canes ambled across that 'Hallowed Ground' at Gettysburg. Former opposition forces recounted those horrible days. The captain and John again shared individual stories. The scene was the 50th celebration of the Battle of Gettysburg.

That was the last time John and Captain Steele saw each other. The captain died shortly.

With the completion of the home, Jonas and John visited each other annually. During one trek to the south, John discovered Andersonville, Georgia and Jonas' father's former slave plantation were just 10 miles apart. Jonas successfully developed his own law firm before he died in 1920.

The aftermath years brought little comfort to John but he would have been proud to hear his great grandson, a recent graduate from West Point, recite The Gettysburg Address at the 100 anniversary of its reading November 19,1963. John Trenton died of pneumonia in 1925 in his own Soldier's Home in Clinton, Tennessee. He was 81, and a very proud American!

CPSIA information can be obtained
at www.ICGtesting.com
Printed in the USA
FSHW010750170519
58218FS